T0319746

# DYNAMICS OF UNEVEN DEVELOPMENT

# Dynamics of Uneven Development

*Lynn Mainwaring*

*Senior Lecturer in Economics*
*University College of Swansea*

Edward Elgar

© Lynn Mainwaring 1991

All rights reserved. No part of this publication may be reproduced, stored in a retrieval system, or transmitted in any form or by any means, electronic, mechanical, photocopying, recording, or otherwise without the prior permission of the publisher.

Published by
Edward Elgar Publishing Limited
Gower House
Croft Road
Aldershot
Hants GU11 3HR
England

Edward Elgar Publishing Company
Old Post Road
Brookfield
Vermont 05036
USA

**British Library Cataloguing in Publication Data**
Mainwaring, Lynn
  Dynamics of uneven development.
  1. Economic development
  I. Title
  330.9

**Library of Congress Cataloguing in Publication Data**
Mainwaring, Lynn, 1949–
  Dynamics of uneven development / Lynn Mainwaring.
    p.   cm.
  1. Autarchy. 2. Economic development. 3. International trade.
  I. Title.
  HD82.M344 1991
  338.9–dc20
                                                              90–45398
                                                                   CIP

ISBN 1 85278 319 2

Printed in Great Britain by
Billing & Sons Ltd, Worcester

*For Ann*

# Contents

# Acknowledgements

Though they probably do not remember it, an informal discussion I had with Heinz Kurz and Stan Metcalfe was the inspiration for this book. They suggested that a brief note that I had published some years earlier, on 'International investment and the Pasinetti process' would bear further elaboration. My efforts in this direction, at first tentative, took on a more earnest character after I discussed my ideas with Edward Elgar. My principal debt (as usual) is to Ian Steedman who found time, in a busy period, to read through the entire manuscript. I have also benefited from the more particular suggestions of John Bennett, David Evans and Adrian Wood. It goes without saying that responsibility for what follows is entirely mine. The manuscript was typed with speed and accuracy by Siân Davies.

Parts of the book draw on previously published articles in the *Journal of Development Studies, Kyklos,* the *Cambridge Journal of Economics* and the *Journal of Post Keynesian Economics.* I should like to thank Frank Cass and Co. Ltd Kyklos-Verlag, Academic Press Inc. (London) Ltd and Myron E. Sharpe, Inc., respectively, for permission to do so.

# Introduction

*Capitalism itself is, both in the economic and in the sociological sense, essentially one process, with the whole earth as its stage.*

– J.A. Schumpeter (1939, p.666)

Since the work of Prebisch (1950) and Singer (1950), economists have been familiar with the argument that structural asymmetries between the rich, industrialized countries of the global 'North' or 'Centre' and the poor, largely primary-producing countries of the 'South' or 'Periphery' could be responsible for an unequal division of the gains from international trade and investment. Prebisch's version of global Keynesianism and Singer's emphasis on the over-riding role of externalities provided bases for deeper and more radical criticisms of the functioning of the world capitalist economy by the 'dependency' school. Later they were supplemented by neo-Marxian theories of non-equivalent exchange arising out of the contribution of Emmanuel. For a long time neoclassical theorists appeared rather unimpressed by these critiques and even seemed to have difficulty in coming to terms with some of the central concepts of non-neoclassical thought on these issues.

The lack of dialogue may have been partly a consequence of neoclassical suspicion of arguments which, on the whole, are analytically rather weak, the conclusions often appearing to be reached more through assertion than by logical deduction from clearly stated assumptions. In return, neoclassical theory has been attacked for its mechanistic nature, its practitioners accused of abstracting from a rich and varied set of phenomena and processes not susceptible to algebraic formulation, in a single-minded pursuit of rigour. Whatever the merits of these mutual recriminations, there was evidently a need for an approach, or approaches, taking a critical, uncosy view of global economic relations, thus accepting many of the concepts of traditional radical thought, but equally intent on pursuing the impli-

*1*

cations of such a view in a rigorous manner. The last decade has seen the emergence of such a literature, remarkable both for its rapid growth and for its variety. Among the starting points are neoclassical (Findlay, 1980; Burgstaller and Saavedra-Rivano, 1984), structuralist (Taylor, 1983; Darity, 1987; Dutt, 1988a), Kaldorian (Vines, 1984) and 'increasing returns' (Krugman, 1981). Despite their differences, all recognize the basic premise of Prebisch and Singer, that the fundamental long-term asymmetries between the two global regions are not easily erased by freeing international markets in goods and assets and, in many circumstances, free trade may actually consolidate or aggravate these inequalities.

The present study is intended as a further contribution to the debate, choosing yet another starting point, sometimes called neo-Ricardian or post-Sraffian, though it will quickly become apparent that the building blocks of the analysis come from many sources apart from Ricardo and Sraffa, including Leontief, Pasinetti, Lewis, Goodwin and the biologist Manfred Eigen. The justification for yet another approach is simply that each perspective offers fresh insights, not only directly into the subject under investigation but also into the competing and complementary approaches. As Dutt (1988b) remarks:

> ... diversity is perhaps the greatest strength of this literature. The existence of a common approach which dictates the development of a discipline can possibly smother the development of fresh, interesting ways of looking at new issues simply because they do not fit into the accepted theoretical structure. This is particularly important for an area of investigation such as North–South trade, in which different parts of the world may have widely different structures, and different models may be required to understand the functioning of particular structures.

Given that diversity already exists it will perhaps be useful to say something at the outset about the emphases of the present contribution in relation to the other main strands of theorizing on this issue. To do that it will be necessary to offer some critical observations on these other approaches. Because the mushrooming of the literature has been accompanied by an equally rapid growth in the number of survey articles we can afford to be brief and selective in our observations. Readers wishing for more complete background are referred to Findlay (1984), Ocampo (1986), Dutt (1988b) and Evans (1989a), all of which are concerned with the trade–(uneven) development nexus.[1] The survey article by Kanbur and McIntosh (1988) also considers North–South models as a species of 'dual-economy' model (with duality existing between the two global regions).

It is possible to identify in the literature six viewpoints which by now are sufficiently well developed that we can think of them as 'schools'. Needless to say many writers have successfully combined elements from different schools and yet others emphasize features which are not considered essential to any of the six identified here. We shall refer to the schools as: 'dependency', 'unequal exchange', 'orthodox neoclassical', 'neoclassical uneven-development', 'structuralist', and 'Kaldorian'. In what follows and throughout the book the epithets 'Centre' and 'Periphery' will be used in preference to 'North' and 'South', not out of any ideological prejudice but merely to emphasize the structural asymmetry of the regions.

## Dependency

It is worth beginning with the dependency school because its premises and many of its conclusions have been accepted by other schools. What other schools have been more reluctant to take on board are the language and modes of analysis of dependency writers. A useful overview of the school can be found in Blomstrom and Hettne (1984) and a more critical review in Palma (1981).

According to Dos Santos (1970a), the purpose of dependency analysis is to examine development as a historical process and by so doing deduce the laws that govern that process. Dependency itself is defined as 'a situation in which a certain number of countries have their economy conditioned by the development and expansion of another ... placing dependent countries in a backward position exploited by the dominant countries'.[2] In one respect this definition is quite clear. It identifies one economy (the dominant countries) as the 'prime mover' in global economic relations while the other is taken to assume a more reactive role. The definition does, however, raise a number of questions, many of which have been answered in quite different ways by writers all considered to be within the dependency tradition.

What, for example, is meant by 'placing in a backward condition'? Is this a process of general immiserization or *under*development, as Frank (1967) would have it, or is it what Cardoso (1972) calls 'dependent capitalist development' in which rising living standards are accompanied by growing external control of the economy?

Then there is the 'conditioning' process. What is the precise causal connection between the development of the dominant countries and the 'backward condition' of the dependent countries? And how and in what sense do the former 'exploit' the latter? Some, like Sunkel (1973), have placed the emphasis on the monopoly power of transnational enterprises. But while no one would doubt the biases generated by international monopoly power, one would assume that the concept of dependency is intended to survive the absence of widespread monopolies both in theory and in reality. It is difficult to imagine a single dependency theorist proclaiming the virtues of liberal competitive international capitalism. Within competitive capitalism there are only two (not necessarily mutually exclusive) mechanisms which could serve to 'condition' backwardness in the Periphery and bring about its exploitation: international exchange and international investment. But dependency theorists themselves have actually had very little to say about either of these mechanisms. Perhaps the initial appeal of unequal exchange theory was that it offered a way of filling an embarrassing gap in the dependency analysis.

It may be the general lack of rigorous theory and the consequent amorphous and nebulous nature of its concepts that account for much of the frustration of more orthodox economists with the dependency literature (see, for example, Nove's (1974) uncharitable reading of Frank) and an excuse for its easy – even 'cheap' – dismissal.[3] Oddly, some dependency sympathizers like Palma (1981) argue that this is a potential strength of the school. He criticizes those theories within the tradition whose 'mechanical–formal nature renders them both static and unhistorical'. Somewhat ironically, the hapless Frank also gets singled out by Palma for constructing a model 'which is no more than a set of equations of general equilibrium' (which would be news to Nove or any general equilibrium theorist). The view that loose formulation with a heavy dose of reality, as represented by concrete case studies, is preferable to unhistorical rigour seems to me to involve a false dichotomy and a misunderstanding of the role of abstraction in economic theory. Of course dependency and development refer to processes taking place in historical time (and insistence on reflecting this fact in analysis is one of the main contributions of the school). But even real dynamic processes can be captured by rigorously constructed models. The resulting abstraction, as Dutt would argue, should not impose a straitjacket on theorizing but it should aim to provide a broad and flexible framework into which concrete examples could be fitted and related to one another.

## Unequal exchange

The notion of exploitation in Marx is fairly easy to grasp: for performing a certain amount of labour the worker is paid a wage which commands a basket of goods produced with a lesser amount of labour. The objective of unequal exchange theorists, from Emmanuel (1972) onwards, has been to extend a concept initially intended to illuminate the nature of exchange between classes to the issue of exchange between nations. Thus a country is deemed to be the victim of 'non-equivalent' exchange (a concept more readily definable than 'unequal' exchange) if the goods it produces with a certain amount of labour exchange for goods produced abroad with a lesser amount. The extension is not, however, entirely successful.

In the closed-economy class relation, the surplus labour of the worker has a direct counterpart in the form of physical goods, the value of which makes up the profits of the capitalist (provided there is no pure joint production[4]). In the case of exchange between nations it is easy to show that an increasing degree of non-equivalence can be accompanied by an increasing 'gain from trade' as traditionally defined in terms of command over commodities.[5] The question then is what economic or ethical significance, if any, should be attached to the notion of non-equivalent exchanges of labour. These and other issues are discussed in some depth by Evans (1984 and 1989a).

So far as the question of global economic relations is concerned, the potential contribution of unequal exchange theory was to provide a means by which trade allowed the Centre to extract surplus from the Periphery and thus a mechanism for simultaneous development and underdevelopment. The mechanism operates in a world in which the free movement of capital is assumed to equalize rates of profits. While recognition of international capital flows may be regarded as a virtue, there is in this school no rigorous analysis of the direct effects of such flows (as opposed to their implications for the terms of goods exchange)[6] nor any analysis of the process of capital accumulation. Thus the immiserizing mechanism is wholly static and sits awkwardly with the dependency theorists' insistence on viewing (under)development as a historical (and hence dynamic) process.

## Orthodox neoclassical

The twin pillars of neoclassical orthodoxy are the Heckscher–Ohlin and gains-from-trade theories, the first attempting to explain the 'cause' of trade, the second its welfare benefits.

Even as an analysis of trade which has no pretence of illuminating development issues, Heckscher–Ohlin theory is vulnerable to the critique of all neoclassical theories dependent on the concept of aggregate capital (see Metcalfe and Steedman, 1973). But it has additional limitations when applied to the question of development. First, it portrays the potentially trading nations as essentially symmetrical, the only qualitative difference between them residing in their relative factor endowments. 'Distortions' can be introduced into one economy or the other but there is, in general, little attempt to model these distortions as significant, enduring structural features which impinge on the economies in an asymmetrical fashion. Second, the analysis of causation is static in so far as the 'factor' endowments (taken to include capital) are specified exogenously, thus ruling out the possibility that the observable endowments of a nation might be the consequence of the history of the regime(s) (autarky or trade) which it has pursued.

The gains-from-trade literature is not explicitly concerned with the unhindered development process but with policy choice relating to the degree of openness. For static models without distortions the conclusion is unequivocal: the more the freedom to trade the better; free trade is best. For intertemporal models the conclusion carries over provided that the rate of interest (profits) is equal to the rate of social time preference used to discount future gains and losses (Smith, 1984). This finding has been used to criticize not only unequal exchange conclusions but also the neo-Ricardian claim (Steedman and Metcalfe, 1973; Mainwaring, 1974) that failure to comply with the Golden Rule could lead to a consumption loss from trade. The neoclassical equality of profits and time preference rates is an assumption whose importance is not fully appreciated. In my opinion it is this more than anything else (including the treatment of capital) that ultimately distinguishes neoclassical from other schools of thought. For abstinence, the sacrifice of current consumption, can now be held to be the capitalist's contribution to production, and profits accordingly held to be recompense for undertaking this hardship. Then the fact that a worker performs surplus labour can no longer be taken to imply exploitation if the capitalist 'deserves' a share of the product. If, however, capitalists obtain satisfaction from the very act of accumulating (a view consistent with Marx, Keynes and a host of other writers) then there is no reason to identify the social time preference rate with the rate of profits (see Steedman, 1981). Failure to do so would no doubt be seen by neoclassicals as a 'distortion' to be considered, if at all, as an afterthought. For others the desire to accumulate is a defining characteristic of capitalism and should be an integral part of its analysis.

Despite these criticisms, the neoclassical orthodoxy has developed some particularly useful insights that are or can be made relevant to the analysis of Centre–Periphery relations. It is known that growth in the endowment of a factor in the presence of distortions can be immiserizing. One such distortion is size: a large economy which fails to use optimal trade taxes does not gain the maximum benefit from its monopoly power. In this case growth which leads to a deterioration in the terms of trade can be immiserizing. If the growing factor is 'capital' and if its growth is the result of private investment from overseas the possibility of immiserization becomes a necessity as the benefits of the additional capital, the profits, accrue to the foreign investor (Brecher and Choudri, 1982). The same general conclusion is reached in an explicitly intertemporal context, avoiding the use of aggregate capital, by Smith (1984). We then have a neoclassical theorem which states unambiguously that *laissez-faire* may not be the best policy for a capital-attracting country. In the present context it is natural to think of that country as the Periphery.

## Neoclassical uneven development

The idea that factors which might be responsible for negative Peripheral outcomes could be of a structural nature, profoundly entrenched in such economies as a consequence of a long history of colonial and neocolonial development or because of intractable demographic trends, was incorporated into a later generation of neoclassical models. Much credit here goes to Ronald Findlay who developed a theory of international trade between a developed Centre having the properties of the Solow growth model, and a less developed Periphery modelled by elements taken from Ricardo and Arthur Lewis (Findlay, 1980). The basic Findlay model has been extended and modified by himself and by his students, and the contribution of Burgstaller and Saavedra-Rivano (1984) which introduces international capital mobility is of particular interest.

Unlike the neoclassical orthodoxy, the 'Columbia school' makes no attempt to determine the 'cause' of trade, which means that the nature of specialization cannot be inferred from the properties of the notional autarky economies. The pattern of trade thus has to be imposed on the model (a feature shared with unequal exchange models). The methodological absence of autarky *alter egos* also means that the traditional concept of gain (or loss) is inapplicable. What is now relevant is the direction taken by various welfare indices (consumption, employment, etc.) over time. The school is clearly much more oriented towards 'process' rather than 'comparison' and in this respect could be regarded as an attempt to rigorize the dependency perspective. This is explicitly recognized by Findlay (1984, p. 187) and is reflected by the general tendency for the Centre to be the 'engine of growth' in these models. The Periphery's passive role is captured by a recursive structure: the Centre's good (manufactures) is needed in Peripheral production but the Periphery's goods are not needed in Central production. If this particular asymmetry were relaxed the Periphery would come to have greater influence on Central development. This, however, would introduce heterogeneous capital into the framework, running counter to the use of the Solow growth model.[7]

With surplus labour in the Periphery and natural resources and land assumed to be free, the only long-run constraint on development is the supply of labour in the Centre. Thus, in the absence of technological progress, the growth rates in both regions, unequal in the short run, tend to a steady uniform rate equal to that of Central labour-supply growth. The long-run, steady-state tendencies of these models have been criticized by Ocampo (1986, p. 145) as having 'eliminated ... uneven development as such'. This criticism can only be valid if the 'long run' is so short that the 'short-run' properties of the model have little relevance to the understanding of development. It may be that Findlay-type models are insufficiently clear about the length of the long run, but there is nothing wrong in principle in portraying uneven development as a very protracted convergence to even development.

A more substantial criticism of the school concerns the prior imposition of the global pattern of production. This is not necessarily to advocate a comparison-of-regimes approach but simply to suggest that changes in the pattern of production could be endogenized by allowing the pattern to respond to developments within the model.

## Structuralist

Modern Centre–Periphery structuralist models originated with Taylor (1983) and have been developed further by him (1986) and also by Dutt (1988a, 1989). The main characteristic of these models is their portrayal of the Centre in Kaleckian terms, with the price of the manufactured good determined as a mark-up on prime costs in the presence of excess capacity. Investment is determined in the manner of Keynes and Steindl. These models appear to be valuable in examining short-run behaviour, as their Keynesian characteristics imply; Darity (1987) has examined the current debt crisis in this framework. The analysis of long-run capital movements is, however, sketchy (though see Dutt, 1989, Chapter 8). As with Findlay-type models, specialization is pre-specified and dynamic causation runs predominantly from Centre to Periphery.

## Kaldorian

The main contributions here are Vines (1984) and Molana and Vines (1989), successive attempts to develop formally the ideas of Kaldor (1976). In some respects this school represents a structural reversal of Findlay in that labour is assumed surplus in both regions and the long-run constraint on development is now effected by the availability of costly natural resources in the Periphery. Again the pattern of specialization is imposed from outside but a certain amount of two-way influence is present because the Central cost of living depends on the terms of trade. As with the previous school, the Kaldorian model is useful for analysing short-run adjustments to shocks. A significant limitation is that international capital mobility has (so far) not been included.

These observations on alternative approaches are intended merely to put into perspective the contribution which follows. This can be done most easily by outlining briefly the coverage of each chapter and attempting to relate the material to some of the points raised above.

The book is in two parts. The first, shorter part is concerned with a world in which Centre–Periphery economic relations are confined to trade in commodities. By far the largest part of the recent (1980s) literature just discussed deals with this case. In comparison, the potentially interesting and complex issues arising in a world of capital mobility have received very little attention.[8] Unequal exchange writers did assume capital mobility but made no real attempt to analyse the nature or implications of the accumulation process. Of the recent models only Burgstaller and Saavedra-Rivano (1984) and Dutt (1990) have attempted this using models with manufactured capital goods (though Burgstaller's 1985 and 1987 Ricardian models allow mobility of capital construed as a wages fund). Accordingly the second and larger part of the book is devoted to developing a model of international investment.

The first two chapters run in methodological parallel to orthodox approaches to trade theory. The first is largely concerned with 'causation' as reflected in the autarky characteristics of the potential trading partners. The approach is 'neo-Ricardian' in locating the 'cause' of trade in autarky differences in both technology and income distribution. (The textbook 'Ricardian' model neglects the second factor entirely.) Asymmetry is introduced by assuming surplus labour in the Periphery (fixing the real wage) and Central full-employment growth (fixing the rate of profits). Not surprisingly, the properties of the with-trade regime are similar to those of Findlay's model. A tentative welfare conclusion, obtained by comparing autarky and trade outcomes, is that the Periphery may have lower consumption per (employed) worker with trade. The Peripheral growth rate will, however, be greater with trade.

Chapter 2 considers the question of consumption gains in greater depth, by looking at the entire path of the transition from one regime to another. The neoclassical theorem that intertemporal (transition-plus-comparative) gains in total consumption are positive when consumption is discounted using the rate of profits is demonstrated for this particular model, followed by a discussion of the validity of this evaluation procedure. If invalid, then Peripheral immiserization through trade is a possibility.

In most of Chapters 1 and 2, and throughout Part II, Centre and Periphery are considered as aggregations. Chapter 3 represents a departure from this approach, treating the typical Peripheral economy as small in that it faces constant terms of trade. The chapter is concerned with the question of whether Peripheral accumulation is best pursued through the importation of new or of used machines from the Centre.

As analyses of the process of development, the largely 'comparative' approach of Part I has obvious limitations, in some respects the same as those of orthodox neoclassical in relation to neoclassical uneven development theories. But just as neoclassical orthodoxy provides the tools and a framework of thought for the uneven development approach, so the same is intended here of Part I for Part II. It is true that the development implications of the pure-trade model could be deduced by a detailed examination of the with-trade path and examples of this procedure (e.g., analysis of the effects of labour-saving technical progress) are given in Chapter 1. Once a particular pattern of international production is accepted, however, it seems more sensible to proceed directly to a model which also permits international mobility of capital.

The model of free global accumulation begins in Chapter 4 at an aggregate level. This describes the workings of the 'international Pasinetti process' in which (on certain simplifying assumptions) higher-saving Central capitalists gradually take over the entire ownership of the Peripheral capital stock. During this process, capital growth rates in the Centre and in the Peripheral 'enclave' and indigenous sectors will normally differ so that development could be considered as uneven. Nevertheless, both Periphery and Centre growth converge on the same steady rate. Since this convergence goes hand in hand with the working of the Pasinetti process it follows (*à propos* the criticism by Ocampo, noted above) that uneven development will be a very protracted stage of the global accumulation process. Moreover, 'even' development (that is, steady growth) does not imply equality of Centre–Periphery capitalist relations, for here steady growth is associated with complete Central dominance of world capitalism. Chapter 4 is the core of the book. The remaining chapters provide elaborations, modifications, extensions and the occasional digression.

Chapter 5 appends a Sraffa–Leontief production system to the preceding analysis. Both the pattern of specialization and wage rates in both regions are fixed exogenously, leaving differential savings behaviour to carry the burden of asymmetry. On this basis consumption possibilities are traced over time, first for the case in which the Peripheral export sector is socially and technologically homogeneous, then for the case of a 'dual' export sector. It is shown that the Pasinetti process will be restrained if indigenous Peripheral capitalists who entered the 'advanced' part of the export sector adopt the savings behaviour of enclave capitalists. Gradual seepage between backward and advanced sub-sectors provides a means by which dualism, both within the Peripheral export sector, and between Periphery and Centre, is gradually eliminated.[9]

In Chapter 6 the Central wage is allowed to rise in response to a full-employment constraint, thus imparting some Findlay-like properties to the model. Rising wages could elicit a number of responses but, importantly, they provide a means for endogenous change in the global pattern of production. Rising labour costs in the Centre create an inducement to locate part of manufacturing production in the Periphery. The symmetrical possibility of a natural-resource constraint in the Periphery stimulating primary production in the Centre is also, though briefly, considered (so defining a point of contact with the Kaldorian approach). Thus, given initial conditions (of specialization), the internal dynamics of the model could be allowed to dictate the way in which the global division of labour evolves over time.

Although Part II is mainly concerned with 'process', Chapter 7 returns to more orthodox ways in attempting to evaluate the gains to a switch from an investment-autarky regime to one with free investment. The immiserizing insights of neoclassical orthodoxy are relevant here, as are remarks made earlier about the appropriate rate of discount. Chapter 8 takes advantage of the framework developed previously to make some critical observations on the theory of non-equivalent exchange. It has already been noted that the relation between the exchange of labour values and the exchange of physical commodities is tenuous. In this chapter it is shown that even if attention is confined to exchange of labour values nothing can be said *a priori* about which region extracts labour from the other. Chapter 9 returns to the basic development theme and introduces various forms of technical progress, particularly those provoked by incipient shortages of labour and natural resources.

The final chapter first summarizes the contribution by listing the main propositions which arise from it, and then (albeit crudely) examines the consistency of some of these propositions with particular episodes in the history of global accumulation.

Part of what follows reproduces or draws freely on previously published work. Chapters 3 and 8 are amended versions of Mainwaring (1986) and (1980b), respectively. Chapter 1 draws on (1974). The material of Chapters 4 and 5 represents the most recent phase in the evolution of ideas previously marked by (1980a), (1982) and (1988a).

## Notes

1. Dutt and Evans have also recently published books bearing directly on these issues. Dutt (1990) develops a deterministically incomplete framework, allowing different 'closures' to correspond to different models. Evans (1989b) offers a synthetic approach to the analysis of trade and development.
2. The quotation is from Dos Santos (1970b); the English translation by Valenzuela and Valenzuela (1979, p. 44).
3. Consider, for example, Little's (1982) attempt to enlighten his readers as to the meaning of 'underdevelopment': 'As I understand it, one takes the worst features of LDCs and ascribes them to the intrusion of capitalism and the integration of LDCs within "the world capitalist system"!'
4. See Steedman (1975).
5. See, for example, Findlay (1984) pp. 192–3.
6. In Bacha's (1978) reformulation, for example, balanced trade is assumed despite the fact that capital flows exist.
7. Alternatively the Peripheral good could be considered as an intermediate which is not advanced in production and is thus not a capital input. Though unsatisfactory, this is the typical way in which intermediates are treated in neoclassical trade theory.
8. Metcalfe and Steedman (1979) is an important contribution (in the tradition of this study) but it deals only with the case of a single, small open economy.
9. Cf. Kanbur and McIntosh's (1988, p. 109) critical comment that 'As with standard dual economy models, North–South models do not entertain to any great extent the end of dualism itself as the world economy progresses.'

# PART I

# WORLD TRADE IN GOODS ALONE

# 1 Autarky and trade in steady growth

## 1.1 Introduction

A tendency to think of 'capital movements' as synonymous and contemporaneous with the removal of physical capital from one country to another persists in the orthodox literature on international economics. This may be a legacy of the representation, in the simpler and most widely used models of neoclassical theory, of each nation's capital stock as an 'endowment'. As such, capital exists as an input into production without having been an output. If capital (like land) exists simply because 'it exists', it may be natural to think of capital movements as a transfer of part of one nation's endowment to another nation. In reality, of course, the matter is nowhere nearly as simple. Capital movements are movements of finance, giving the borrower temporary claim over physical goods (which may or may not be capital goods) and the claim is normally surrendered with interest. Movements of financial assets may thus induce trade in capital goods but trade in capital goods can take place and, indeed, almost certainly would take place in the absence of international capital mobility. The two phenomena must therefore be kept conceptually distinct.

This and the following chapters consider trade in goods in the absence of trade in financial assets. The goods may be consumed directly or they may be used as inputs into production and thus constitute capital. The basic production model used in this chapter (and also in the chapters on international investment in Part II) involves only circulating capital and thus rules out any explicit consideration of the use of or trade in durable capital goods such as machinery. In Chapter 3, a fixed-capital model is employed to develop a specific analysis of trade in machines.

The present analysis is relevant to a world of little capital mobility (the assumption of zero mobility being a defensible simplification) though its limitations as a description of historical reality will be explicitly acknowledged. In this chapter our main purpose is to develop the basic techniques of analysis and the theoretical 'viewpoint' adopted throughout the book, in a context that is familiar to all theorists of international economics. That context consists in comparing a world whose component economies exist in autarky equilibrium with a world in which the economies engage in free international trade. Apart from the existence or absence of trade, and the consequences arising therefrom, the individual economies are alike in all respects in the two states of the world. Chapter 2 covers slightly less familiar territory by looking at the implications of transitions from one equilibrium state to another. Despite its admitted descriptive limitations such an analysis may nevertheless have considerable prescriptive relevance.

## 1.2   Distribution and prices in autarky

The world is assumed to consist of two large economies, Centre and Periphery, labelled I and II respectively. In each, production takes place according to a single-products Sraffa–Leontief technology which is unchanging over time. Since the absence of joint products rules out durable capital then, necessarily, all capital is of the circulating variety: capital stocks are used up completely over a specified time period and are replaced, and possibly augmented, at the beginning of the following period out of the outputs of the current period. The assumption of zero technical progress is dropped in 1.7. The assumption of constant returns is an important limitation. Superficially, it may seem to be unproblematic in a large country model since, in the long run, plants of the most efficient scale (assuming such a scale exists – in other words, assuming that average costs do not fall indefinitely) can be replicated. This, unfortunately, leaves the large-country assumption taking the strain. The Periphery is not, in fact, one large economy and individual components of the Periphery may be too small fully to exploit economies of scale. As these economies grow, so returns increase. If 'the Periphery' is intended to represent this aggregation of individual countries then the assumption of constant returns is potentially restrictive.[1] The nature of the difficulty is, however, similar to that of exogenous technical progress, since both allow a reduction in input:output coefficients over time, and the matter will not be explicitly considered further.

In autarky, each country produces two commodities (1 and 2) by means of labour and the same two commodities. (Each commodity is thus 'basic' in the sense of Sraffa, 1960.[2]) In country $Z(Z = \mathrm{I}, \mathrm{II})$, $l_j^z$ is the input of labour into a unit of $j$ ($j = 1,2$); and $a_{ij}^z$ is the input of commodity $i$ into a unit of $j$. The wage is assumed to be paid at the end of the period, at a rate $w^z$, though nothing of substance hinges on the timing of the payment. Writing the price ratio as $p^z (= p_1^z / p_2^z)$, $r^z$ as the rate of profits, and expressing the wage in terms of good 2, then the price equations for the two processes are:

$$p^z = (1 + r^z)(p^z a_{11}^z + a_{21}^z) + w^z l_1^z \tag{1.1}$$
$$1 = (1 + r^z)(p^z a_{12}^z + a_{22}^z) + w^z l_2^z \tag{1.2}$$

Competition ensures the uniformity of $r^z$, $w^z$ and $p^z$ throughout the autarkic economy.

Since there is no risk of ambiguity in the present discussion, we shall drop the $z$ superscripts in the interests of simplicity. Equations (1.1) and (1.2) are easily solved to obtain a relationship between the wage rate and the rate of profits, henceforth referred to as the *w–r* frontier:

$$w = \frac{\det(\mathbf{I} - \mathbf{RA})}{(1 - Ra_{11})l_2 + l_1 a_{12} R} \tag{1.3}$$

where $R = 1 + r$, and

$$\mathbf{A} = \begin{bmatrix} a_{11} & a_{12} \\ a_{21} & a_{22} \end{bmatrix}$$

and $\mathbf{I}$ is the identity matrix. Similarly, the price ratio may be written as a function of $r$:

$$p = \frac{(1 - a_{22}R)l_1 + l_2 a_{21} R}{(1 - a_{11}R)l_2 + l_1 a_{12} R} \tag{1.4}$$

Differentiating (1.4) with respect to $R$ gives:

$$dp/dR \lesseqgtr 0 \text{ as } (pa_{11} + a_{21})/l_1 \lesseqgtr (pa_{12} + a_{22})/l_2 \tag{1.5}$$

The terms in parentheses are the values of commodity inputs into a unit of each process, and the denominators are the labour requirements per unit. When these capital:direct labour ratios are the same the processes have what Marx called 'equal organic compositions of capital'. In this case relative prices do not vary with $r$, but in general they do so, increasing or decreasing monotonically. By taking the second derivative of $w$ with respect to $R$ in (1.3), it can be shown that

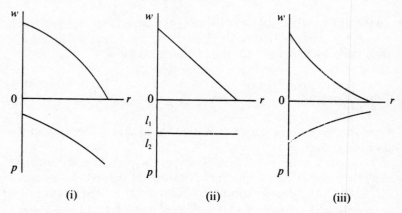

*Figure 1.1*

each of these possibilities is associated with a particular shape of the $w–r$ frontier. When $dp/dR > 0$, the $w–r$ frontier is concave to the origin; when $dp/dR = 0$, it is a straight line; and when $dp/dR < 0$ it is convex to the origin (Figure 1.1).

We define a 'technique' of an economy as a combination of processes that will satisfy the demands of the economy. In autarky, the technique must, of necessity, consist of the processes for producing both commodities – of necessity because in the no-trade economy any one activity is not sustainable on its own. But once the possibility of international trade is admitted it then becomes possible to have a single process supported by imported inputs of the other commodity. The possibility of trade thus presents two additional techniques, each consisting of a single process. The problem of technical choice is often presented by superimposing the $w–r$ frontiers of each technique to obtain an 'outer frontier'. Then, for a given value of $r$, say, the technique that is chosen under competitive conditions is the one which allows the maximum $w$, i.e., the one on the outer frontier. An intersection of frontiers on the outer frontier is known as a 'switchpoint'. At such a point the corresponding techniques are equally profitable. In order to approach the problem in this way it is necessary to derive the $w–r$ relations for the with-trade techniques. We continue to denote the frontier for the no-trade economy by $w–r$; the single-process 'trade-offs' representing possible with-trade techniques will be denoted by $(w–r)_1$ and $(w–r)_2$. For process 1, the trade-off is given by:

$$w = [p - R(pa_{11} + a_{21})]/l_1 \qquad (1.6)$$

a straight line of slope

$$-k_1 = -(pa_{11} + a_{21})/l_1$$

where $k_1$ is the capital:labour ratio in process 1. For process 2,

$$w = [1 - R(pa_{12} + a_{22})]/l_2 \qquad (1.7)$$

a straight line of slope

$$-k_2 = -(pa_{12} + a_{22})/l_2$$

As may be seen from Figure 1.1, movements along the $w$–$r$ frontier are, in general, accompanied by changes in relative prices. Since $p$, itself, is a function of $r$ it need not appear explicitly in the equation of the $w$–$r$ frontier, Equation (1.3). On the other hand, the $(w$–$r)_i$ trade-offs, Equations (1.6) and (1.7), are defined for specific values of $p$. Indeed, for each process there will be an infinity of trade-offs, each one corresponding to a different price ratio, and thus having a different slope from every other one. There are two important points to note:

1. From (1.5) it follows that $k_1 \gtreqless k_2$ as $dp/dR \gtreqless 0$.
2. The $(w$–$r)_i$ trade-offs 'bracket' the $w$–$r$ frontier in a particular manner.[3] Differentiating Equations (1.6) and (1.7) with respect to $R$ gives:

$$\frac{dw}{dR} = \frac{1}{l_1} \cdot (1 - a_{11}R)\frac{dp}{dR} - k_1$$

and

$$\frac{dw}{dR} = -k_2 - \frac{a_{12}}{l_2} \cdot \frac{dp}{dR} \cdot R$$

It follows that if $dp/dR > 0$, then $k_1 > -(dw/dR) > k_2$; and in general:

$$dp/dR > 0 \text{ when } k_1 > -(dw/dR) > k_2,$$

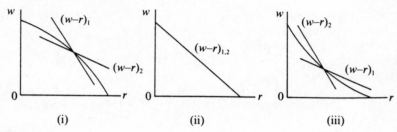

*Figure 1.2*

$$dp/dR = 0 \text{ when } k_1 = -(dw/dR) = k_2 \qquad (1.8)$$
$$dp/dR < 0 \text{ when } k_1 < -(dw/dR) < k_2$$

The possible configurations are shown in Figure 1.2. When $dp/dR \neq 0$, it can be seen from (1.6) and (1.7) that an increase in $p$ raises the (absolute) slope of both $(w-r)_i$ trade-offs; it also changes their vertical intercepts, raising that of $(w-r)_1$ and reducing that of $(w-r)_2$. Thus, excepting the singular case in which $dp/dR = 0$, no $(w-r)_i$ frontier drawn for a given value of $p$ will intersect the $(w-r)_i$ frontier drawn for some different value of $p$ (in the positive quadrant).

### 1.3   Consumption and growth
Continuing to dispense with the $z$ superscripts, write gross output per worker (p.w.) as $x_i$, total consumption (wages plus capitalist consumption) p.w. as $c_i$, and the uniform period-by-period rate of growth as $g$. Then under autarky:

$$x_1 = (1+g)(a_{11}x_1 + a_{12}x_2) + c_1 \qquad (1.9)$$
$$x_2 = (1+g)(a_{21}x_1 + a_{22}x_2) + c_2 \qquad (1.10)$$

Equation (1.9) says that the gross output of good 1 in any period must, in equilibrium, be such as to allow for the replacement of 1 as means of production at the existing levels of output, plus growth (net investment) at the rate $g$, plus consumption. The uniformity of $g$ reflects long-run steady growth. In the (assumed) absence of changes in the structure of demand this is an equilibrium requirement and implies constant relative prices; otherwise the faster growing sector will need to reduce its price if it is to balance supply with demand.[4] Since that reduces the profitability of the faster growing sector, it will attract less investment and its growth will be retarded.

Assuming for expositional simplicity that all consumption is in the form of commodity 2,[5] setting $c_1 = 0$ and solving Equations (1.9) and (1.10) for $c_2$ gives:

$$c(=c_2) = \frac{\det(\mathbf{I} - \mathbf{GA})}{(1 - Ga_{11})l_2 + l_1 a_{12}G} \tag{1.11}$$

where $c$ is consumption p.w. of good 2 (and hence the value of consumption p.w.), and $G = 1 + g$. Equation (1.11) is the mathematical dual of Equation (1.3): that is, the relationship described in Equation (1.3) between $w$ and $r$ is identical to the relationship in Equation (1.11) between $c$ and $g$.[6] This latter relationship will be referred to as the 'consumption-growth', or $c$–$g$ frontier. Thus the curves in Figures 1.1 and 1.2 which represent the economy's $w$–$r$ frontier in autarky can also be taken to represent its $c$–$g$ frontier.

The next step is to show that duality also applies to the $(w$–$r)_i$ and $(c$–$g)_i$ trade-offs for processes operated in isolation, a matter of relevance only to completely specialized international trade. To see how the $(c$–$g)_i$ frontier is constructed, consider process 2. In value terms, consumption p.w. is equal to gross output p.w. minus the value of inputs required for next period's production. Everything is in the form of good 2 except $a_{12}x_2$ which must be obtained from imports. It can be converted into an amount of good 2 through exchange at the ruling international price ratio, $p^T$; then, with balanced trade (and assuming no costs of international transport):

$$c = x_2 - G(p^T a_{12} x_2 + a_{22} x_2)$$

This is an expression relating consumption p.w. as a homogeneous physical quantity, and the rate of growth. This procedure is valid so long as one bundle of goods can be transformed into another bundle by means of exchange at a given price ratio. It is not valid (in general) in the incompletely specialized or no-trade economy where net output and consumption combinations are transformed according to a technical relationship. Since, for each process operated in isolation, $x_i = 1/l_i$, then:

$$c = [1 - G(p^T a_{12} + a_{22})]/l_2 \tag{1.12}$$

Similarly, for process 1,

$$c_1 = p^T x_1 - G(p^T a_{11} x_1 + a_{21} x_1)] l_1$$
$$= p^T - G(p^T a_{11} + a_{21})] / l_1 \qquad (1.13)$$

Comparison of Equations (1.12) and (1.13) with (1.6) and (1.7) shows that the $(c-g)_i$ and $(w-r)_i$ single-process trade-offs are identical under balanced trade.

## 1.4   Distributional closures

The $c-g$ relationships are completely independent of any assumptions concerning the financing of accumulation and, hence, concerning the source of savings. The same is therefore true of the duality between the $w-r$ and $c-g$ relationships. Even so, throughout most of this book we shall employ the simplifying assumption that all savings come from profits and that profits are received entirely by capitalists (the so-called 'classical' savings assumption).[7] Specifically, it is assumed that in country $Z$ capitalists save a fixed proportion $s^z (0 \leqslant s^z \leqslant 1)$ of their profits.

In the absence of government expenditure and taxation, and without overseas investment, domestic equilibrium in a balanced-trade regime requires that investment equals savings. Since savings are a proportion of profits and profits are what is left after this period's capital has been replaced (i.e., depreciation has been made good), the equilibrium condition, stated more precisely, is that savings from profits should equal net investment. If the present value of the capital stock is $K$, net investment, the growth in the value of capital stock from one period to the next, will equal $gK$. Profits on capital at the rate $r$ equal $rK$ and, if a proportion is saved, aggregate savings are $srK$. The equilibrium condition is thus:

$$gK = srK$$

or

$$g = sr \qquad (1.14)$$

(1.14) is the so-called 'Cambridge' growth equation; since $s$ is fixed it implies a proportional relationship between $g$ and $r$. Given this relationship, the dual $w-r$ and $c-g$ relations imply a relationship between $w$ and $c$. Since $s \leqslant 1$, $g$ can never exceed $r$ and (because the dual relations slope downwards) $w$ can never exceed $c$.

Equation (1.14) is an equilibrium condition (viewed *ex ante*, of course). It says nothing about how any of the four variables $r$, $g$, $w$ and $c$ is determined. It is in the determination of distribution that we shall locate the fundamental asymmetry between Centre and Periphery. In country I, the Centre, it is supposed that there is full employment of labour. Thus, in the absence of technological change, the long-run rates of growth of capital and output are determined by the growth rate of the labour force, exogenously fixed at $n^I$. With $g^I$ thus fixed, $s^I$ determines the rate of profits that is necessary to finance accumulation; $g^I$ and $r^I$ then determine $c^I$ and $w^I$, respectively. Although Equation (1.14) in itself does not imply a causative mechanism, a plausible out-of-equilibrium adjustment process can be sketched out. For example, should the wage rate be above its equilibrium value (and hence $r^I$ below equilibrium), the pace of accumulation will fall relative to the growth rate of the workforce. The resulting excess supply of labour will then put downward pressure on the wage rate. The process of convergence to equilibrium thus involves a supply–demand mechanism in the labour market and its stability may depend on assumptions which are not considered here but merely taken for granted.[8]

In country II, the Periphery, it is supposed that the supply of labour is perfectly elastic at some conventionally defined subsistence wage rate. This is true under any circumstances, which means that the growth rate of the labour force is greater than the growth rate of capital in either the autarky or the trade steady-state equilibrium. In this case the causative sequence is straightforward: $w^{II}$ determines $r^{II}$ which, in conjunction with $s^{II}$, determines $g^{II}$ and hence $c^{II}$. Here supply and demand conditions in the labour market do not need to operate indirectly via the accumulation rate.

Throughout, it will be assumed that under any circumstances the wage rate in I exceeds that in II.

## 1.5 International trade
We are now in a position to introduce trading possibilities between the two economies. Apart from a short digression in the next section our interest will be in the comparison of positions of long-run dynamic equilibrium. Since, in the free-trade regime, the world may be regarded as a unified, closed economy, this implies that the output of each good must grow at the same steady rate. If each country is fully specialized (which will be shown below to be a

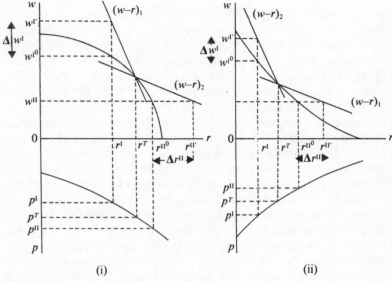

*Figure 1.3*

necessary outcome for steady growth) this, in turn, implies that each country grows at the same steady rate. This rate is dictated by the condition of full employment in the Centre. Since, for the purposes of comparison, $n^1$ and the $s^z$ are all taken to be the same as between the two regimes (autarky and trade), it follows that $g^1$ is also the same with and without trade, as is $r^1$. Long-run equilibrium thus implies, for each good:

$$g_1 = g_2 = g^w = g^1 \tag{1.15}$$

(where $g^w$ is the world average growth rate) and, in the case of complete specialization:

$$g^1 = g^{11} = g^w \tag{1.16}$$

So far as the Periphery (only) is concerned, $w^{11}$ is taken to be the same in both equilibria.

It is assumed that there are no impediments to trade in the form of transport costs or artificial trade barriers.

To begin, suppose that I and II have the same autarky technique, whose $w-r$ frontier is represented by the curve in Figure 1.3(i) (with

$dp/dR > 0$). Given $r^I$ and $w^{II}$, the implied autarky price ratios may be read off the $p$–$r$ function in the lower quadrant. Provided these price ratios are different, there will be an inducement to trade, the profitable direction of trade being indicated by the relation between the ratios. Here, since $p^I < p^{II}$, capitalists in I will be induced to export good 1 and import good 2 and capitalists in II to do the reverse. The precise determination of the international terms of trade (which, in the absence of impediments is the same for both countries) will be considered shortly. For now, suppose that it lies at some point strictly between $p^I$ and $p^{II}$. In this case it can be shown that specialisation will be complete.

This can be done by superimposing on the autarky $w$–$r$ frontier the $(w$–$r)_i$ trade-offs for each good, defined at prices $p^T$. These, we know, intersect the $w$–$r$ frontier at that $(w,r)$ combination for which $p = p^T$. This combination thus defines a switchpoint between the two trade-offs and the frontier. Moreover, when $dp/dR > 0$, $(w$–$r)_1$ has greater (absolute) slope than $(w$–$r)_2$. In effect, capitalists in each nation are now confronted with a choice of technique, each technique having its own $w$–$r$ relation. As is well known, the most profitable technique is the one whose $w$–$r$ relation is 'outermost', that is to say, for a given rate of profits, the one which pays the highest wage rate, or, for a given wage rate, the one returning the highest rate of profits. It is clear from Figure 1.3(i) that capitalists in I prefer the technique which consists only of process 1, so long as prices $p^T$ prevail, since it pays a wage rate which is higher than the two-process technique by an amount $\Delta w^I$. Capitalists who persisted with the production of good 2 would simply not be able to compete in the labour market and would go out of business. In country II it is equally apparent that, at the fixed wage rate $w^{II}$, those capitalists who concentrate entirely on the production of good 2 earn a higher rate of profits (by the amount $\Delta r^{II}$). Figure 1.3(ii) shows that when in autarky $dp/dR < 0$, the pattern of specialization is reversed. It is evident from Figure 1.2(ii) that when $dp/dR = 0$, then no matter how different the autarky profits rates, trade does not allow the attainment of a superior $w$–$r$ combination.

How precisely is $p^T$ determined? The exact value of the terms of trade follows directly from the condition for steady growth with specialized trade (1.16). When the economies are linked together through trade (but not through investment), the with-trade value of $r^{II}(= r^{II'})$ becomes determined by the savings-investment condition.

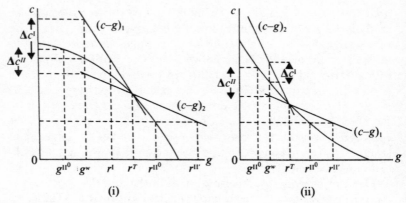

*Figure 1.4*

$$r^{II'} = g^w/s^{II} = (s^I/s^{II}) \, r^I \tag{1.17}$$

The with-trade price equations (one for each country) are thus left to solve for the two remaining unknowns, $w^{I'}$ and $p^T$. In terms of the geometry, $p^T$ must be such that (in Figure 1.3(i), for example) the position of the $(w-r)_2$ trade-off, in conjunction with the given value of $w^{II}$, allows the attainment of the value of $r^{II'}$ specified in (1.17). A lower value of $p^T$, representing more favourable terms of trade from the point of view of the Periphery would give rise to a more favourable $(w-r)_2$ trade-off and a higher rate of profits with trade. Given the Periphery's savings rate this would generate too high a rate of accumulation and a disproportionate growth of good 2. Some implications of non-equilibrium outcomes are briefly considered in the following section in conjunction with the analysis of incomplete specialization.

Although it has been shown that specialized trade is more profitable than autarky, it does not follow that levels of consumption p.w. are higher in the free-trade equilibrium than they are without trade. The comparative effects on consumption p.w. are illustrated in Figure 1.4 which exploits the duality properties of the $w-r$ and $c-g$ relations. (The lower quadrants are the same as in Figure 1.3 and are not reproduced here.)

Consider Figure 1.4(i) (where $dp/dR > 0$). In I the growth rate is the same in each regime so that the change in consumption p.w., $\Delta c^I$, can be obtained by comparing the vertical heights of the relevant c-g

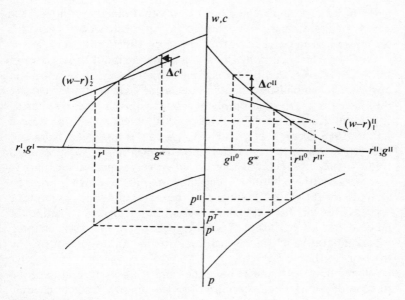

*Figure 1.5*

relations at $g^w$. In the case shown, it is clear that $\Delta c^I > 0$ and, moreover, that it exceeds $\Delta w^I$. It follows that capitalist consumption p.w. must be higher with trade. In the case of II the growth rate will be higher with trade ($g^w > g^{II0}$). Nevertheless, since $g^w < r^I < r^T$, the $(c-g)_2$ trade-off lies below the $c–g$ frontier at $g^{II0}$ and, since it is downward sloping, with-trade consumption p.w. at $g^w$ must be less than no-trade consumption p.w. at $g^{II0}$: $\Delta c^{II} < 0$. With a constant wage rate, the reduction is borne entirely by capitalists. The reverse specialization (Figure 1.4(ii)) can be similarly interpreted.

So far, it has been assumed that the two countries share the same autarky technique. Trade between countries with different techniques can be represented in the back-to-back diagram of Figure 1.5. On the left are the $w–r$, $c–g$ and $p–r$ functions for I; on the right those for II. As is apparent from the diagram, once autarky techniques are allowed to differ, there is no difficulty in constructing examples in which both countries have lower levels of consumption p.w. with trade. It is equally easy to construct examples in which with-trade consumption p.w. is higher in both countries. In neither case is it necessary that $dp/dR$ take different signs in I and II. But there is nevertheless a sense in which one can say that the 'more similar' the autarky techniques, the more difficult is it to construct cases in which the consumption outcomes are in the same direction.

We finish this section by briefly restating the main conclusions of the analysis so far and by adding one further result. It is important, however, to emphasize that the conclusions are tentative because they have been arrived at simply by comparing outcomes on alternative equilibrium paths. This gives an incomplete picture because it fails to take account of what happens in the transition from one equilibrium to another. A transition from autarky to specialized trade (or *vice versa*) could, in principle, be very short, taking place in one or two periods. On the other hand, as will be shown in the next section, the new steady state may be reached by an asymptotic process. But whether a transition is short or long its effects cannot be ignored and a fuller account will be given in the following chapter. The comparative effects nevertheless provide an important part of the story in their own right.

When countries I and II have the same autarky technique, comparison of autarky and specialized-trade equilibria leads to clearcut conclusions concerning differences in wage rates, profit rates, consumption p.w., and growth rates. With $w^{II}$ given, trade will always imply a higher rate of profits in II; and, with $r^I$ given, a higher wage rate in I. With the $s^z$ given it also follows that the rate of growth will be higher in II but the same in I. Consumption p.w. will be greater with trade for country I, lower for country II. Welfare benefits are unambiguously positive for the Centre; less so for the Periphery. Here, the negative effects are borne entirely by the capitalists, who suffer the entire reduction in consumption p.w., while workers as a whole benefit from a faster rate of employment growth. Where autarky techniques differ, the conclusions relating to consumption differences may fail to hold.

The comparative consequences of technical progress are discussed in 1.7, but one further comparative result can be considered here. Up to now it has been assumed that $s^{II}$ is given. It would be understandable if, in the interests of raising the rate of growth, Peripheral governments were to encourage capitalists to save more. Within the context of this model it is clear that such a policy could not succeed because the with-trade equilibrium growth rate in the Periphery is determined by the rate of labour force growth in the Centre. Increasing the savings rate would thus necessitate a reduction in the rate of profits, in turn implying a deterioration in the terms of trade. Since this would reduce consumption p.w. without increasing the growth rate, its comparative effects are wholly negative.

## 1.6 Incomplete specialization

Equation (1.17) provides the link between the global steady growth requirement and the terms of trade. Complete specialization requires that the value of $r^{II'}$ determined by Equation (1.17) be such that $p^T$ lie between $p^I$ and $p^{II}$. But with $g^w$ given (by $g^I$) the value of $r^{II'}$ depends only on $s^{II}$ which itself may lie anywhere in the open range $(0,1)$. In principle, therefore, the value of $r^{II'}$ which satisfies Equation (1.17) could be such as to imply a value of $p^T$ lying outside the closed range $[p^I, p^{II}]$.[9] For example, in Figure 1.3(i), a very low value of $s^{II}$ (and hence a high value of $r^{II'}$) would require $p^T > p^{II}$, in which case II-capitalists would not specialize. Yet, in either case, a return to autarky must also be ruled out since different autarky prices will always provide an inducement to trade so long as there are no impediments to trade.

A value of $p^T$ lying outside $[p^I, p^{II}]$ implies that capitalists in both countries would want to export the same good, an outcome which clearly cannot be sustained. The only remaining possibility is that trade takes place at the autarky price ratio of one of the countries and that that country is incompletely specialized. If this happens it may be necessary to dispense with global steady growth as can be seen by considering further the case already discussed. We know that a low value of $s^{II}$ will thwart the satisfaction of Equation (1.16): country II cannot 'keep up' with the production of good 2. On the face of it, however, the more general condition (1.15) appears to be satisfied if I were to produce a proportion (increasing over time) of II's export good. This is the outcome depicted in Figure 1.6(i) where I remains incompletely specialized at its autarky price ratio. But steady growth is not possible. In I, the growth rate of 2-output will have to be faster than the growth rate of 1-output in order to make up for the sluggishness of II's contribution. Yet, so long as II is making a contribution the world growth rate will be a weighted average of $g^I$ and $g^{II}$ and, therefore, necessarily greater than $g^{II}$. That being so, over time I's economy becomes proportionately larger and the weights which determine $g^w$ shift progressively in favour of $g^I$. Thus $g^w \to g^I$; in other words, I's economy tends, in the limit, to complete dominance of the world economy.[10]

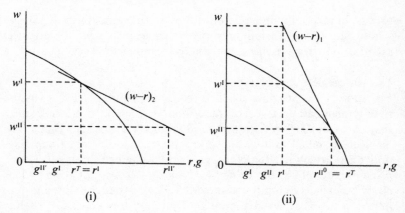

*Figure 1.6*

If $g^w$ is rising over time then we no longer have steady growth. Instead, we have an infinite sequence of period-by-period transitions from one form of global productive organization to another with higher investment requirements. These additional investment needs must be accommodated by drawing more heavily on the net outputs of the previous period. But with given consumption proportions,[11] the amounts available for additions to net investment will not normally be in the proportions required for steady growth. Thus, as a general rule the output of one commodity will grow faster than that of the other. Given the rate of growth in II, the necessary adjustment will have to be made through changes in the composition of output in I.

Figure 1.6(ii) illustrates the case where country II is incompletely specialized. This is the consequence of a relatively high $s^{II}$ leading to $g^{II} > g^I$. In this case country II will come to dominate the world economy.

One issue may still require clarification. Why should the incompletely specialized economy continue to trade if it cannot obtain a superior $(w,r)$ combination compared to autarky? It has already been noted that a return to autarky would recreate an inducement to trade by restoring the divergence of international prices. Indeed, starting from a position of incomplete specialization in I, say (as in Figure 1.6(i)), a move toward self-sufficiency, replacing imports of good 2 by domestic production, would temporarily increase that abundance of good 2, lowering its price and pushing down the $(w–r)_2$

trade-off. This would encourage a retreat from 2-production. The production of both goods in one of the economies is thus in the nature of a competitive equilibrium. It is the only self-sustaining outcome whenever $s^{II}$ is too low or too high to allow completely specialized trade. But it is not a steady-state equilibrium.

## 1.7 The effects of technical progress
For our purposes, technical progress may be thought of as the innovation of a new process, or the improvement of an existing one, that leads to an outward movement of the 'outer' $w-r$ frontier in the neighbourhood of the prevailing $(w,r)$ combination. Technical progress thus increases system profitability in the sense of allowing an increase in $w$ without a fall in $r$, or *vice versa*, or an increase in both. At this level of abstraction and aggregation there exists no satisfactory theory of technical progress and no attempt is made to offer one here, the intention being simply to analyse the consequences of exogenously determined technical progress. (In Chapter 9 technical progress is endogenized by relating it to the scarcity of labour in the Centre.) To begin we follow the conventional procedure of supposing that technology progresses at some 'neutral' rate, whereby particular production coefficients fall over time at a constant rate. For the sake of simplicity formal discussion is confined to the case of direct savings in labour. Technical progress thus proceeds in a globally Harrod-neutral manner implying continuous and uniform reduction of the $l_i$ coefficients. This is formally equivalent (in its effect on outputs) to an additional growth of the labour force. That is, if $n$ is the rate of growth in the number of workers and $q$ is the rate of technical progress (productivity growth), then $n+q$ is the rate of growth of labour capacity in efficiency units.

To begin, suppose that the countries have the same autarky technique. Differences in techniques and different rates of technical progress can easily be considered subsequently.

From Equation (1.3) it can be seen that a uniform reduction in the $l_i$ has the effect of raising autarky $w$ in proportion, at any rate of profits. This means that the $w-r$ frontier shifts upwards each period by a constant proportion. The maximum value of $r$ (corresponding to $w=0$) remains the same because, when wages are zero, labour-saving technical progress has no beneficial effect on profitability. From Equation (1.4) it can be seen that proportionate changes in the $l_i$ leave $p$ unaffected for a given level of $r$. Then, taking some value of

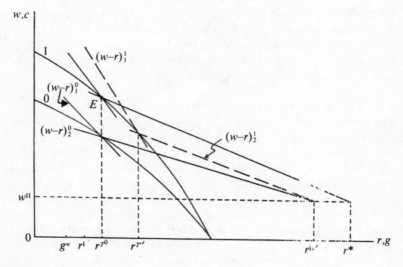

*Figure 1.7*

$r$ (and hence of $p$), consider the $(w-r)_i$ trade-offs which intersect the $w-r$ frontier at that level of $r$. From Equations (1.6) and (1.7) it is seen that the slopes and the vertical and horizontal intercepts of the trade-offs all increase as the labour coefficients fall. With these changes in mind it is possible to see the implications of globally Harrod-neutral technical progress for trading equilibrium.

In Figure 1.7 (where $dp/dR > 0$), the curves marked 0 and 1 represent the $w-r$ frontier in successive periods; $r^{T0}$ corresponds to $p^{T0}$, the terms of trade in period 0; $(w-r)_i^0$ are the trade-offs corresponding to these prices as they appear in period 0. If $p^{T0}$ is an equilibrium price ratio, the $(w-r)_2^0$ trade-off allows the Periphery to attain a rate of profits $r^{II0}$ such that equation (1.17) is satisfied and in which

$$g^w = g^{I} = n^{I} + q \tag{1.18}$$

It can now be seen that the terms of trade in period 0 cannot be the equilibrium prices of period 1. The $(w-r)_i$ trade-offs at these prices in period 1 intersect the $w-r$ frontier for that period at point $E$, corresponding to $r^{T0}$, and are indicated by continuous straight lines. If $p^{T0}$ were sustained the $(w-r)_2$ trade-off would allow the Periphery to reach a higher rate of profits ($r^*$) and thus to 'over-accumulate'. This is rectified by a deterioration in its terms of trade: an increase in $p$ to $p^{T^1}$ (corresponding to $r^{T^1}$). These new prices define the trade-offs ($w$–$r$)$_i^1$ indicated by the dashed lines. Note that the extent of deterioration necessary to bring about equilibrium depends on $w^{II}$. If $w^{II} = 0$, then $r^{II^0} = r^*$ and no deterioration would be necessary.[12]

The diagram illustrates changes occurring from one period to the next. The same qualitative behaviour occurs in all periods so long as technical progress is taking place. There is thus a continuous deterioration in the terms of trade of the Periphery. This does not mean that the Periphery fails to benefit from productivity growth: ($w$–$r$)$_2^1$ lies above ($w$–$r$)$_2^0$ in the relevant range.[13] Technical progress does not affect the duality properties of the model and so, at the growth rate given by (1.18), the Periphery experiences increasing consumption p.w. over time. Nevertheless, consumption p.w. would have risen faster had it not been for the terms of trade change. In the Centre, the benefits from productivity growth are compounded by the improvement in the terms of trade. The gains from technical progress are thus unequally divided. The intuitive explanation for this outcome is that the saving of labour is more beneficial to the economy in which labour is scarce. The Periphery doesn't benefit as much as it would have were labour fully employed because with surplus labour its excessive tendency to accumulate is not choked off by rising domestic wages (and thus 'internalized') but has to be restrained by a deterioration in the terms of trade. The consequence is similar to that of an increase in the savings rate, except that here it is only partially self-defeating: the growth in productivity does have some impact. It goes without saying that compared to a world with zero technical progress, $q > 0$ implies a corresponding reduction in the rate of growth of Peripheral employment.

This analysis is readily adapted to allow for a difference in autarky techniques and for different rates of progress in Centre and Periphery. In the case of different techniques the outcome is not affected in any essential way. In Figure 1.7 we could simply imagine that the $w$–$r$ frontiers shown apply only to the Periphery. In period 0 the Periphery trades at $p^{T^0}$, specializing in good 2. The relevant ($w$–$r$)$_1$ trade-offs now belong to another quadrant (as in Figure 1.5), but since $g^w$ is independent of I's technique the previous argument holds without modification.

The consequences of different rates of progress can be illustrated by supposing that $q^I > 0$ but $q^{II} = 0$. In Figure 1.7 the $w–r$ frontier for the Periphery remains fixed at, say, position 0, whereas that for the Centre moves outwards. One might suppose that after a period of steady growth with technical progress, the Centre's frontier would be a long way from that of the Periphery, but a shift from 0 to 1 will nevertheless illustrate the basic principles. In this case there is no deterioration in the Peripheral terms of trade because, without domestic technical progress, $r^{II}$ has no tendency to increase. But the $(w–r)_1$ trade-off does rise (as indicated by the steeper line through $E$) and all the benefits of I's technical progress are reaped by workers in that country. International trade does not transmit any of the Centre's productivity gains to the Periphery. Nor does $q^I > q^{II}$ imply a divergence in the size of the economies. Where $q^I > q^{II} > 0$, the outcome lies between that just described and that in which rates of progress are equal. By repeating the analysis for $q^I = 0$ and $q^{II} > 0$ it is easily seen that the Periphery's productivity gains do benefit the Centre via the terms-of-trade effect.

In the case of savings on commodity inputs, conclusions are less clearcut, even if the savings are uniform. Indeed, it is easier analytically to consider the case in which savings are so distributed among the input coefficients as to maintain a constant price ratio at $r^{T0}$. The main departures from Figure 1.7 are then that (i) the $w–r$ frontier moves outwards in all directions, and (ii) the $(w–r)_i$ trade-offs at constant prices become flatter, as input coefficients fall. In this case the necessary deterioration in the Periphery's terms of trade leads to immiserization in the sense that the $(w–r)_2^1$ trade-off will lie below the $(w–r)_2^0$ trade-off for $r < r^{II0}$. On the other hand, employment continues to grow at the same rate as capital and output.

Finally it is worth noting that inequality of gains from technical progress does not arise where the Centre is unable to specialize fully because of the slow growth rate of the Periphery. In this case there is scope for the Periphery to increase its rate of accumulation without damaging its terms of trade. With Centre gains going to enhanced consumption, global technical progress is a means by which the Periphery can catch up with the Centre's growth rate.

## 1.8   Concluding remarks

It is worth emphasizing that some important results in this chapter have been derived by use of a very particular methodology, that of comparing steady-growth equilibrium paths. This method does provide useful insights. Even so, it paints only part of the picture. If countries have a choice between free trade and autarky or, more realistically, between more trade and less trade, then the consequences of going from one state to the other must be assessed by examining the whole history of the switch, including the path of transition. A fuller analysis of the 'gain from trade' will be conducted in the next chapter.

Throughout this chapter it has been assumed that Centre and Periphery behave as single unified entities. If both economies are 'large' neither is able to take the terms of trade as given. Instead, the long-run terms of trade are defined by the need for balanced Centre–Periphery trade at a common growth rate. But Centre and Periphery are both aggregations and many of their component economies may be regarded as 'small' in the conventional sense that the participation in trade by any one has an insignificant effect on world prices. An alternative analytical approach would be to regard each of the economies as small. They could still be considered as representative of Centre and Periphery if the rate of profits were exogenous in one and the wage rate in the other. There is, however, a difficulty in following this approach if the analysis is confined to steady-state comparisons.

On the face of it, the implications of smallness appear straightforward. First, the comparative gain from trade (in per-worker terms) is likely to be greater because the additional supply of goods on to the world market does not depress the terms of trade. Second, and as a consequence, the small economy is not confined to growing at the pace of the world as a whole since faster growth is no longer penalized by deteriorating terms of trade. But this is where the difficulty arises. A small economy growing more rapidly than the average rate will sooner or later become a large economy. Allowing an excessive growth rate, even for an initially small economy, effectively runs counter to the methodology of steady-growth equilibrium. The development of the small economy should really be seen in terms of a (very long) transition to a steady state. It would, though, be excessively pedantic to insist that a comparative analysis could not be used to shed some light on the shorter-term outcomes for small economies. (In Chapter 3, the analysis of trade in fixed capital explicitly focuses on a small Peripheral economy.)

Once the composite nature of the Periphery is recognized, the policy implications of the analysis become immediately confused.

Thus, the expansion of one economy in isolation may be deemed a sensible policy from the point of view of that economy. But a collective expansion which undermines the Peripheral terms of trade might prove self-defeating. The problem of strategic interdependence calls for a collusive approach to relations with the Centre so as to prevent the fragmentation of monopoly power: a clearly defined area for South–South cooperation.

## Notes

1. The representation of many small economies by one large 'region' is also problematic in the consideration of policy. This will be discussed further in 1.8.
2. For an introduction to the Sraffa system and the Sraffa–Leontief growth model, see Mainwaring (1984).
3. The $w–r$ frontier can be considered as the locus of the $(w–r)_i$ intersections. From Equations (1.1) and (1.2) can be obtained expressions for relative prices. These are simply re-arrangements of the $(w–r)_i$ expressions; equating and solving for $w$ yields Equation (1.3).
4. If there is no substitutability in final demand a commodity subject to persistently faster growth will become a 'free good', as in the von Neumann model.
5. The assumption can be relaxed considerably. All that is required is that the proportions in which the two commodities enter the wage are the same as the proportions in which they enter capitalist consumption. This ensures that the wage and consumption p.w. can be measured in terms of the same commodity bundle. Restrictions on capitalist consumption can be removed entirely without substantially affecting conclusions but at the cost of considerable complexity.
6. This is a well-known result in modern capital theory; see, for example, Bruno (1969).
7. The present model of international trade has been generalized to incorporate workers' savings, by Chang and Chiang (1986). This leads to a much greater variety of outcomes in terms of the relationship between patterns of specialization and autarky distribution.
8. It may also take a cyclical path. This possibility is explicitly considered in the context of international investment, in Chapter 6.
9. There are also technical reasons why specialization may fail: if one country is very small relative to the other, it may not be able to provide all the inputs required for specialized production in the larger country. This issue is discussed in the following chapter.
10. Dominance here is to be understood in the relative sense. II's economy is growing but its proportionate contribution to the world economy tends towards zero. The dynamics of relative dominance are analysed more fully in the case of international investment, in Chapter 4.

    Unlike the case of complete specialization where attempts to raise $s^{II}$ were self-defeating, here it is possible to raise the Peripheral growth rate without giving rise to a negative effect on the terms of trade.
11. For ease of exposition it has been assumed above that only one commodity is consumed. In this case a sequence of transitions of the type discussed here will be impossible (see 2.2). However, nothing in this chapter hinges on this assumption. (See footnote 5.)

    Note also that even if world relative consumption demands are a function of relative price, the latter is fixed and so, therefore are the former.

12. Changing prices do create a problem for this analysis which means that the conclusions reached need to be treated with a little caution. The problem is that under these circumstances the growth of capital stocks in physical terms is no longer equal to growth in value terms. If the physical growth rate in I is $\gamma^I$ then (1.18) should read $\gamma^I = n^I + q$.[1] Increasing $p$ leads to continuous upward revaluation of capital stocks so that $g^I > \gamma^I$. Full-employment growth in the Centre will require that savings out of profits in both regions (and hence the precise rates of profits in both regions) be such as to maintain physical capital growth at the rate $\gamma^I$.

13. This follows because both the horizontal intercept and the slope of $(w-r)_2^1$ are less than those of the $(w-r)$ frontier passing through $E$, whereas the horizontal intercept of $(w-r)_2^0$ is the same as that of the frontier passing through $E$.

# 2 The transition from autarky to trade

## 2.1 Introduction

This chapter is concerned with the nature and implications of a transition from one global regime to another. This represents a significant and necessary extension of the analysis of Chapter 1. Even so, it is important to recognize at the outset that the resulting theory still has limited descriptive value.

Its limitations are those of all orthodox trade theories. The essence of international trade theory, from Ricardo to the present day, has been to try to explain the pattern of trade on the basis of the inherent characteristics of the non-trading economies. The problem with this approach, which is common to neoclassical and classical economics, is that it neglects history entirely in favour of a purely logical, mechanical and generally unidirectional explanation of trade patterns. Countries are first depicted in their pure autarky states and then free trade is allowed to enter into the picture, the lack of further qualification implying in the reader's mind a *historical* transition from one state to another. There is, though, little doubt that many of the characteristics which are considered relevant to the description of the autarky state never existed *in vacuo* but, by the time of the Industrial Revolution and the development of capitalism, were themselves conditioned by a history of colonial external economic relations. Very few of the countries at the centre of the modern capitalist world can have begun the era of capitalist international exchange in a state of near autarky.

In his classic, yet nevertheless neglected, critique of the conventional methodology, J. H. Williams (1929) cites the example of 'England' (meaning 'Britain'):

> England provides us today with the best illustration of the ultimate logical effects of international trade upon national economic organisation. Through specialisation in production for world markets, fostered by export of capital and labour from early colonial times down to the war of 1914, and by a free trade policy, she has been able to concentrate capital and labour on a small amount of land in 'increasing returns' industries, and to buy the products of 'increasing cost' industries, from abroad. By such specialisation she has achieved, of course, enormous

*40*

advantages of territorial division of labour; but in so doing *she has no less clearly committed herself to a particular organisation of her productive effort*. International trade is her *raison d'être* (p. 204, emphasis added).

Then, in a critique of J. S. Mill's *Principles of Political Economy* Williams draws attention to the limitations of a comparative statics methodology or, as he calls it 'cross-section value analysis'. Mill, says Williams,

> failed to see the relation of international trade to national economic development, spread over time. For him the problem was one of cross-section value analysis upon particular assumptions about mobility of factors. He failed to see that England's capital and labour were *products* (results) of international trade itself, but for which they would not have existed in any comparable degree (p. 205, original emphasis).

There is a great deal to be said in favour of Williams's viewpoint. At the present level of abstraction one is strongly inclined to argue that the two overriding determinants of national economic characteristics are historical and geographical: in the first case, technological and capital bases and social framework; in the second, the global distribution of natural resources. This is why, in the analysis of international investment in Part II, the basic pattern of specialization is initially taken as given: a pattern which, in broad outline, could be regarded as that inherited by post-colonial capitalism from an earlier period. Any subsequent changes to that basic pattern will be seen to be the result of a historically recognizable process.

It would however, be foolish to abandon the orthodox method entirely. Trade patterns do change as certain characteristics of the trading partners change, or are made to change as a matter of policy. Theoretical analysis can be used to determine the consequences of change and to judge the effectiveness of policies. Despite its descriptive deficiencies the theory may still have useful prescriptive content. But there do remain important matters of interpretation. It is, for example, unusual for countries to go, in relatively short periods, from a pure autarky regime to a free-trade regime, or *vice versa*. On the whole, changes which do take place are in the nature of greater or lesser degrees of openness. A larger multi-country, multi-commodity analysis is needed to deal fully with these more subtle changes. Such analyses may be possible but they are avoided here in the belief that consideration of wholesale changes of regime in a relatively simple model provide a basis for inferring the direction of the effects of smaller-scale changes in a complex world.

We begin by looking briefly at the structural mechanics of transition; that is, the way in which an economy's sectoral composition can be changed while maintaining the intersectoral consistency of quantities implied by the technology matrix. A particular problem will arise where the two autarky economies are of such different sizes that a speedy transition to a free-trade steady state is not possible. This eventuality will be considered in 2.3. In 2.4–2.7 the welfare effects of trade are examined in some detail by comparing a continuous autarky path with one involving a transition from autarky to free trade.

## 2.2   Transitional mechanics

The first significant analysis of the transition between techniques in a multi-sector model is that of Solow (1967). Two important adaptations are necessary in order to apply Solow's analysis to international trade. The first, and most obvious, is that transition now requires the coordinated changes of two, or more, economies.[1] The second is that, unlike the case discussed by Solow, the transition need not occur at a switchpoint: indeed at least one of the economies must be involved in a non-switchpoint change. The second adaptation need not bother us here though we shall return to it in 2.5. This section is concerned merely with the problem of maintaining intersectoral consistency during the period of transition and for this Solow's argument can easily be modified to the two-economy context.

The potential complications that can arise out of an analysis of transitions are endless and so, in order to get a feel for the process, some brutal simplifications will be employed (not all of which are necessary to the subsequent analysis). We begin by examining the case in which two independent autarkic economies adjust to a fully specialized free-trade equilibrium in the space of a single production period. Specifying the conditions necessary for such a straightforward transition will throw into relief the kinds of problem that are likely to arise in more realistic circumstances.

Consider one economy. (The $Z = $ I, II superscripts will be avoided wherever possible.) The intersectoral quantity relations in autarky may be written in matrix notation as:

$$\bar{\mathbf{X}} = \mathbf{A}\bar{\mathbf{X}}(1 + \bar{g}) + \bar{\mathbf{Y}} \tag{2.1}$$

Here $\bar{\mathbf{X}}$ and $\bar{\mathbf{Y}}$ are the vectors of gross and net outputs, respectively. (The 'bar' indicates autarky: capital letters refer to total, as opposed to per-worker, magnitudes.) In autarky, the net output vector is necessarily the same as the vector of consumption quantities. Equation (2.1) is therefore a compact version of Equations (1.9) and (1.10).

It may be supposed that the outputs in Equation (2.1) are those in existence at the end of period 0. If, instead, a trading equilibrium had already been established and in period 0 was employing the same amount of labour as the autarky system (an assumption to be reconsidered shortly), the corresponding equation would be:

$$\mathbf{X} = \mathbf{A}\mathbf{X}(1+g) + \mathbf{Y} \tag{2.2}$$

On this path, period $-1$ inputs would be $\mathbf{A}\mathbf{X}(1+g)$. If there is to be a single-period transition from autarky to trade these inputs must be obtainable from the gross outputs of the autarky economy. At this point it becomes necessary to look at the matter from a global perspective. Taking the economies together the structural adjustment requires that:

$$\bar{\mathbf{X}}^{\mathrm{I}} + \bar{\mathbf{X}}^{\mathrm{II}} \geqslant (\mathbf{A}^{\mathrm{I}}\mathbf{X}^{\mathrm{I}} + \mathbf{A}^{\mathrm{II}}\mathbf{X}^{\mathrm{II}})(1+g) \tag{2.3}$$

For this to be possible the full weight of adjustment is borne, in just one period, by changes in the world consumption vector.

For one of the economies, net output available at the end of period 0 when a transition occurs is:

$$\tilde{\mathbf{Y}} = \bar{\mathbf{X}} - \mathbf{A}\mathbf{X}(1+g) \tag{2.4}$$

and the global consumption vector is $\tilde{\mathbf{Y}}^w = \tilde{\mathbf{Y}}^{\mathrm{I}} + \tilde{\mathbf{Y}}^{\mathrm{II}}$. Equation (2.3) implies that no single element of $\tilde{\mathbf{Y}}^w$ can be negative. There must, in other words, be sufficient 'slack' available in each element of the net output vector to allow the necessary quantitative adjustment in the means of production.

Although the net output and consumption vectors in the separate economies are necessarily the same in autarky, balanced trade at long-run equilibrium prices, $\mathbf{p} = [p_1, 1]$, requires only that:

$$\mathbf{p}\mathbf{Y} = C$$

(where $C$ is the *value* of consumption). Similarly, balanced trade during the transition implies:

$$\tilde{\mathbf{p}}\tilde{\mathbf{Y}} = \tilde{\mathbf{C}}$$

($\tilde{\mathbf{p}}$ ruling at the end of period 0).

The value of $\mathbf{p}$ must be consistent with supply and demand. In general this will be a complex matter, but it can be simplified by supposing that world relative consumption demands are a direct function of the price ratio.[2] Then the terms of trade must be such that consumption demands are equal to consumption supplies:

$$\mathbf{Y}^w = \mathbf{Y}^w(\mathbf{p}) \tag{2.5}$$

If the levels of employment are predetermined, $\mathbf{Y}^w$ follows directly from $\mathbf{Y}^I + \mathbf{Y}^{II}$ in Equation (2.2); Equation (2.5) then determines $\mathbf{p}$. This way of looking at the matter is, however, inconsistent with the analysis of Chapter 1. For the existence of surplus labour in the Periphery gives a degree of freedom to the determination of employment and hence the magnitude of $\mathbf{Y}^{II}$. In this case the direction of causation in Equation (2.5) is reversed. The equilibrium terms of trade are determined, as in the previous chapter, by the need to sustain those rates of profits which, given the $s^z$, imply steady uniform growth. (With $r^I$ given and $r^{II}$ determined by Equation (1.17), the two price equations, (1.1) in I and (1.2) in II, are left to determine $w^I$ and $\mathbf{p}$.) Equation (2.5) then determines $\mathbf{Y}^{II}$ and hence Peripheral employment.

The principles by which the free-trade steady-state terms of trade are detemined do not, however, apply to the determination of price in the transitional period. For this period $r^I$ is no longer given since it is not the product of steady growth (*via* the equation $n^I = s^I r^I$). The savings–investment conditions in the transition are given by:

$$\tilde{\mathbf{p}}(1+g)\mathbf{A}^z\mathbf{X}^z = \tilde{\mathbf{p}}(1+s^z r^z)\mathbf{A}^z\bar{\mathbf{X}}^z \tag{2.6}$$

The price ratio and the two rates of profits are then determined jointly by the two equations (2.6) and the net output supply–demand equation:

$$\tilde{\mathbf{Y}}^w = \tilde{\mathbf{Y}}^w(\tilde{\mathbf{p}})$$

where the $\tilde{\mathbf{Y}}^z$ are themselves determined from Equation (2.4) given the need to attain the steady-growth path by period 1. In general, there is no reason why $\tilde{\mathbf{p}}$ and $\mathbf{p}$ should be the same.

This account of an unimpeded single-period transition raises many questions, only a few of which will be discussed here.

First, what happens if there is not enough slack in current consumption to allow the needed adjustments in the means of production? Even if $\tilde{Y}^w \geqslant 0$ is attainable it could still be that consumption of one of the commodities becomes so low that the workforce cannot be sustained. (Imagine that one of the commodities is a non-food good and the other is corn. If almost all of the last year's corn net output is taken for means of production it will be impossible to feed the workers needed to effect the transition.) This problem is easily overcome (at least, in principle) by undertaking a slower transition so that the adjustment burden which is thrown on consumption is spread over time. In each period the economy can be depicted as a weighted average of Equations (2.1) and (2.2), the weight on (2.1) gradually shifting from unity to zero (*see* Solow, 1967). Much more problematic is the case in which transition implies increased requirements of some commodity whose entry in the autarky net output vector is zero. A possible response to this difficulty would be to employ, during the transitional stage, a different method of production (for example, one using a substitute for the scarce input). The method would be abandoned, perhaps gradually, as the necessary structural transition became effected. If no alternative technique were available to accomplish this then it might be necessary either to undergo a period of non-steady growth or to reduce the scale of the free-trade economy, the maximum scale being dictated by the availability of the scarcest input.[3] This leads into the enormous question of how a decentralized economy accomplishes a structural change of this sort. No completely satisfactory answers to this question are available and none will be attempted here.[4]

The final point concerns the relative magnitudes of the two economies and the duration of the transitional process. The one-period transition discussed above takes the world directly to a net output vector at which the balance of supplies and demands yields terms of trade consistent with steady growth. This, again, is a tremendously simplified view of a potentially complex process. If the autarky level of employment in the Periphery is a long way from its free-trade steady-growth level then the transition is going to have to take a much longer time and specialized trade will not be a short-run possibility. This case is discussed in more depth in the following section.

## 2.3  Physical limits to specialization

In Chapter 1 it was seen that fully specialized trade may not always be possible. This issue can be given a general treatment taking Equation (2.2) as a starting point. For simplicity of exposition suppose that the two countries have the same autarky technique and that in autarky $p^I < p^{II}$ so that the tendency would be for I to specialize in good 1. With full specialization the only positive component of I's gross output vector would be $\mathbf{X}^I_1$ which would be equal to total employment divided by the labour coefficient in process 1:

$$\mathbf{X}^I_1 = L^I/l_1$$

In terms of the requirements for means of production, (2.2) then implies that specialization is possible if[5]

$$(L^I/l_1)[1 - a_{11}(1 + g^I)] \geqslant (L^{II}/l_2)(1 + g^{II})a_{12}$$

and

$$(L^{II}/l_2)[1 - a_{22}(1 + g^{II})] \geqslant (L^I/l_1)(1 + g^I)a_{21}$$

The first inequality says that outputs of good 1 (in I) which remain after replacement and net investment in 1–production are sufficient to provide for replacement and net investment needs in 2–production (in II). The second inequality is similarly interpreted. These are, of course, necessary conditions for complete specialization but they may not be sufficient because they take no account of constraints on consumption. Writing $G^z = (1 + g^z)$, they can be compactly combined into the double inequality

$$(1 - a_{22}G^{II})/a_{21} \geqslant l_2 L^I/l_1 L^{II} \geqslant (1 - a_{11}G^I)/a_{12} \qquad (2.7)$$

Condition (2.7) is of general applicability. The problem discussed in Chapter 1 represents a failure of the condition because any terms of trade lying strictly between the autarky price ratios, together with a sufficiently low value of $s^{II}$, yields too slow a rate of growth in II. As a result the middle term in Equation (2.7) gets bigger over time and eventually the left-hand inequality becomes violated.

Equation (2.7) is also of relevance to the discussion of transitions because a problem arises, as was noted at the end of the last section, if there is a marked difference in the sizes of the autarky economies. Suppose, for example, that in period 0 output in the Periphery is very much smaller than that in the Centre. Capital transfers are ruled out by assumption. Then even if country II adjusts completely in a single period to specialized production it will not, at the end of period 1, be able to produce sufficient good 2 for global requirements: Equation (2.7) is again violated because of the magnitude of the middle term. As in the previous case, the Centre will be unable to specialize and the terms of trade will be the same as I's autarky price ratio. Correspondingly, the rate of profits in II is equal to $r^{II'}$ in Figure 1.6.

What happens subsequently depends on the value of $s^{II}$. If the savings rate is sufficiently large that $s^{II}r^{II'} > g^I$ then, over time, the Periphery can 'catch up' with the Centre. It will be some time (perhaps a very long time) before Equation (2.7) becomes satisfied and during that time the terms of trade and $r^{II}$ will remain at their earlier values. Even when Equation (2.7) is satisfied, consumption rigidities may prolong the period of incomplete specialization. Eventually, however, the faster growth of the Periphery will make itself felt in deteriorating terms of trade and falling rate of profits which, in turn, moderates the rate of accumulation. This process continues until the steady-growth condition with complete specialization, Equation (1.16), is satisfied.

If $s^{II}r^{II'} = g^I$, the countries grow at the same rate indefinitely and the initial size differential is maintained. If $s^{II}r^{II'} < g^I$, the Periphery falls progressively further behind, its relative significance falling continuously toward zero. This is the case discussed in Chapter 1.

## 2.4 The gains from trade

In Chapter 1 it was shown that the level of consumption p.w. could be higher or lower with trade compared to autarky. Such differences are referred to by Metcalfe and Steedman (1974) as 'steady-state' gains (or losses) from trade. They note, however, that if an economy moves from autarky to trade then a complete or 'inclusive' measure of the gains from trade needs to take account of occurrences during the transition. In 2.2 it was seen that the transition would normally require a re-adjustment of the capital stocks of the participating countries. These re-adjustments could, on balance, require a reduction in the value of capital, or an increase. Since the capital stocks are replaced from the annual outputs of the economy, a transitional reduction (say) of the stock would mean that more output is (temporarily) available for consumption purposes. There is, thus, also a 'transitional' gain (or loss).

In order to evaluate the 'inclusive' gains from trade, therefore, it is necessary to compare the entire stream of consumption along the transition-plus-trade path with that along the autarky path. There is a difficulty however: consumption along one path may be higher at some time (for example, along the steady state) and lower at another (during the transition, say). An obvious way to overcome this is to compare the present value of the streams by choosing an appropriate discount factor. But the crucial question then becomes: what is the appropriate rate of discount? The neoclassical answer is immediate and straightforward. In competitive intertemporal equilibrium the interest rate is equal to the marginal rate of time preference of all individuals and hence of society. The interest rate (which in general intertemporal equilibrium is equivalent to what we have been calling the profits rate) on the transition-plus-trade path should thus be used to compare the present values of the alternative streams. It turns out that if the rate of profits is used to discount future consumption the gains from trade are non-negative in all circumstances.

We shall now prove the neoclassical proposition under fairly general assumptions concerning the transitional path.[6] Because of its generality, however, the demonstration fails to bring to light the precise nature of the gains. In an attempt to give a slightly clearer picture the simple case of a one-period transition will subsequently be discussed in some depth and represented geometrically. This will also permit an understanding of the crucial role played by the choice of discount factor. The neoclassical conclusions will then be reconsidered in the light of this analysis.

Consider then an economy which up to period 0 exists in autarky. During period 0 it undergoes a transition (lasting any number of periods) to a regime of free international trade. The value of consumption in period 0 and in each subsequent period can then be compared with the values that would have obtained had no transition occurred. The valuations are undertaken at prices, wage rates and interest rates prevailing on the with-trade path.[7] In what follows, superscripts refer to time periods until otherwise stated. Quantities in autarky are indicated by a bar (for example, $\bar{X}$); variables expressed in value terms on the autarky path are indicated by a 'hat' when evaluated in the prices of the with-trade regime (for example, $\hat{C}$ and $\hat{K}$, where $K$ is the value of the capital stock). Variables on the with-trade path carry no special distinction.

Begin by considering the alternative values of consumption at the end of period 0. These are

$$C^0 = p^0 X^0 - K^1 \tag{2.8}$$

and

$$\hat{C}^0 = p^0 \overline{X}^0 - \hat{K}^1 \tag{2.9}$$

for transition-plus-trade and autarky, respectively. Here $p^0 X^0$ is the value of the gross output of period 0 and since this is the same for both regimes it follows that

$$p^0 X^0 = p^0 \overline{X}^0 \tag{2.10}$$

$K^1$ is the value of the following period's capital requirements on the transitional path:

$$K^1 = p^0 A X^1$$

and $\hat{K}^1$ the value of next period's autarky capital stock. Subtracting Equation (2.9) from Equation (2.8), and bearing in mind Equation (2.10), gives the difference in consumption in period 0 in terms of with-trade prices:

$$C^0 - \hat{C}^0 = \hat{K}^1 - K^1 \tag{2.11}$$

At the end of period 1, consumption with trade is given by

$$C^1 = p^1 X^1 - K^2 \tag{2.12}$$

Writing

$$p^1 X^1 = (1 + r^1) K^1 + w^1 L^1 \tag{2.13}$$

Equation (2.12) can be rewritten as

$$C^1 = (1 + r^1) K^1 + w^1 L^1 - K^2 \tag{2.14}$$

Consumption in autarky, valued at trade prices is, corresponding to Equation (2.9), given by

$$\hat{C}^1 = p^1 \bar{X}^1 - \hat{K}^2 \qquad (2.15)$$

Assuming (as is appropriate for the Centre) that the level of employment is the same on both paths, the first term on the right-hand side of Equation (2.15) may be expressed by the inequality:

$$p^1 \bar{X}^1 \leqslant (1 + r^1) \hat{K}^1 + w^1 L^1 \qquad (2.16)$$

(The inequality arises out of the evaluation of the quantities of one regime by the profit-maximizing prices and wage rate of another.[8]) Thus Equation (2.15) can be rewritten as

$$\hat{C}^1 \leqslant (1 + r^1) \hat{K}^1 + w^1 L^1 - \hat{K}^2 \qquad (2.17)$$

Comparing (2.14) and (2.17):

$$C^1 - \hat{C}^1 \geqslant (1 + r^1)(K^1 - \hat{K}^1) - K^2 + \hat{K}^2 \qquad (2.18)$$

And, in general,

$$C^t - \hat{C}^t \geqslant (1 + r^t)(K^t - \hat{K}^t) - K^t + \hat{K}^t \qquad (2.19)$$

The present value of the difference in consumption streams up to time $\tau$ is

$$C(\tau) = C^0 - \hat{C}^0 + \sum_{t=1}^{\tau} (C^t - \hat{C}^t)/\Delta^\tau \qquad (2.20)$$

where

$$\Delta^\tau = (1 + \rho^1)(1 + \rho^2) \ldots (1 + \rho^\tau)$$

$\rho^t$ being the social rate of discount in period $t$. If, on the neoclassical assumption, we put $\rho^t = r^t$ then from Relations (2.11) and (2.19), Equation (2.20) becomes

$$C(\tau) \geqslant (\hat{K}^{\tau+1} - K^{\tau+1})/\Delta^\tau \qquad (2.21)$$

which may be evaluated as $\tau \to \infty$. The paths of the $K^{tz} (Z = \text{I,II})$ are determined by the savings–investment, Equation (1.14):

$g^{tz} = s^z r^{tz} < r^{tz}$ (for $s^z < 1$)

Thus the numerator of inequality (2.21) grows more slowly than the denominator as $\tau \to \infty$ so that the discounted values of the $K^z$ converge to zero over time and we may conclude that

$$C(\tau) \geqslant 0 \tag{2.22}$$

Note that an equality holds in Relation (2.16) if autarky and trade prices are the same, and that will also be true in Relation (2.22). In other words, there will only be a gain from trade if there is a change in the terms of trade.

For the Centre this is all that needs to be said. For the Periphery, however, a small modification to the argument may be required. With a constant subsistence-determined wage but with different employment levels due to superior growth with trade, inequality (2.16) needs to be amended by substituting $\bar{L}^t$ for $L^t$. The right-hand side of Relation (2.21) is correspondingly supplemented by the term $\sum^{\tau}_{t=1} w(L^t - \bar{L}^t)/\Delta^{\tau}$. The net consumption gain $C(\tau)$ thus contains an additional term. Care is needed in interpreting this result. If the subsistence-determined wage in formal employment is the same as the remuneration in the subsistence sector (the source of surplus labour) then all that happens as a result of faster growth of the former is a transfer of primary income from one part of the economy to another. A subsistence-determined wage is not, however, necessarily the same thing as a pure subsistence wage, the former perhaps involving a conventionally determined mark-up on the latter. Even so, the supplementary term given above still overstates the consumption gains from faster growth, the correct term being

$$\sum^{\tau}_{t=1} (w - \underline{w})(L^t - \bar{L}^t)/\Delta^{\tau}$$

where $\underline{w}$ is the rate of remuneration in the subsistence sector. There may, of course, be external social benefits (and costs) from the faster growth of the formal sector which this analysis is unable to quantify.

## 2.5 A single-period transition

Inequality (2.21) provides us with a fairly general statement of the gain from trade. While it proves the basic proposition it does not illuminate the result as clearly as one might wish. In this subsection we shall attempt to pinpoint the nature of the gain, first by finding a geometrical representation of the gain and then by relating it to the literature on the rate of return to transition in a closed economy. To do this requires two considerable simplifications. First, we confine discussion to a single-period transition to a regime of specialized trade. Second, we consider an economy that enters world trade as a price-taker so that the free-trade equilibrium price rules during the transitional period (which would not generally be the case for two large economies initiating trade). Because the argument is to be expressed geometrically it will be conducted throughout in per-worker terms (reflected in the use of lower-case notation).

Following Metcalfe and Steedman, we may think of the gain as being the sum of the steady-state and transitional components, $Q$ and $T$, respectively. $Q$ and $T$ are measured in terms of the free-trade commodity prices. The analysis is developed initially for a Centre-type economy (that is, one for which the rate of profits does not change) which, for the sake of argument, is assumed to benefit from a constant steady-state gain, $c - \hat{c}$ for all periods 1, 2, ... ,$\infty$.

Since trade and autarky consumption streams grow at the same rate $g$, the present value of this infinite series of gains is given by

$$Q = (c - \hat{c}) \left[ \frac{1+g}{1+\rho} + \frac{(1+g)^2}{(1+\rho)^2} + \cdots \right] \tag{2.23}$$

This sum will converge if $g < \rho$, in which case it can be written more succinctly as

$$Q = (c - \hat{c})(1+g)/(\rho - g) \tag{2.24}$$

$T$, the increase or decrease in the value of consumption p.w. during the transition, is obtained either from Equations (2.1) and (2.4) or by reinterpretation of Equation (2.11):

$$T = p(\tilde{y} - \overline{y}) = (\hat{k} - k)(1+g) \tag{2.25}$$

Both $k$ and $\hat{k}$ may be represented geometrically. It has already been established that with specialized trade the value of capital p.w. is the (absolute) slope of the appropriate $(w-r)_i$ trade-off corresponding to the terms of trade. In the case depicted in Figure 2.1 it is the slope of the line $(w-r)_1$:

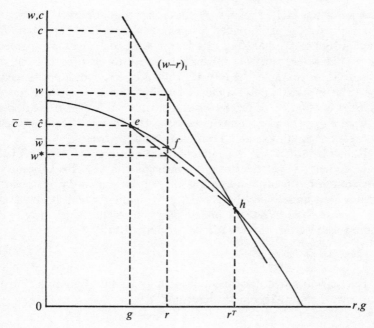

*Figure 2.1*

$$k = (c-w)/(r-g) \tag{2.26}$$

Finding a representation of $\hat{k}$ is somewhat more difficult and we proceed in two stages, the first involving the determination of the value of autarky capital p.w. at autarky prices, $\overline{k}$. Net national income p.w. at autarky prices may be written as

$$\overline{py} = \overline{w} + r\overline{k} = \overline{c} + g\overline{k}$$

from which it follows that

$$\overline{k} = (\overline{c}-\overline{w})/(r-g)$$

which is given by the slope of the line passing through points $e$ and $f$ on the autarky $w$–$r$ frontier. The next stage is to allow for the revaluation of autarky quantities by free-trade prices. This can be done by noting that a movement along the $w$–$r$ frontier (because of a change in the rate of profits) would imply a continuous change in autarky prices. Yet, provided $g$ remained constant in this exercise, there would be no change in autarky quantities. Changes in the value of capital would thus be attributable solely to changes in relative prices. If, for example, the rate of profits were $r^T$, with $g$ unchanged, the value of capital p.w. would be given by the slope of the line *eh*. Since $r^T$ is that rate of profits which corresponds to free-trade prices and since $g$ does, in fact, remain the same, the slope of *eh* can be taken as measuring autarky capital p.w. at free-trade prices: $\hat{k}$.

It may be noted that the value of consumption p.w. in autarky is independent of the prices used to measure it: $\bar{c} = \hat{c}$. This is because consumption is measured as a quantity of the standard of value (an assumption underlying the geometry of duality) which is constant between regimes.[9] That the line *eh* passes through the point $(g,\hat{c})$ is merely a reflection of the national product identity

$$p\bar{y} = \hat{c} + g\hat{k}$$

But, as was noted in connection with inequality, Equation (2.16), the corresponding income statement is

$$p\bar{y} \leqslant w + r\hat{k}$$

(where $w$ is the price of labour with free trade). If this inequality is converted into an equation by replacing $w$ with $w^* \leqslant w$, then we may write

$$\hat{k} = (\hat{c} - w^*)/(r - g) \tag{2.27}$$

$w^*$ is that level of the wage which would be needed in order for autarky net output $\bar{y}$, valued at free-trade prices $p$, to yield a rate of profits, $r$. It is a purely notional concept.

Using Equations (2.26) and (2.27), the transitional gain, Equation (2.25), can be expanded as

$$T = (\hat{c} - c + w - w^*)(1 + g)/(r - g)$$

which, added to Equation (2.24), yields an expression for the inclusive gain from trade:

$$Q + T = (c - \hat{c}) \left[ \frac{1}{\rho - g} - \frac{1}{r - g} \right] (1 + g) + \left[ \frac{w - w^*}{r - g} \right] (1 + g) \tag{2.28}$$

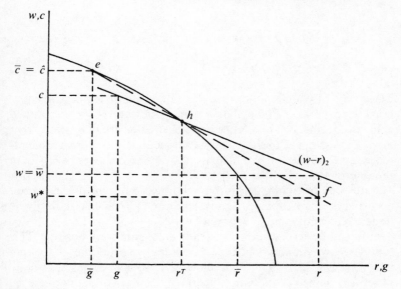

*Figure 2.2*

If the discount rate $\rho$ is set equal to the rate of profits it can be seen immediately that the first term on the right-hand side of Equation (2.28) becomes zero. In the second term, $(w - w^*)$ is the notional 'increase' in the wage rate resulting from a restructuring of net outputs at constant prices. This second term represents the present value of the infinite sequence of the difference $(w - w^*)$ subject to growth at the rate $g$ and discounted at the rate $r$. It may be regarded as a measure of the p.w. gain from trade under neoclassical assumptions, and is necessarily non-negative.

The same kind of argument can be applied to the Periphery (Figure 2.2, where the symbols correspond to Figure 2.1), though here there is the added complication that profits rates and growth rates differ between regimes. Corresponding to Equations (2.24), (2.25) and (2.28) we now have

$$Q = \frac{c(1+g)}{\rho - g} - \frac{\hat{c}(1+\overline{g})}{\rho - \overline{g}}$$

$$T = \hat{k}(1+\overline{g}) - k(1+g)$$

and

$$Q + T = c(1+g)\left[\frac{1}{\rho - g} - \frac{1}{r - g}\right] - \hat{c}(1 + \bar{g})\left[\frac{1}{\rho - \bar{g}} - \frac{1}{r - \bar{g}}\right] +$$
$$\frac{w(1+g)}{r-g} - \frac{w^*(1+\bar{g})}{r-\bar{g}} \tag{2.29}$$

These are, of course, more general statements of the earlier equations. Here, if $\rho = r$, the inclusive gain from trade is the discounted value of the notional difference in wage streams growing at different rates. But, as noted in the previous subsection, with positive subsistence-sector wages the real benefits of faster growth will be less than those implied by the sum of $Q + T$.

Returning to Figure 2.1, it may be noted that had the transition occurred at a switchpoint (that is, had $r$ and $r^T$ coincided), implying no terms of trade change, $w$ and $w^*$ would coincide and the inclusive gain would be zero, even if the steady-state gain were positive. This is precisely what one would expect from known properties of the rate of return. Spaventa (1972) has shown that at a switchpoint the rate of return, defined as the ratio of perpetual gain to initial sacrifice, is, in the case of a single–period transition, *identically* equal to the rate of profits at the switchpoint. Thus, if the rate of profits is used to discount the perpetual gain, it is hardly surprising that it should be equal to the transitional sacrifice, implying zero overall gain.

At a switchpoint there is no potential increase in primary income and the return is entirely a return to capitalist consumption. Where, as in the cases discussed above, the transition occurs away from a switchpoint there is the additional effect of a potential increase in primary income. (In the case of the Periphery these potential benefits are diverted into the form of extra profits.) The second term of Equation (2.28) is a measure of this perpetual gain. It follows that a transition from autarky to trade involving a terms of trade change will always entail a gain from trade provided the rate of profits is used to discount future consumption.[10]

## 2.6 The neoclassical perspective

From the rate-of-return property of transitions it follows that the country obtaining a steady-state gain also suffers a transitional loss (reflected in Figure 2.1 by the build-up of capital stock). The country losing in steady state likewise gains in transition. In the case in which two large countries have the same autarky technique then, as was seen in Chapter 1, if they trade together one will obtain a steady-state gain and one a loss. The steady-state gainer has a lower autarky rate of profits than the loser. The neoclassical view is that these rates of profits (interest) are equal to rates of time preference which, in turn, measure individuals' 'impatience' to consume now rather than later. Smith (1976) sums up this line of argument as follows: 'An "impatient" high-interest-rate country uses trade to obtain more of its preferred goods: it sacrifices future consumption for present consumption.' It is important to remember, however, that equating the private rate of time preference of current-generation individuals to a social rate connecting many generations is a value judgement and one which is not universally shared (even by neoclassical economists). This is something which will be considered in more depth in the next subsection.

There is, however, a way of avoiding the value judgement concerning the relative social weights of gains and losses of different generations implied in a choice of discount rate. This alternative, and from a neoclassical point of view, more satisfactory procedure is to show that by some appropriate redistribution from initial gainers to initial losers everyone can be made better off (or, at any rate, no-one is left worse off). If that were so, and if the redistribution were actually undertaken,[11] the transition-plus-trade path would be Pareto-superior.

This second, more robust argument is the one now usually pursued by neoclassical theorists. As normally applied in the atemporal context it demonstrates that lump-sum transfers within each country can allow gainers to compensate losers. Dixit and Norman (1980) have also proved that compensatory transfers can be achieved by the much more practical devices of commodity and factor taxes and subsidies. By applying this argument to the usual intertemporal interpretation of Walrasian general equilibrium they obtain precisely the same conclusions in the case of gains and losses spread over time. In this way Dixit and Norman have rigorously demonstrated, what was previously asserted by Smith (1976, 1979) and Samuelson (1975, 1978), that with appropriate redistribution free trade is Pareto-superior to autarky in an intertemporal context.

It is, perhaps, a touch ironic that to obtain the optimistic 'gains-for-all' outcome from this second approach it is necessary to rely heavily on the willingness of governments to supplement the workings of *laisser-faire* capitalism by instituting a system of optimal transfers. 'Formally', says Smith (1984), 'there is no difficulty: if the achievement of Pareto superiority requires a lump sum transfer between groups of individuals who are members of different generations, then the transfer will require the temporary creation of public debt or the temporary public acquisition of assets'. But turning from formalism to realism, he concedes: 'Nonetheless, the intertemporal aspect of the problem gives good ground for scepticism about whether the required redistributions would actually be effected'. This indeed, is the nub of the matter. If (say) the losses of future generations continue indefinitely then the redistributive arrangement will also need to continue indefinitely. Future generations would have to be bound by an intertemporal social contract not to appropriate for themselves what should be passed on to their successors. This requires a very active and very far-seeing succession of governments. The design, magnitude and endurance of the redistributive mechanism makes the pursuit of this first-best policy extremely improbable (which is not to say that second- or other-best policies, including autarky, could easily be sustained either). At this point, therefore, it may be useful to turn away from potential Pareto comparisons and return to arguments based on social welfare judgements, taking as a point of reference the case in which there are no intergenerational redistributions.

## 2.7 Discounting future consumption

Translating a positive present value into a social welfare gain implies a set of weights attached to the value of consumption of each generation, those weights being implicit in the choice of discount rate. In the neoclassical view, at least as represented in the literature on international trade, the social rate of discount is taken to be the interest rate, the market price at which future and present consumption are traded. This procedure is subject to a number of well-known criticisms.

The view that the concept of consumers' sovereignty has little applicability in an intertemporal context has a long tradition in economics.[12] Pigou (1932), for example, saw discounting on the basis of private time preference as a consequence of a 'deficiency of the telescopic faculty'. This is a criticism of individual rationality which is valid here. But the real issue goes beyond individual rationality because it concerns the whole of society understood as a (conceivably) infinite set of succeeding and overlapping generations. And it is the implicit undervaluation of the welfare of succeeding generations that most concerns us here. Because future generations do not have a vote in present decisions, discounting on the basis of pure time preference is, as Ramsey (1928) put it, 'ethically indefensible'.

Even if one were to confine oneself to the preferences of the present generation, it is still probable that society, in general, will undertake insufficient savings if they are guided solely by private market signals. The suboptimality of savings (implying a private rate of discount in excess of the socially optimal rate) is a logical consequence of Sen's (1961) and Marglin's (1963) 'isolation paradox' for reasonable assumptions concerning individual orderings of the alternatives (Sen, 1967). The isolation paradox is an extension of the 'prisoner's dilemma' of two-person, non-zero sum game theory. Paraphrasing Sen, it can be explained as follows. Given the actions of others, the individual is better off not saving one extra unit than saving the unit. But given the choice between everyone saving an extra unit and no-one saving an extra unit each individual prefers that everyone save. If saving is purely an individual decision then no-one will undertake the extra saving and the outcome will be suboptimal even if judged solely on the basis of the preferences of those currently doing the saving.[13]

What are the implications of such arguments for the neoclassical gains from trade conclusions? Even from the limited point of view of one generation, the private rate of discount (equal in neoclassical equilibrium to the rate of interest) overdiscounts (that is, undervalues) future gains and losses. Precisely how the use of a discount rate $\rho < r$ affects the evaluation of the inclusive gain depends on whether the transition from one regime to another leads to a change in the growth rate.

Consider first the case in which the growth rate remains unchanged, as in Figure 2.1. Here the Centre has a steady-state gain which is undervalued when overdiscounted at the rate $r$. Discounting at $\rho < r$ increases the evaluation and hence, also, the inclusive gain. This is easily confirmed by inspection of Equation (2.28). If the Centre had suffered a steady-state loss (a possibility illustrated in Figure 1.5), the present value of that loss discounted at $\rho$ could exceed the transitional gain and so give rise to an inclusive loss from trade. For the Periphery a corresponding result can only be obtained (with a fixed savings ratio) when the growth rate in both regimes is zero (implying $s^I = s^{II} = 0$). Then, as can be seen from Equation

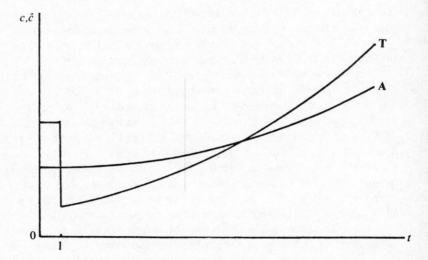

*Figure 2.3*

(2.29), a sufficiently low value of $\rho$ will again reverse the standard neoclassical result.

When a switch to trade is accompanied by a rising growth rate, as will generally be the case for the Periphery, the last result requires considerable qualification. Initially, a lowering of the discount rate from $r$ favours the autarky path and may, as before, reverse the standard result. But a further lowering will reinstate the trade path to the superior position. Indeed, as can be seen from Equation (2.29), as $\rho \to g, Q + T \to \infty$. The reason for this reversal is clearly related to the well-known problem of multiple internal rates of return, as can be seen by inspecting the alternative consumption profiles (Figure 2.3). A high discount rate places heavy weight on the transitional gain relative to subsequent differences in the paths. A slightly lower rate shifts the emphasis to the period of comparative loss (and may therefore generate an inclusive loss). But this period is of finite duration because of the superior growth of the trade path and this long-term superiority is given prominence by a yet lower discount rate.

The discussion may be summarized briefly. When countries have the same, or sufficiently similar, autarky techniques, the Centre will necessarily gain from trade, the Periphery may gain or lose depending on the appropriate social discount rate. When countries have sufficiently different techniques one or both may gain and one or both may lose.

## 2.8 Conclusion

This chapter has been concerned largely with the welfare consequences of a change in regime. Attention was drawn in the introduction to the limited relevance of this question to an understanding of the historical process of development. There are important, historically imposed constraints on regime switching. Colonialism created a pattern of productive specialization in which the colonies became providers of raw materials and markets for the manufacturers of colonial powers. Political and social impediments to change are powerful and long-lasting: 'Britain's Colonial Empire established what was in effect an artificial world division of labour that has lasted down to our times' (Barratt Brown, 1974, p.96).

It has to be admitted that important internal and international social and political relations that serve to perpetuate the neocolonial patterns of international specialization are largely beyond the reach of pure trade theory. Nevertheless, to the extent that contemporary Peripheral economies have some room for manoeuvre and are searching for appropriate strategies in their economic relations with the rest of the world, the current analysis is of relevance. It has been seen that if the Periphery has access to the same technologies as the Centre (as is assumed, for example, in Heckscher-Ohlin theory), the steady-state level of consumption p.w. is necessarily lower with trade. Under some circumstances the inclusive gain may also be negative. These circumstances are more likely to occur the higher the return to labour in the subsistence sector since this reduces the opportunity cost of foregoing the faster growth implied by trade. If social discount rates in the Periphery fall short of the rate of profits it may be perfectly sensible to restrain involvement in international trade.

## Notes
1.  A theoretical exception arises in the case of a 'small' economy whose entry into international trade has insignificant effects on the rest of the world. The small-country assumption is useful in international economic theory and will be employed later in this chapter.
2.  Note that a downward-sloping relative demand function does not conflict in any serious way with the analysis of Chapter 1 in which a closed-economy consump-

tion–growth frontier is used (see also 2.5). Although a single consumption good was assumed for simplicity of exposition, essentially the same conclusions can be deduced for the case in which consumption consists of both commodities in any positive proportions.

3.  Spaventa (1972) discusses alternative transitional routes when there are problems of obtaining means of production.
4.  The growing literature on the classical adjustment process (the convergence of prices to natural values) is an obvious starting point. On this see, for example, Dumenil and Levy (1987).
5.  This is a simple modification of the zero-growth condition stated in Steedman and Metcalfe (1973).
6.  The demonstration is due to Smith (1984) which in turn is a generalization of Metcalfe and Steedman (1974). Smith's proof is more general, compact and elegant than ours. These are virtues which may be lost on the less mathematical reader, one reason why a more laboured and specialized approach is taken here.
7.  The use of with-trade prices and interest rates (which in neoclassical terms are simply intertemporal prices) for evaluation follows from standard revealed-preference reasoning. The point is illustrated in the diagram illustrating the textbook 'Ricardian' model.

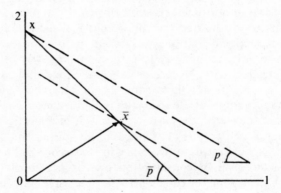

Valuing autarky and free-trade output vectors, $\bar{X}$ and $X$, respectively, at autarky price, $\bar{p}$, implies zero gain. Valuing at free-trade prices correctly indicates the enlarged consumption possibilities allowed by trade. (Valuing alternatives in terms of their own prices would also imply zero gain if good 2 is used as standard of value.)

8.  Competitive pricing implies that no firms can make profits beyond the normal rate. In matrix notation,

$$\mathbf{p} \leqslant (1+r)\mathbf{pA} + w\mathbf{l}$$

If $p$, $r$ and $w$ are applied to the quantities of the same regime then complementary slackness implies

$$\mathbf{pX} = (1+r)\mathbf{pAX} + w\mathbf{lX}$$

In other words, since those firms which fail to make normal profits go out of business, multiplying the price inequality by the corresponding quantity vector converts it into an equation. (One can then re-divide by quantities to obtain the price equations of those firms still in business – Equations (1.1) and (1.2).) But if the prices of one regime are applied to the quantities of another (which are competitively viable at the prices of that other regime), the inequality must, in general, remain:

$$\mathbf{p}\overline{\mathbf{X}} \leqslant (1+r)\mathbf{p}\mathbf{A}\overline{\mathbf{X}} + w\mathbf{1}\overline{\mathbf{X}}$$

Thus

$$\hat{C}^t = \mathbf{p}^t\overline{\mathbf{X}}^t - \mathbf{p}^t\mathbf{A}\overline{\mathbf{X}}^{t+1} \leqslant (1+r^t)\mathbf{p}^t\mathbf{A}\overline{\mathbf{X}}^t + w^t\mathbf{l}\overline{\mathbf{X}} - \mathbf{p}^t\mathbf{A}\overline{\mathbf{X}}^{t+1}$$

which translates back to the text as Equation (2.17).

The argument can again be illustrated with reference to the simple 'Ricardian' diagram of the previous footnote. The value of autarkic consumption *at autarky prices* is

$$\overline{C} = \overline{\mathbf{p}}\overline{\mathbf{X}} = \overline{w}L$$

But the same bundle evaluated at free-trade, profit-maximizing prices is

$$\hat{C} = \mathbf{p}\overline{\mathbf{X}} \leqslant wL$$

because the real wage with trade ($=\mathbf{p}\mathbf{X}/L$) is higher. (The plane $\hat{C} = \mathbf{p}\overline{\mathbf{X}}$ lies below the plane $C = \mathbf{p}\mathbf{X}$.) A strict equality would hold only if: (i) free trade and autarky prices were the same; or (ii) autarky consumption consisted only of the good in which the economy also specializes with trade (a condition which does not carry over to the Sraffa-based model).

9. This is also true of the autarky wage *bundle* but it is not true of the wage as a measure of the value of a unit of labour time. A unit of labour time in autarky measured at free-trade wages has value $w$ and not $p$ times the autarky wage bundle.

10. If the price ratio during transition is not the same as that in free-trade equilibrium (that is $\tilde{p} \neq p$), as will normally be the case for a large economy, the analysis and its interpretation will need to be modified slightly to take account of revaluation effects within the transitional period.

11. There is no merit in applying the Kaldor–Hicks criterion here (or anywhere else for that matter). If redistribution is not undertaken then we are back to the first procedure.

12. For a more thorough account, see Steedman (1989).

13. As Sen (1967) notes there is a closely related, yet distinct reason why savings may be suboptimal, known as the 'assurance problem'. Each individual would save more if others also would save more. If not, the individual's contribution to future welfare is negligible but the loss of current welfare may be significant. To save more, each needs assurance that others will save more. The two forms of market failure, isolation and lack of assurance, have different policy consequences, though, as far as we are concerned they serve to reinforce each other.

# 3 International trade in machinery

## 3.1 Introduction

The preceding chapters have made use of a circulating-capital model of production. Given the degree of generality of the questions that have been addressed such an approach is quite appropriate. Confinement to a circulating-capital model does, however, mean that some interesting but more particular issues have to be glossed over. This chapter digresses from the circulating-capital approach in order to focus on one such issue. Despite its use of a fixed-capital model many of the techniques of analysis are related to those already used. Readers unfamiliar with the basic model may, however, find this chapter rather more difficult than the others. Such readers can skip directly to Part II without loss of continuity since the present chapter also digresses from the main theme of the book – the long-run pattern and consequences of global accumulation – in its concern with an independent, but related matter: the appropriate *method* of accumulation for the Peripheral economy.

Following an extensive literature on the choice of techniques in underdeveloped countries, some writers have considered the more specific question of whether such countries should augment their capital with new or second-hand imported machinery. From a theoretical point of view, the most important contributions are by Sen (1962), Schwartz (1973) and Smith (1974).[1]

In his seminal contribution, Sen showed that a low-wage underdeveloped country would benefit most by importing the oldest available second-hand machines from the high-wage industrialized country. If market and shadow wage rates are equal, this socially preferred allocation coincides with the market allocation. Sen's partial equilibrium analysis, however, deals only with the case of machines having a pre-specified physical lifespan. His advocacy of imports of second-hand machines is echoed by Schwartz who uses a simple neoclassical approach to criticize the prohibition that some underdeveloped countries have applied to such imports. The most general theoretical approach is, however, that of Smith who employs a vintage capital model 'in the Heckscher–Ohlin tradition'. In this partial equilibrium analysis two 'large' countries trade in machines.

In the spirit of Sen, Smith concludes that the high-wage country will use only young machines; the low-wage country will use only old machines.

This chapter develops a more explicitly classical analysis of international machinery trade, taking advantage of Sraffa's model of fixed capital.[2] For the most part it reflects the spirit of Sen's conclusions, though we shall see that the precise age-pattern of machine trade depends on a number of factors which do not appear in previous discussions. Unlike Smith, we follow Sen and Schwartz in the assuming that the machine importing country is a small Peripheral economy. The only source of supply of machinery is the Centre, considered as a large homogeneous economy. Thus all machine prices are determined domestically within the Centre.

The small-country assumption has an important theoretical implication. Since the small country is a price taker it is possible to value capital in that country (but only in that country) independently of income distribution and so talk, unambiguously, of 'capital' and 'capital intensity'. This feature of the analysis is not the result of the slipping in of some neoclassical postulate but is solely the consequence of the small-country assumption.

## 3.2 The technological possibilities

Let I be the large, potentially machine-exporting Centre, and II the small, potentially machine-importing Peripheral economy. Being small, II will normally[3] specialize in a single traded good which we shall call 'food'. Other Peripheral countries, III, IV, etc. will specialize in food or other goods according to their own circumstances. Country I may be partially specialized (since the Periphery, in aggregate, may be able to provide some of its requirements). Nevertheless, it is assumed to be a large producer of food and also to produce a machine which may be employed in the manufacture of food.

Given the wage in I($w^1$), the technique chosen to produce food is one which involves the use of the machine. Then taking a unit of food as the standard value, the price equations of the various processes used to produce food in I are:

$$1 + \pi_1 = R^l(e_0 + \pi_0) + w^l\lambda_0 \qquad (3.1.0)$$
$$1 + \pi_2 = R^l(e_1 + \pi_1) + w^l\lambda_1 \qquad (3.1.1)$$

$$1 + \pi_{m+1} = R^l(e_m + \pi_m) + w^l\lambda_m \qquad (3.1.m)$$

Equation (3.1.0) says that one new machine of price $\pi_0$, together with materials of value (at equilibrium prices) $e_0$, and $\lambda_0$ homogeneous labour, produce a unit of food plus a one-year-old machine of value $\pi_1$. (A unit of food is obviously defined as the product of one machine-year). $R^l = 1 + r^l = $ one plus the equilibrium rate of profits. Equation $(3.1.t)$ $(t = 1 \ldots m)$ may be interpreted in a like manner: a $t$-year-old machine, price $\pi_t$, together with an appropriate value of materials, $e_t$, and quantity of labour $\lambda_t$, produces a unit of food plus a $1 + t$-year-old machine.

In general, $\lambda_t$ and $e_t$ will change over time as machine efficiency changes. Changing efficiency could also make itself felt, in principle, through changes in the machine:output ratio but, for simplicity, it is assumed that one machine of whatever age produces one unit of food. Thus changes in machine efficiency are reflected solely in the intensity of repair and maintenance (indicated by changes in $\lambda_t$) and the use of spare parts and material wastage (changes in $e_t$). One particular case, of purely theoretical interest, is that of constant lifetime efficiency. In that event, $\lambda_t$ and $e_t$ are constant throughout.

The number of machine processes used (that is, the value of $m + 1$) is, in general, not determined technologically but is a matter of profitability. Thus the optimal *truncation* in I, as determined in the usual competitive fashion,[4] will be taken as given. The price of the machine output from the last process used, $\pi_{m+1}$, may, in principle, be positive (where it has scrap value), negative (where it involves costly disposal) or zero. This price is not affected by any disposals that may be made to country II, because the latter is small. It is assumed throughout that $\pi_{m+1} = 0$.

Each of equations $(3.1.t)$ may now be rearranged to define a $w$–$r$ trade-off associated with each machine-using process:

$$w = [(1 + \pi_{t+1} - \pi_t - e_t)/\lambda_t] - r(\pi_t + e_t)/\lambda_t \qquad (3.2.t)$$

Since, under competitive conditions, each process must pay the same wage and rate of profits, the intersection of these trade-offs defines

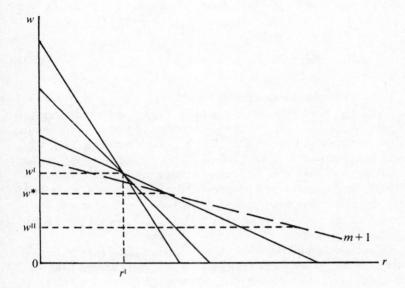

*Figure 3.1*

the equilibrium point $(w^I, r^I)$ on the economy's $w$–$r$ frontier (see Figure 3.1). If the exogenously determined $w^I$ should change then so, in general, would equilibrium prices and, therefore, the slopes, intercepts and intersection of the trade-offs.[5] It may be seen from (3.2.$t$) that the absolute value of the slope of each trade-off $(\lambda_t + e_t)/\pi_t$ measures the capital:labour ratio in process $t$, where capital is valued at the equilibrium prices.

To produce food, country II has a choice of techniques. One, which will be referred to as the 'indigenous' technique, has a price equation

$$1 = (1 + r^{II})a + w^{II}l \tag{3.3}$$

Here $l$ units of labour plus '$a$' units of food (as capital) jointly produce a unit of food. In principle, one could imagine a rather more sophisticated indigenous technique using a machine produced by food and labour. Such a technology could be regarded as 'intermediate', though whether it is 'appropriate' is another matter. Nevertheless, nothing is gained by making Equation (3.3) any more complicated than it is. Rearranging Equation (3.3) gives the $w$–$r$ frontier for this technique:

$$w^{\text{II}} = [(1 - a)/l] - r^{\text{II}}.a/l \qquad (3.4)$$

Throughout it is assumed that $w^{\text{II}} \leqslant w^{\text{I}}$.

The alternative way of producing food involves the use of imported machinery together with imported complementary inputs (raw materials and spare parts). The prices of machines, of all ages, and the prices of materials are all fixed (relative to food), on the small-country assumption. Transport costs are initially assumed to be zero. In addition, it will be assumed throughout that the nature of the deterioration (or improvement) of machines is identical wherever they are used, so that a $t$-year-old machine has the same world price whether it has been used in I or II or both.

Considered from the standpoint of II, then, machines of all ages are available, at known prices $\pi_0, \pi_1 \ldots 0$. A process using a $t$-year-old machine has a $w$–$r$ trade-off given by Equation (3.2.$t$). In general, all trade-offs have different intercepts and different slopes. Thus, whenever $w^{\text{II}} < w^{\text{I}}$ only one process will normally be used. (In the absence of transport costs, only in exceptional circumstances will machines of successive ages operate side-by-side.) The purchase of a $t$-year-old machine will be followed, a year later, by its replacement with a machine of identical age, the superseded machine being scrapped. If $w^{\text{II}} = w^{\text{I}}$ then machines of all ages are equiprofitable and some or all will be used side-by-side. It goes without saying that private producers will only import machines, if, at $w^{\text{II}}$, the implied rate of profits exceeds that yielded by the indigenous technique.

Having outlined the technological possibilities their implications for the world pattern of trade can now be considered. It is assumed that food is the most profitable commodity to produce in II, even with the indigenous technique. In that case the food is exchanged for other final commodities. It may, however, be that the availability of machines makes food production yet more profitable, in which case the food is exchanged not only for other final commodities but also, of course, for the machines and their complementary inputs. The initial form of specialization, then, is a consequence of both technology and income distribution. The same will be true of the choice between machines and the indigenous technique.

### 3.3 Machines of constant efficiency

In the very particular case of constant efficiency it is necessary to specify in advance the lifetime of the machine. For if $\lambda_t$ and $e_t$ are constant, there is no reason why machine use should be truncated unless, after some finite time, the machine collapses beyond economic repair. We shall suppose that this break-down takes place at year $m+1$ when the machine has zero value. (It is also assumed that it is beyond economic repair in country II.)

Subtracting Equation ($3.1.t+1$) from ($3.1.t$) gives, in this case:

$$\pi_t - \pi_{t+1} = R^{\mathrm{I}}(\pi_{t-1} - \pi_t) \tag{3.5}$$

Since $\pi_0 > 0, \pi_{m+1} = 0$ and $R^{\mathrm{I}} > 1$, this is the well-known result that machines of constant efficiency decline in price at an increasing rate.

In this case, following Sen (1962), we can show that, under competitive conditions, only machines of the oldest usable age ($m$) will be imported into II whenever $w^{\mathrm{II}} < w^{\mathrm{I}}$. From Equations ($3.2.t$) and (3.5) it can be seen that the $w$–$r$ trade-off for a process using an older machine has a smaller $w$-intercept and smaller slope than one for a newer machine. It follows that the Peripheral economy will use only the oldest available machine. This machine, not surprisingly, is associated with the process having the lowest capital:labour ratio, where capital is valued at prices associated with the higher wage $w^{\mathrm{I}}$. For country II, these prices are given so that an unambiguous meaning can be attached to 'the value of capital'. The machine will run for one year. It will then collapse and be replaced by an identical $m$-year-old machine. If wage rates are the same in both economies, capitalists in II would be indifferent to machine age.

Taking this last case, Sen supposes that in II there is considerable underemployment of labour so that the shadow wage rate ($swr$) falls short of the market wage rate ($mwr$). If that is so, the socially optimal outcome would again be the use of the oldest machine. (In Figure 3.1 it is as though $swr = w^{\mathrm{II}}$ and $mwr = w^{\mathrm{I}}$.) For a given investment in machines, more old machines could be purchased which would create greater output and employment. In this case, decisions based on private profitability lead to a socially suboptimal outcome.

In his analysis, however, Sen compares only the alternatives of buying younger and older machines. In many underdeveloped countries there may be an alternative indigenous (either 'traditional' or

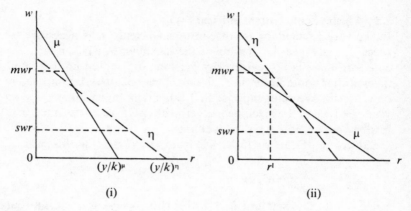

Figure 3.2

'intermediate') technique. The social profitability of machine use should then be compared to the social profitability of the alternative process, represented by Equation (3.4). If *mwr* diverges from *swr*, capitalists may fail to adopt the indigenous technique when that is socially optimal, or they may employ it when it would be better not to. These possibilities are shown in Figure 3.2 where μ is the machine-using, and η the indigenous technique. In the first case:

$$a/l < (\pi_n + e)/\lambda$$

whereas the inequality is reversed in the second case. Note that if the indigenous technique is available in country I then the second case can be ruled out. For at $mwr = w^I$ this technique repays a higher rate of profits in I and so would be adopted there. In that case no second-hand machines would be available to II in the first place. The second case is thus only possible if, either η is not available to I for environmental reasons, or $w^I > mwr > swr$. Even then there may be a presumption that a technique using imported machines (albeit second-hand) has a higher capital intensity. If the situation is as it is shown in Figure 2(i), there will be a socially undesirable use of imported machinery. The indigenous technique would yield greater output per unit of investment: $(Y/K)^\eta > (Y/K)^\mu$; greater employment: $(L/K)^\eta > (L/K)^\mu$; and, if a proportion of the surplus were reinvested, a faster growth rate. In this case, the indigenous technique would also be an 'appropriate' technique.[6]

### 3.4 Machines of variable efficiency

The case of constant efficiency is really only of theoretical significance. In reality the efficiency of machines varies over their lifetimes. In most cases machines could live indefinitely if owners were willing to pay increasing bills for repair and maintenance. Not that efficiency necessarily declines with age, for in the early stages of a machine's life 'running in' and overcoming of teething troubles may be important. We shall, however, begin with the case of constantly declining efficiency. The decline will be reflected in successive increases in either $\lambda_t$ or $e_t$ or both[7] and we shall consider the cases separately beginning with $\lambda_t$.

It hardly needs saying that in the case of monotonically declining efficiency machine prices also fall with age.[8] It follows immediately from equation (3.2.$t$) that a process using an older machine (with lower $\pi_t$ and higher $\lambda_t$) has a $w$–$r$ trade-off with a smaller slope (and necessarily, therefore, a smaller $w$-intercept). As one would expect, then, increasing costs of labour maintenance gives support to Sen's conclusion, but with one slight qualification. This arises from the fact that the truncation is now a consequence of profit considerations in country I rather than of the physical collapse of the machine. The $m+1$-year-old machine can still function if enough spares and maintenance are expended on it. Its unattractiveness to capitalists in I is reflected by the fact that the $w$–$r$ trade-off for this process passes below the point ($w^1$, $r^1$) as shown by the dashed line in Figure 3.1. An extension of the truncation to include this process would reduce the rate of profits associated with the given wage, $w^1$. The $m+1$-year-old machine is cheaper ($\pi_{m+1} = 0$) than a machine of age $m$. On the other hand it requires greater labour costs. Thus, assuming no divergence between *swr* and *mwr* in II, the chosen machine now depends on whether $w^{11} \gtrless w^*$ in Figure 3.1. If the younger machine is chosen then it will still, of course, be run for a single year.

Sen's conclusions also follow, perhaps a little more surprisingly, in the case where the entire maintenance burden is in the form of additional imported spare parts and complementary materials. This is because the period-by-period increase in $e_t$ can never exceed the period-by-period decline in $\pi_t$, so that older processes remain more labour-intensive. This can again be seen by taking the differences between successive price equations, to give

$$\pi_t - \pi_{t+1} = R^1(e_{t-1} - e_t) + R^1(\pi_{t-1} - \pi_t) \tag{3.6}$$

Since the left-hand side of Equation (3.6) is positive, it follows that

$$|(e_{t-1} - e_t)| < |(\pi_{t-1} - \pi_t)| \tag{3.7}$$

Equations (3.7) and (3.2.$t$) indicate that the $w$–$r$ trade-off slope terms decline for successive processes. This argument applies, however, only to those processes which are profitable in I. The price equation for process $m + 1$ could be written

$$1 = \bar{R}^1 e_{m+1} + w^1\lambda_{m+1} \tag{3.1.$m+1$}$$

where, at $w^1$ and equilibrium prices, $\bar{R}^1 < R^1$. Subtracting (3.1.$m + 1$) from (3.1.$m$) and setting $\lambda_m = \lambda_{m+1}$, yields

$$e_{m+1}/(e_m + \pi_m) = R^1/\bar{R}^1 > 1$$

In this case, then, the $m + 1$-year process is more capital-intensive and unambiguously inferior to the $m$-year process.

The efficiency of machines may not decline monotonically with age. In the early years of its life a machine may require 'running-in'. It is as though it is still being perfected but is able to produce some final good even if not, technically, as efficiently as it will later on. In this case expenditures $e_t$ and $\lambda_t$ may first decline with age and then rise. Since the machine is not yet at its peak, its value may rise with age before it finally declines.

If the expense of running-in falls entirely on complementary inputs this does not affect any of our conclusions. The ratio of capital expense of a young machine to that of an $m$-year-old machine is

$$\frac{\pi_t + e_t}{\pi_m + e_m} = \frac{1 + \pi_{t+1} - w^1\lambda_t}{1 - w^1\lambda_m}$$

Since $\lambda_t = \lambda_m$ and $\pi_t > 0$, the m-year process will always be less capital–intensive.

The same conclusion does not apply if the burden of running-in falls entirely on labour. This is because the much higher initial labour cost makes the earlier process labour-intensive and, possibly more labour-intensive than the $m$-year or $m+1$-year process.[9] This implies the leasing out of new machines to low-labour-cost countries, the (partly) run-in machine returning to I after one period. It is not easy to think of examples from reality in which new machines are temporarily removed to low-labour-cost countries for running-in. Transport costs, to be discussed below, may have something to do with this, but even allowing for such costs this does not seem to be a particularly interesting case. Yet it is the only reason that has been uncovered so far why a low-wage country would import any machine younger than age $m$.[10]

A more interesting and realistic possibility does, however, exist even in the absence of transport costs. Up to now it has been assumed that the techniques of production are identical in I and II. The machine is obviously a common component of machine-using processes in I and II, but the complementary inputs could differ. A vehicle, for example, can be maintained by a more intensive use of spare parts or a more intensive use of labour. In one economy it may make sense to replace dirty spark plugs with new ones; in another it may be more profitable to expend labour time cleaning the old plugs.

If the technology allows, one would expect that where labour is relatively cheap there would be a switch in the use of complementary inputs away from materials and towards labour. For each $t$, $e_t$ would be smaller, $\lambda_t$ higher. Of course, the machine prices $\pi_t$ would still be determined by the technique adopted in country I. But the $w$–$r$ trade-offs in I and II would be different for processes using a machine of given age.[11] From Equation (3.2.$t$) it can be seen that the trade-off for a $t$-year process in II will have a lower slope. It will also have a lower $w$-intercept. This is necessarily the case because each trade-off for an alternative process must pass below the point $(w^{\mathrm{I}}, r^{\mathrm{I}})$; if this were not so then at least one alternative process would be profitable in I also.

There now arises the possibility that the profitability ranking of processes (defined by machine age) at $w^{\mathrm{II}}$ will differ from the Sen-ranking. The possibility is illustrated in Figure 3.3. Machines of two ages (0 and 1) are available. The bold lines refer to the (capital-intensive) technique adopted in I; the narrow lines to the alternative processes in II. The substitution of labour for materials has made

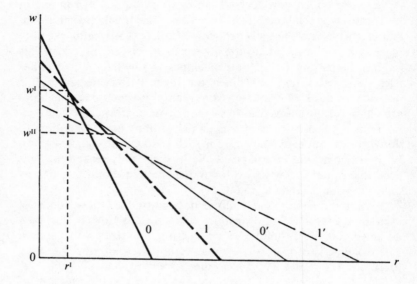

*Figure 3.3*

both processes more labour-intensive. But, given the level of $w^{II}$, the older process has become too labour-intensive while the younger process has shifted into the 'right' intensity range.[12]

Thus quite plausible changes in the methods of operating machines in the Periphery can make the acquisition of new (or, at any rate, newer) machines profitable. This possibility is not considered by Sen (1962), though it would seem to be a logical extension of his arguments based on the relative cheapness of labour in underdeveloped countries. Smith (1974) considers technical differences between low- and high-wage countries but since labour is the only complementary input included in his model he is unable to analyse the sort of substitution considered above. He is, therefore, forced to conclude that 'the essential plausibility of the argument for low wage countries to specialise in used machines is maintained' (p. 273).

### 3.5   The effect of transport costs

In all the cases studied so far, capitalists in II purchase a machine and operate it for one period, replacing it with another machine of precisely the same age. The old machine is either discarded, because it is worthless, or resold to country I. Since the discrete-period model is a theoretical simplification of what is actually a continuous process, the image conjured up by this analysis is scarcely credible: a continuous flow of machines from I to II, each being used for an instant, then returned or discarded, and succeeded by the next. One reason for this fantastic outcome is that costs of shipment are zero. Smith (1974) also concedes that the expected consequence of including transport costs in his model is that his results 'are very considerably weakened'. He consoles his readers, however, by quoting Kindleberger (1962) to the effect that costs of international transport on 'heavy manufactures such as machine tools' are typically no more than 2 per cent so that, in Kindleberger's words, 'they can be safely ignored by economists'.

The quotation from Kindleberger is not, however, as consoling as was intended by Smith. Transport costs which add 2 per cent to the price of a *new* machine may perhaps be 'safely ignored'. But the same absolute level of transport costs will add a considerably greater percentage to the prices of second-hand machines. Indeed, the price of discarded machines of zero scrap value will increase infinitely as the result of positive transport costs. Nor is that all. Total shipment costs include, not only surface transport, but dismantling costs in I and re-erection costs in II. Dismantling costs will not figure in the shipment costs for new machines since these can be packaged straight off the production line. Second-hand machines may require not only dismantling (think of the costs of dismantling, say, an electric-arc furnace) but are likely to be more 'delicate' the older they are and so require greater care (and cost) in the three shipment operations. These considerations suggest that transport costs can be expected to rise with machine age, not only in percentage terms, but in absolute terms as well. Despite this, in the formal discussions which follow it will be assumed that absolute shipment costs are the same for machines of all ages. Also, for simplicity, the costs of transporting food and other finished goods will be assumed to be insignificant.

We shall suppose that transport costs are paid in the form of a quantity (and hence value) of food: $z$ per machine per trip. Thus if $\pi_t$ is the price of a $t$-year-old machine in I, the c.i.f. import price in II is $\pi_t + z$, whereas the price received in II for an exported machine is $\pi_t - z$.

If $w^I = w^{II}$ then, in the absence of transport costs, all processes are equiprofitable in II and all, or any combination, may be used. We first show that, when $z > 0$, the use of all processes is superior to the use of any subset. We then show that a gradual lowering of the ratio $w^{II}/w^{I}$ leads to the elimination of younger machine imports (in the absence of technical substitutions). It is assumed throughout that machine efficiency declines with age, with $e_t \leqslant e_{t+1}$ and $\lambda_t \leqslant \lambda_{t+1}$. To keep things simple, the formal analysis is confined to the case of a machine which, in I lasts only two years.

*(a)*   $w^{II} = w^{I}$

In the absence of transport costs, the two processes represented by the following equations are equiprofitable in II:

$$\pi_1 + 1 = R^0(e_0 + \pi_0) + w^{II}\lambda_0 \tag{3.8^0.0}$$
$$1 = R^0(e_1 + \pi_1) + w^{II}\lambda_1 \tag{3.8^0.1}$$

where $R^0 = 1 + r^{II}$ when transport costs are zero. If the same two processes are used with transport costs, these equations become

$$\pi^0_1 + 1 = R'(e_0 + \pi_0 + z) + w^{II}\lambda_0 \tag{3.8'.0}$$
$$1 = R'(e_1 + \pi^0_1) + w^{II}\lambda_1 \tag{3.8'.1}$$

Apart from the inclusion of $z$ in (3.8'.0), the only difference in the two sets of equations is that the price of the second-hand machine in II becomes divorced from its world (f.o.b.) price. From now on, $\pi^i{}_j$ will refer to the price in II of a machine acquired at age $i$ and used for $j$ subsequent periods, the total age of the machine being $i + j$.

Equations (3.8'), unlike (3.8⁰), do not refer to separate processes since Equation (3.8'.1) is determined by Equation (3.8'.0) and cannot exist without it. Alternative processes are, however, possible. These consist of:

(i)   The acquisition of a new machine, run for one year only, then returned to I;
(ii)   the acquisition of a second-hand machine, run for one year, then scrapped;
(iii)   an extension of the system of Equations (3.8') to a third or subsequent year;
(iv)   a similar extension of alternative (ii).

We first show that, of these, only (iii) can prove to be profitable.

Since the system of Equations (3.8′) is more costly than (3.8⁰), it follows directly that $R' < R^0$ and, by comparison of Equations (3.8⁰.1) and (3.8′.1), that $\pi^0_1 > \pi_1$. We can now quickly dispose of alternative (i), the process represented by the equation

$$\pi_1 - z + 1 = R^i(e_0 + \pi_0 + z) + w^{II}\lambda_0 \tag{3.9}$$

Since $\pi^0_1 > \pi_1$, it can immediately be seen, by comparing Equations (3.8′.0) and (3.9), that, although it uses the same inputs, alternative (i) creates less value and, therefore, pays a lower rate of profits than system (3.8′).

Alternative (ii) implies the equation

$$1 = R^{ii}(e_1 + \pi_1 + z) + w^{II}\lambda_1 \tag{3.10}$$

Comparing Equations (3.10) and (3.8′.1), $R' > R^{ii}$ if $\pi^0_1 < \pi_1 + z$; or if $\pi^0_1 = \pi_1 + z + x$, where $x < 0$. We now show that this is so. Subtracting Equation (3.8′.0) from Equation (3.8⁰.0) gives

$$-(z + x) = (R^0 - R')(e_0 + \pi_0) - R'z \text{ or}$$
$$e_0 + \pi_0 = [z(R' - 1) - x]/(R^0 - R') \tag{3.11}$$

Subtracting Equation (3.10) from Equation (3.8⁰.1),

$$0 = (R^0 - R^{ii})(e_1 + \pi_1) - R^{ii}z \text{ or}$$
$$e_1 + \pi_1 = R^{ii}z/(R^0 - R^{ii}) \tag{3.12}$$

For all cases in which $\lambda_1 \geqslant \lambda_0$ we know from Equation (3.7) that

$$(e_0 + \pi_0)/(e_1 + \pi_1) > 1$$

Thus, dividing Equation (3.11) by Equation (3.12), it follows that

$$(zr' - x)/(r^0 - r') > R^{ii}z/(r^0 - r^{ii})$$

or, rearranging,

$$\frac{1 + r^{ii}}{r' - (x/z)} < \frac{r^0 - r^{ii}}{r^0 - r'} \tag{3.13}$$

Now if $r^{ii} > r'$, then the right-hand side of Inequality (3.13) is less than 1 and $x > 0$. But, as can be seen from the left-hand side, this is a contradiction; $r^{ii} = r'$ is similarly impossible; and so we must conclude that $R' > R^{ii}$. Alternative (ii) may, therefore, be ruled out.

The increase in the acquisition price of a machine may make it profitable to extend the truncation (alternative iii)) and thus help to spread the burden of the price increase over a greater production run.[13] For the same reason, (ii) may be improved by extending the truncation (this is option (iv)), but since $\pi^0_1 < \pi_1 + z$, one-year-old machines may be acquired more cheaply via system (3.8').

To sum up the discussion so far, if $w^{ii} = w^{i}$ then machines of all ages which are profitable in I will be used and, indeed, so may machines of greater age; that is, the truncation may be extended.

### (b)  $w^{i} > w^{ii}$

Alternative (ii) which is not feasible when wages are equal may become so when $w^{i} > w^{ii}$. Its disadvantage is that, compared to system (3.8'), it has to bear an extra burden of transport costs – it now bears outward carriage every one year instead of every two. It is, however, a more labour-intensive method than system (3.8') and this weighs increasingly in its favour as we notionally reduce $w^{ii}$. When transport costs are zero we know that $R^{ii} > R'$. It follows from the continuity of the rate of profits with respect to the input coefficients that there exists some $z > 0$ sufficiently small that $R^{ii} > R'$ still holds. Of course, if $z$ is large, or the differences $w^{i} - w^{ii}$ small, alternative (ii) will remain unprofitable. On the other hand, if $z$ is sufficiently small and if labour can be substituted for material inputs, alternative (i) can be the most profitable even though the machine bears outward carriage every year and return carriage every year.

All of these results can be extended, in a straightforward fashion, to cases in which system $(3.8^0)$ consists of more than two processes. The resulting configurations are illustrated in Figure 3.4. Here, the line marked (0) represents machine prices f.o.b. in I; uniformly above it are indicated the corresponding c.i.f. prices, $\pi_t + z$; and, uniformly below, the received prices in II, $\pi_t - z$. The dashed curve shows the profile of machine prices when $w^{i} = w^{ii}$. This profile may extend to $m + 1$ or beyond. Here machine prices are such that

$$\pi_t < \pi^0_t < \pi_t + z \tag{3.14}$$

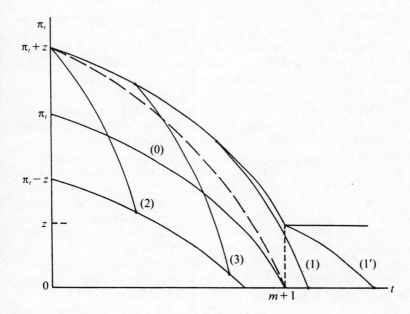

*Figure 3.4*

The curve marked (1) relates to the case $w^I > w^{II}$; here an earlier acquisition is profitable if $\pi_1^{t-1} < \pi_t + z$. (1') is a special case in which II acquires discarded machines at the cost of shipment only. In this case, the standard closed-economy analysis of truncations holds without modification. Along (1) and (1'), Inequality (3.14) also holds but along curves (2) and (3) it becomes violated. These curves show profiles of machine prices when the Peripheral economy uses a more labour-intensive process with each machine. In principle, this could lead to re-export if machine use in II is truncated at a positive 'received price'.

For simplicity, it has been assumed that $z$ is constant. If, more realistically, $z_t$ increases with $t$, the consequences are straightforward: acquisition dates can be expected to move forward; truncation dates can be expected to be postponed.

### 3.6 Technological progress and obsolescence
We now consider some possible consequences of technological progress in country I on the initial assumption that shipment costs

are zero. It is also assumed, for simplicity, that the wage rate in I is given. As a result of innovation a new method of food production is introduced which thus allows the economy to pay a higher rate of profits, $r^{I'} > r^I$. Capitalists in I who are still in possession of outdated machines will not cease production with those machines if, to quote Sraffa, they 'are worth employing for what they can get' (1960, p. 78). What this means is that the prices of superseded machines will drop to that point at which they can pay the new, higher rate of profits. In other words, the price profile of such machines (Figure 3.4) will shift vertically downwards. The older obsolete machines are less able to bear the higher profit burden, so that discarding will now occur at some age $h + 1 \leqslant m + 1$.

As a result of the improvement in production and the consequent increase in $r^I$, relative prices in I will change. If the material inputs consists of a number of commodities combined in proportions which vary from age to age of machines, the magnitudes of the changes in values of the $e_t$ will depend on $t$: that is, the original ranking of the $e_t$ may not be preserved. To keep things tractable, therefore, we shall assume that materials, spares, etc. are used in unvarying proportions. Then, if there are no elements of jointness in the system, apart from fixed capital, and if the technical progress occurs only in the production of food, the prices of all other goods will rise relative to that of food.[14] Thus the $e_t$ will all increase in proportion. The price equations in I, after revaluation are now:

$$1 + \pi'_1 = R^{I'}(e'_0 + \pi'_0) + w^I\lambda_0 \qquad (3.15.1)$$

$$1 = R^{I'}(e'_h + \pi'_h) + w^I\lambda_h \qquad (3.15.h)$$
$$1 = \bar{R}^I(e'_{h+1}) + w^I\lambda_{h+1} \qquad (3.15.h+1)$$

Inspection of Equations (3.15.1) – (3.15.h) shows that, although $e_t$ has risen (to $e'_t$), the value of capital ($e'_t + \pi'_t$) must have fallen as a result of the revaluation of machines, which means that the slopes of the $w$–$r$ trade-offs for all processes $1 \ldots h$ have fallen. Process $h + 1$ is no longer viable in I, and at the newly estimated prices is unable to pay the competitive rate of profits: $\bar{R}^I < R^{I'}$.

In addition to the simplifying assumptions already made, suppose that, at the new prices, the process corresponding to the newest modern machine has a capital:labour ratio in excess of the revalued ratios of any of the obsolete processes. Similarly, the oldest modern machine process has a higher capital:labour ratio than the oldest obsolete process (process $h$). With these assumptions we can hardly lay claim to a general treatment of the issue, but they are the most plausible ones that can be made while maintaining some degree of simplicity. Let us now reconsider the previous cases:

(a) $w^{\mathrm{I}} = w^{\mathrm{II}}$. In this case, II-capitalists are indifferent to using modern machines or obsolete machines, up to age $h$, at their revalued prices. The rate of profits in II increases to $r^{\mathrm{I}'}$.

(b) $w^{\mathrm{II}} < w^{\mathrm{I}}$. Here obsolete machines are preferable to new ones, but the choice of machine age and the impact on the rate of profits depend on technical circumstances and the level of $w^{\mathrm{II}}$.

Suppose that older machines ($h + 1$, onwards) unambiguously decline in physical efficiency; that is $e'_{t+1} \geqslant e'_t$, and $\lambda_{t+1} \geqslant \lambda_t (t = h + 1 \ldots m + 1)$ with at least one strict inequality holding. Now since $\pi_{h+1} = \pi_{h+2} = \ldots 0$, this means that, whatever the given level of $w^{\mathrm{II}}$, processes $h + 2 \ldots m + 1$ are physically less productive and, therefore less profitable than process $h + 1$. Thus, the only two processes which are eligible on profitability grounds are $h$ and $h + 1$. Although the $w$–$r$ trade-off for $h + 1$ passes below $(w^{\mathrm{I}}, r^{\mathrm{I}'})$ it may have a smaller slope ($e'_{h+1} \geqslant e'_h$ but $\pi_h > \pi_{h+1} = 0$) and so be viable at a low level of $w^{\mathrm{II}}$. (The conclusion here resembles that relating to the earlier choice between $m$ and $m + 1$, illustrated in Figure 3.1)

The question remains, however, whether or not $r^{\mathrm{II}}$ will increase as a result of the obsolescence of machinery. For $w^{\mathrm{II}}$ sufficiently close to $w^{\mathrm{I}}$ there is little doubt that it will. There exists some range of $w^{\mathrm{II}}$ for which the revalued process $h'$ is unambiguously more profitable than process $m$ at the old prices. (See Figure 3.5 where the primes indicate new values.) On the other hand, for low levels of $w^{\mathrm{II}}$ the conclusion is not clear-cut. Compare, for example, process $m + 1$ at old prices and $h + 1'$ at new. If $e_{m+1} = e_{h+1} < e'_{h+1}$ and $\lambda_{m+1} > \lambda_{h+1}$ then the trade-offs may appear as they are in Figure 3.5. Since the intercepts on the $r$-axis are $(1/e_{m+1}) - 1 > (1/e'_{h+1}) - 1$, it follows that if $w^{\mathrm{II}}$ is sufficiently low, the rate of profits may decline as a consequence of obsolescence.

The last result may be understood as a consequence of technical progress leading to a deterioration in the terms of trade of the food

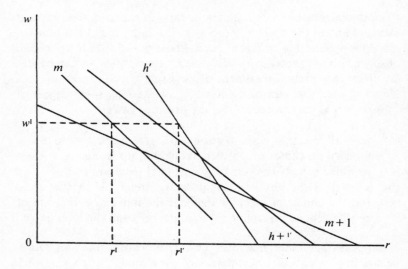

*Figure 3.5*

exporter. Because II is small it suffers from the relative price changes brought about by innovation. Since capitalists there are already using a machine which is free, or very cheap, they benefit little from the downward revaluation of machine prices, but they do suffer from the increased prices of other materials. Improvements in farming techniques in rich countries may have the effect of depressing world food prices to an extent which outweighs the benefits to poor countries of being able to obtain the older techniques more cheaply. Of course, if innovations in other sectors of I's economy were keeping pace with that in food, this terms-of-trade effect would be neutralized and II could not suffer reduced profitability.

Whether $r^{II}$ rises or not, capitalists in II will have to make the best of the new situation. The small-country assumption implies that the stock of machines of any age is infinitely large compared to II's annual requirements. If machines of zero price are chosen (that is, age $h + 1$) then, in the absence of storage costs and machine deterioration, the entire stock would be acquired and would last indefinitely. This unlikely story is not so much a reflection of the limitations of the small-country assumption as of the importance of including realistic costs in the analysis. But, even with positive storage costs, the stock of acquired machines may be in excess of annual requirements. Only when that stock is depleted will more costly second-hand machines be employed. A low-cost stock of machines will allow the low-wage country to maintain a relatively high profits rate until modern machines are about to be discarded (though, by that time, they too may be obsolete).

The effect of transport costs, it may be noted, will be to delay changes which would otherwise have taken place immediately in order to spread the overhead costs of shipping the machines already *in situ*.

The analysis of this section so far may be summed up as follows. At relatively high levels of $w^{II}$, $r^{II}$ will rise through the purchase of obsolete machines. It will then fall once the stock of obsolete machines is exhausted but will remain above its initial level. Obsolescence gives a windfall boost to the rate of profits. At low levels of $w^{II}$, $r^{II}$ may fall in two stages: first, due to the switch to a younger obsolete machine and then to the switch to a second-hand modern machine. This last result is not, however, inevitable and no clear-cut conclusions can be stated, even on the assumptions that have been made. With a fixed savings ratio, the rate of growth in II will follow the course of $r^{II}$.

This leaves a final point. We have considered technical improvements that were innovated on behalf of I's food producers. Their effects on II are ambiguous. It may, however, be that research and development skills in I could allow the development of technologies particularly suited to low-wage countries. The adoption of *new* low-capital techniques in II could be more profitable than employing second-hand machines left over from more capital-intensive methods. If II-capitalists are incapable of developing indigenous appropriate technology, entrepreneurs in I could do it for them. Because of the smallness of II's market a successful 'appropriate innovation' would not affect the natural rate of profits in I, but short-run competitive pressures could still induce such efforts.

## 3.7 Conclusions

This section summarizes the main results of the chapter, compares them with the findings of other writers and ends on a brief theoretical note.

It has been seen that where the operating costs of machines are constant or increasing with age, then, in the absence of transport costs, low-wage countries will purchase the oldest machines available. It was this finding that Sen emphasized. The case of decreasing operating costs was also examined. If labour costs fall it may make sense for poor countries to buy new machines, but if the lower operating costs are due to lower commodity inputs the Sen result is unaffected. Here we are in disagreement with Smith (1974, p. 276) who concludes that 'If the lower operating costs are due to lower requirements of freely traded inputs, no producer will find it advantageous or disadvantageous to use older rather than new machines'. The Sen conclusions are upset where the possibility of input substitutions is admitted. If, as one might expect, low-wage countries use more labour and less commodity inputs with a machine of given age, then it is not possible to say *a priori* which age is most profitable.

Where transport costs are zero only one age will be chosen (by a small economy) in all but very exceptional circumstances where two ages may be equiprofitable. But with positive transport costs the neat conclusions become rather blurred. The acquisition–truncation period now becomes extended so as to spread the burden of shipment. In combination with input substitutions this can give rise to a wide variety of import–export patterns. It is not so surprising, on the basis of this analysis, to find one observer[15] reporting that a large proportion of low-wage country imports were of new machines. Smith prefers to attribute this to market imperfections though his justification for ignoring transport costs, we have already argued, is rather weak.

Sen regards trade in second-hand machinery due to obsolescence as 'easy to understand' and does not analyse the problem. Schwartz similarly argues that machines which are depreciated because of obsolescence 'will be bargain priced'. Our analysis suggests that obsolescence is a more complicated matter than these remarks would lead one to believe. The technological advance which is the source of obsolescence may give rise to a terms-of-trade effect which reduces profitability in the low-wage country. Such countries may continue to purchase used machines but the possibility of reduced profitability could make indigenous or intermediate techniques more attractive. Conclusions relating to obsolescence appear to be a lot less 'easy to understand' than conclusions relating to machine depreciation at constant or increasing operating costs.

The entire analysis has been expressed in positive terms on the assumption that decisions in II are taken by competitive capitalists. It can easily be recast in normative terms by regarding $r^{II}$ as the rate of surplus on capital at the appropriate shadow wage rate $w^{II}$. Government policy should then be directed to a machine import structure which maximizes the rate of surplus. This could imply no imports at all if a superior indigenous technique is available or it could imply imports of brand-new 'appropriate' machines. There are no straightforward recommendations. Schwartz is surely right to call for the removal of simple rules preventing imports of second-hand machines. There is a danger, though, that a presumption that market wage rates exceed shadow wage rates will lead economists to call for imports of old machines in the naive belief that this is always rational.[16] Insistence on the use of second-hand machinery irrespective of circumstances could be as damaging as prohibitions.

We finish on a theoretical note. The relative simplicity of our analysis is due mainly to the small-country assumption. If I and II were both large countries, and both incompletely specialized, it would not be possible to refer with theoretical ease (and accuracy) to the capital–intensity of techniques. Explanations of trade patterns in these terms would almost certainly be impossible. Since, no doubt, second-hand machinery is extensively traded between large economies, such an analysis would be desirable. But it would, in full Sraffian generality, be an extremely complex affair.

## Notes

1. For a simple exposition, see Sau (1978). Gabisch (1975) also addresses this problem; Smith (1976) has shown, however, that Gabisch's conclusions are flawed by a crucial error in his analysis.
2. See Sraffa (1960, Ch.X). On the modern development of Sraffian fixed-capital theory, the classic reference is Schefold (1980); see also the essays by Baldone and Varri in the same collection: Pasinetti (1980). For a simplified account, see Mainwaring (1984).
3. It is assumed that, apart from machine use, there are no elements of joint production in II. Labour is the only primary input. Only by coincidence would two or more traded goods then be equiprofitable. The inclusion of non-traded goods in II would not affect the results provided that they are not used as means of production in food.
4. See references cited in note 2.
5. The trade-offs are thus completely analogous to those of the single-products system used in Chapters 1 and 2. It may be noted that for a fixed-capital system the outer $w$–$r$ frontier (that is, the relation between $w$ and $r$ allowing for a choice of techniques) will be monotonically downward sloping. (See references cited in note 2.)
6. This analysis gives (conditional) support to Todaro's (1970) view, summarized by Smith (1974), that 'using second-hand machines ties underdeveloped countries to the labour-saving technical progress of the developed countries, where the introduction of capital-saving domestic technologies would give a better

prospect for the long-run solutions of the problems of underdeveloped countries'. Smith, however, appears more sceptical of this view.

7.  It is, of course, possible that one of these costs may increase as the other falls. Since the effects are 'additive', however, nothing of interest would be gained by considering this possibility separately.

8.  No machine used in a profitable process can have a non-positive price (see references cited in note 2). A zero price will obtain for discarded machines on the zero-scrap-value/free-disposal assumption: that is $\pi_{m+1} = 0$. Then, comparing Equations $(3.1.m-1)$, with $\pi_m > 0$, and $(3.1.m)$, with $\pi_{m+1} = 0$, it can be seen that $e_m \geqslant e_{m-1}$ and $\lambda_m \geqslant \lambda_{m-1}$ imply $\pi_m < \pi_{m-1}$. Working backwards along the series of equations reveals that $\pi_t > \pi_{t+1}$.

9.  The algebraic conditions for this occurrence are not especially illuminating, but there is no difficulty in constructing numerical examples.

10. Non-monotonic labour costs also imply the theoretical, though very exceptional, possibility of machines of different ages operating equiprofitably in II.

11. It is assumed that the quality, and hence price, of a machine of given age is independent of the way it has been maintained.

12. A simple numerical example which conforms to the diagram is as follows: In I, the machine is discarded after two years. The data are: $\pi_0 = 1$, $\lambda_0 = \lambda_1 = 0.05$, $e_0 = 0.2$, $e_1 = 0.25$. If $w^I = 1.564$, then $R^I = 1.2$ and $\pi_1 = 0.518$. In country II, the alternative coefficients are $\lambda_0 = 0.2$, $\lambda_1 = 0.4$, $e_0 = 0.04$, $e = 0.05$. Machines are traded at prices already established in I. Then for the approximate limits $0.6 < w^{II} < 1.2$, the new machine is the most profitable purchase.

13. Extending system $(3.8')$ by one year requires a modification of Equation $(3.8'.1)$ and the addition of a new equation:

$$1 + \pi^0{}_2 = R'(e_1 + \pi^0{}_1) + w^{II}\lambda_1$$
$$1 = R'(e_2 + \pi^0{}_2) + w^{II}\lambda_2$$

Taking, for simplicity, the case of a fixed $r$ and variable $w$, the changes in wages for 2- and 3-year truncations are:

$$\frac{dw_2}{dz} = \frac{-2Rz}{\lambda_0 R + \lambda_1} \text{ and } \frac{dw_3}{dz} = \frac{-3Rz}{\lambda_0 R^2 + \lambda_1 R + \lambda_2}$$

If $\lambda_2 \geqslant \lambda_1 \geqslant \lambda_0$ and $R > 1$, wages fall faster with the 2-year truncation.

14. See, for example, Mainwaring (1984), p. 139.

15. James (1970), reported in Smith (1976).

16. Sen comes close to this, while James (1975) offers the following advice (emphasis added): 'The case now seems to favour *overwhelmingly* the promotion (or at least allowance) and the judicial use of second-hand machines in LDCs.'

# PART II

# WORLD TRADE IN GOODS AND ASSETS

# 4 The international Pasinetti process

## 4.1 Introduction

It was shown in 1.6 that under certain circumstances free trade in goods would enable one of the economies to grow at the expense of the other. This possibility arose, however, only where the faster growing economy was unable to specialize completely, an outcome which in the context of the model might be regarded as a somewhat special case. But once free international investment is permitted the growing dominance of one economy becomes the general rule. This chapter is largely concerned with a demonstration of this assertion and a preliminary examination of some of its implications. The process of economic domination is nevertheless the thread which runs through most of Part II. To begin, the analysis is conducted at a highly aggregated level, the specification of production relations being postponed till the following chapter.

As in the example in Chapter 1, the growing dominance of one economy cannot normally co-exist with global steady growth. It thus becomes necessary to find an alternative framework within which to discuss the evolution of the world economy and the general process of uneven development. While an evolutionary process cannot be adequately represented by a system in stationary equilibrium or in steady growth, it may, as in some biological theories, be regarded as a movement towards a steady, albeit very distant, state. Indeed, the biological concepts of evolution and selection are suggestive ways of modelling economic development. A potentially fruitful approach to the analysis of global accumulation is provided by the 'self-organization' theory of Manfred Eigen (1971) which models the selection of biological information carriers.[1]

In Eigen's theory, the simplest case of 'constant overall organization', without feedbacks is represented by the equation

$$\dot{z}_i = \varepsilon(s_i - \tilde{s})z_i \tag{4.1}$$

where $z_i$ is the relative importance of carrier $i$ in conveying information ($\dot{z}_i = dz_i/dt$); $s_i$ is the 'selective value' of carrier $i$, a measure of its competitiveness against other carriers, $\tilde{s}$ is average selective value weighted by the $z_i$; and $\varepsilon$ is an adjustment parameter.

The implication of Equation (4.1) is that only those information carriers will grow whose selective values are greater than $\tilde{s}$ and, as a consequence of this growth, they shift the 'threshold value', $\tilde{s}$, to steadily higher levels, so that

$$\tilde{s} \rightarrow s^m{}_i \tag{4.2}$$

where $m$ 'refers to the species with maximum selective value relative to all competitors in the final phase' (Eigen 1971, p. 477).[2]

The self-organization theory could be applied to the issue of economic development and underdevelopment by an appropriate reinterpretation of the variables of Equation (4.1). If, instead of information carriers, our competing agents are national economies or, more accurately, national capitals, then the $z_i$ would refer to the relative share of nation-$i$ capital in total world capital. The selective values would then have to be an index of the aggressiveness in the pursuit of capital accumulation ('animal spirits', perhaps) of the competing groups of capitalists. Again, neglecting feedbacks, the interpretation of Equation (4.1) and process (4.2) would then be that the more aggressive national capitals would come to dominate the less aggressive and that, in the limit, one, and only one, such capital would assume economic significance, the relative importance of all the others tending to zero. Interestingly, there already exists a dynamic economic model which, as we shall show below, has all the relevant properties of the simple self-organization model. Luigi Pasinetti has shown that in a closed economy where there are several groups of capitalists characterized by different savings propensities, 'the thriftiest group of capitalists will in the end dominate all the others' (1974, p.141). Considering the world as a closed economy, this process of domination should also apply to capitalists of different nations if these, too, have different savings ratios.

Of course, the actual historical time needed for these asymptotic tendencies to reach something approaching complete economic dominance by one population of capitalists may be enormous, far in excess of the epoch of world capitalism from early colonial times to the present. But the asymptotic states are not our direct concern. What are of interest are the properties of the evolutionary path at any point in time. The changes that take place over decades, or even years, may still be sufficiently large to be of interest.

The purpose of this chapter is to develop a particularly simple model of capitalist self-organization based on the international Pasinetti process. The world is again divided into two countries, or regions, Centre and Periphery, labelled from this chapter on as 1 and 2, respectively. No assumptions are made about the nature of international specialization though, in the production model of the next chapter, such assumptions will be unavoidable. It is assumed that there are no political or institutional obstacles to the free movement of capital between the two regions. The model, in other words, is one of perfect capitalist development.

## 4.2 International investment and the Pasinetti process
The capital flows may take the form of foreign direct investment (for example, the establishment of multinational branch plants), or of portfolio investment (the purchase of titles to real capital), or of credits which are not tied in any direct way to particular items of capital equipment but which, nevertheless, imply claims on wealth. In the case of portfolio investment and credit, the 'capital' flows are financial, though the transfer of purchasing power will normally induce a corresponding flow of goods, or real capital. In the case of direct investment, the flows of finance and physical capital are generally coincident (though not necessarily so). In either case, capital flows change the pattern of ownership of a country's total capital stock, measured in value terms, and it is with such stocks that we are concerned in this chapter.

Starting from an arbitrary point in time, the analysis considers the dynamic behaviour of capital stocks (i.e., growth rates of capital), the ownership of capital and flows of profits remittances. At the starting date it is assumed that the (hypothetical) rates of profits that would obtain in each country in the absence of international investment, $r_1$ and $r_2$, are such that $r_1 < r_2$. This means, of course, that the direction of investment flow is from 1 to 2. The rate of flow is just sufficient to equalise the rates of profits actually obtaining, at the rate $r$. The conditions for the convergence of $r_1$ and $r_2$ are not investigated, merely assumed.

Within country 1, we assume a simple class division between workers and capitalists. Initially, it is supposed that workers do not save out of their incomes, whereas capitalists save a constant proportion, $s_1$ $(0 < s_1 \le 1)$, of profits. Also, for the time being, government economic activity is ignored. Country 2 also has a worker–

capitalist division, but there is also a division based on capital ownership. Since investment flows from 1 to 2, some part of the capital stock in 2 is owned by capitalists in 1. (Depending on the type of investment, the ownership may be of actual physical assets, of titles to assets or of claims on wealth.) That part of the means of production of 2's economy which is foreign-owned we refer to as the *enclave*. Note that, in the case in which all foreign investment is of the direct variety, this term bears some resemblance to the way it is generally used in the literature on underdevelopment. Allowing for portfolio investment (or even joint ventures), however, means that the term, as used here, is rather more abstract, many enterprises in country 2 being partly domestically owned, partly foreign-owned. Allowing for credits increases the degree of abstraction even further. Capital outside the enclave is, by definition, domestically owned. It is assumed that the indigenous capitalists of country 2 save out of domestic profits a proportion, $s_2$ $(0 \leq s_2 < s_1)$; workers in country 2 save nothing.

Since we have abstracted from government activity in the form of revenue raising, expenditure or international transfers, the national income accounts for each country may be written as:

$$I_i + E_i + F_i = S_i + M_i \quad (i = 1, 2) \tag{4.3.i}$$

where I is the value of net domestic investment; $E$, the value of exports; $M$, the value of imports; $F$, net foreign income from abroad; and $S$, savings. The equation of external balance is

$$E_i + F_i = M_i + B_i \tag{4.4.i}$$

where $B$ is the current balance, equal in magnitude but opposite in sign to the capital account balance. Equations (4.3) and (4.4) together imply

$$I_i = S_i - B_i \tag{4.5.i}$$

while the restriction to two countries implies that

$$B_1 = -B_2 \text{ and} \tag{4.6}$$
$$F_1 = -F_2 \tag{4.7}$$

A problem now arises concerning the way to deal with the flows of financial investment and remitted profits. It is assumed that the proportion saved out of overseas profits earned by 1-capitalists is the same as the proportion saved out of their domestic profits. Overseas profits which are not saved are repatriated and there is no further saving out of this income; the portion saved is reinvested abroad, in addition to the continued outflow, $B_1$. Let $K_i$ be the value of the capital stock in country i, and $\alpha$ the proportion of $K_2$ owned by 1-capitalists. Then $F_1$, the amount of profits remitted, is given by

$$F_1 = (1 - s_1)r\alpha K_2 \tag{4.8}$$

Note that, with this way of modelling financial flows, outward net investment from country 1 $(-B_1)$ is occurring at the same time as inward profits remittances $(F_1)$. Would it not make more sense if 1-capitalists were to retain more (and possibly all) of their profits earnings in country 2, reinvesting them there, and correspondingly reducing investment funding out of home profits? Clearly, as long as there is no cost in moving funds (which we assume), it makes no logical difference how we approach this matter, since the net outflow, $-B_1 + F_1$, is the same in either case. The chosen procedure has the advantage, however, of leaving the savings ratio on foreign and domestic profits the same, whereas the alternative would require that the savings ratio on foreign incomes be greater than on domestic profits. This is purely a matter of accounting definitions and in no way affects the generality of the analysis.

Since all savings come from profits, total savings in country 1 are $S_1 = s_1 r K_1$. Thus, dividing Equation (4.5.1) by $K_1$ gives

$$g_1 = s_1 r - \beta_1 \tag{4.9}$$

where $g_1$ is the rate of growth of the capital stock in country 1, and $\beta_1 = B_1/K_1$, the ratio of capital outflow to capital stock. Substituting Equation (4.6) into Equation (4.5.2) and dividing by $K_2$ yields

$$g_2 = \bar{s}_2 r + \beta_2 \tag{4.10}$$

where

$$\beta_2 = B_1/K_2 \tag{4.11}$$

is the ratio of capital *inflow* to capital stock in country 2, and

$$\bar{s}_2 = s_1\alpha + s_2(1 - \alpha) \tag{4.12}$$

is the average of 1-capitalist and 2-capitalist savings ratios, weighted according to their shares in the ownership of 2-capital. Note that $g_2$ measures the rate of growth of all capital in country 2, irrespective of ownership.

The Pasinetti process suggests that provided $s_1$ remains greater than $s_2$, then, over time, $\alpha$ approaches unity as 1-capitalists come to dominate the ownership of the world's capital. In the present context, this result may be obtained formally, as follows. In period $t + 1$, 1-capitalist's ownership of 2-capital may be written as

$$\alpha^{t+1}K_2^{t+1} = \alpha^t K_2^t + s_1 r^t \alpha^t K_2^t + B_1^{t+1} \tag{4.13}$$

That is, capital ownership in period $t + 1$ is equal to capital ownership in period $t$ plus additions through net investment financed by savings out of profits in country 2, plus the capital inflow financed by savings out of profits in country 1. Dividing through Equation (4.13) by $\alpha^t K_2^t$ gives (by way of Equation (4.11)) and the fact that $1 + g_2^t = K_2^{t+1}/K_2^t$,

$$\frac{\alpha^{t+1}}{\alpha^t} \cdot (1 + g'_2) = 1 + s_1 r^t + \frac{\beta^t_2}{\alpha^t} \tag{4.14}$$

where

$$\beta^t_i = B_i^{t+1}/K_i^t$$

Substituting for $g_2^t$ from Equation (4.10) allows Equation (4.14) to be written

$$\frac{\alpha^{t+1}}{\alpha^t} = \frac{1 + s_1 r^t + (\beta^t_2/\alpha^t)}{1 + \bar{s}_2 r^t + \beta^t_2} \tag{4.15}$$

Since $\bar{s}_2$ is a weighted average of $s_1$ and $s_2$ with weights $\alpha$ and $(1 - \alpha)$ then, with $s_1 > s_2$, we must have $s_1 > \bar{s}_2$, as long as $\alpha^t < 1$. So it follows directly from Equation (4.15) that, so long as $\alpha^t < 1$, then $\alpha^{t+1} > \alpha^t$. It is also clear that Equation (4.15) converges to a solution $\alpha^{t+1} = \alpha^t = 1$. In words, if the world capitalist economy evolved according to this model then, over time, ownership of the

Periphery's capital stock by capitalists in the Centre would approach 100 per cent.

### 4.3 Growth paths and comparative growth rates

On the basis of the analysis of the last section we can now consider the growth paths of the world economy, of the Centre and the Periphery and, within the latter, of the enclave and the indigenous sector.

The rate of growth of the world economy, $g_w$, is simply an average of the growth rates of the two countries weighted according to their capital stocks:

$$g_w = \frac{g_1 K_1 + g_2 K_2}{K_1 + K_2}$$

It is clear that, as $\alpha \to 1$, $g_w \to s_1 r$.

To be more precise about the nature of the growth paths it is necessary to specify the assumptions relating to the underlying price and distributional relationships of the model. This is done more fully in succeeding chapters. It will, nevertheless, be helpful to sketch out here the growth behaviour of the two cases to be analysed in depth later:

*Case (i)*, which is more appropriate as a description of the earlier phase of global capitalism, involves the assumption that real wages in both Centre and Periphery remain constant over time. This case will be explored in Chapter 5.

*Case (ii)* allows real wages in the Centre to be determined by the interplay of economic growth and population growth. (Similar considerations arise where the expansion of the Periphery is constrained by the availability of natural resources.)

The transition from case (i) to case (ii) might be thought of as having a historical parallel in terms of the gradual exhaustion of the reserve armies of labour in the Centre, and this is how it will be approached in Chapter 6.

In the first case both the uniform profit rate and relative prices remain constant provided technology displays constant returns, and primary resource constraints and technological progress are absent (or else, exactly offsetting).[3] In the second case these additional assumptions will be insufficient, in general, to prevent $r$ and relative prices varying over time. When prices are constant, capital stock changes are accurately measured in quantitative terms and, with constant returns, the growth rates of value-capital, outputs and employment are all the same. Changing prices mean, however, that capital stocks are subject to period-to-period revaluations and, even with constant returns, the growth rate of value-capital will not, in general, be equal to the growth rate of employment. So far as capital is concerned, however, we can write

$$I^t = g^{t-1} K^{t-1} = \bar{s} r^{t-1} K^{t-1} \pm B^t \tag{4.17}$$

where $I^t$ is an amount of capital purchased at current prices with retained profits (from home and overseas) earned on capital valued at last period's prices. (If the price of the equipment purchased has gone up, this simply means that less can be bought with money available.) It is easy to see from Equation (4.17) that the fundamental growth Equations (4.9) and (4.10) remain intact in value terms even when prices are changing.

In both cases, if demand patterns are constant then the limit path, along which $g_w = s_1 r_1$, will be a steady state in which the means of production will have adjusted themselves to the constant proportions needed to satisfy demands. Along such a path the incentive for international capital movements will, in case (i) and, in certain circumstances, in case (ii), be extinguished, so that $\beta_1 = \beta_2 = 0$. Although such a terminal state may be regarded as exceedingly unrealistic it does provide a starting point for the analysis and allows us to describe the growth behaviour of the model with some degree of precision.

Turning now to the individual countries we have, from Equations (4.9), (4.10) and (4.12)

$$g_2 - g_1 = s_1 r(\alpha - 1) + s_2 r(1 - \alpha) + \beta_1 + \beta_2$$

As compared to a zero-investment world, the movement of capital simultaneously depresses growth in 1 and increases it in 2, the sum of these effects creating the difference, $\beta_1 + \beta_2$. But, over time, there are additional effects due to the growth in $\alpha$ (and also to the changing values of the $\beta_i$ and, since $s_2 < s_1$, it is not possible, in general, to say whether $g_2 > g_1$. Only when $\alpha$ has converged to unity is it possible to write

$$g_2 - g_1 = \beta_1 + \beta_2$$

and, if this limit is a steady-state path with $\beta_i = 0$, we may conclude that $g_1$ and $g_2$ both converge on the value $s_1 r$.

Within country 2 we may now distinguish between the growth of enclave capital $\alpha K_2$ and indigenous capital $(1 - \alpha)K_2$. The growth within the enclave may be obtained directly from Equation (4.13):

$$g^e = \frac{\alpha^{t+1} K_2^{t+1} - \alpha^t K^t_2}{\alpha^t K^t} = s_1 r + \frac{\beta_2^t}{\alpha^t} \tag{4.18}$$

Incremental ownership of capital outside the enclave is given by

$$(1 - \alpha^{t+1}) K_2^{t+1} = (1 - \alpha^t) K_2^t + s_2 r (1 - \alpha^t) K_2^t$$

Rearranging and dividing through by $(1 - \alpha^t) K_2^t$ gives

$$g_2^I = s_2 r \tag{4.19}$$

as the growth rate of the indigenous sector. As will already have been guessed, $g_2$ is the average of $g_2^e$ and $g_2^I$, weighted by $\alpha$ and $(1 - \alpha)$ respectively. It may, however, be worth sounding a slight note of caution in applying these weighting procedures. The determination of the starting points of the free-investment growth paths (which although, in themselves, are only of formal interest, do help in ensuring the consistency of the paths at a later stage) cannot be determined by applying weights involving $\alpha = 0$. If $\alpha = 0$, no investment can have been undertaken which not only implies that $\beta_i = 0$ but also that the appropriate rates of profit are the unequalized rates, $r_1$ and $r_2$. The starting point for the path of $g_2$, for $\alpha$ close to zero, is approximately equal to $s_2 r + \beta_2$.

There are two further points to note. First, the average rate of growth of country 1 and the enclave is, from Equations (4.9) and (4.18),

$$\frac{g_1 K_1 + g_2^e \alpha K_2}{K_1 + \alpha K_2} = s_1 r \tag{4.20}$$

Again, this is not surprising since the enclave is, effectively, the economic territory of $1-$capitalists. From the point of view of

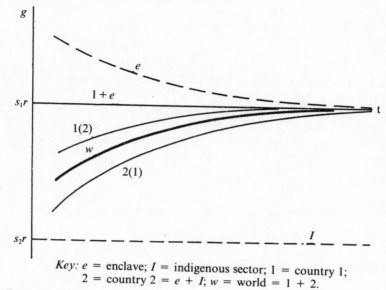

Key: $e$ = enclave; $I$ = indigenous sector; 1 = country 1;
2 = country 2 = $e + I$; $w$ = world = 1 + 2.

*Figure 4.1*

capital movements, country 1 plus enclave may be regarded as a unified closed economy within which only the savings behaviour of 1 − capitalists is relevant for determining the rate of growth. The second point is that $g_w$, being a weighted average of $g_2^I$, $g_2^e$ and $g_1$, must always be greater than the lowest of these rates, $g_2^I$.

Drawing these results together, we may summarize as follows:

$$g_2^e > g_2 > g_2^I$$
$$g_2^e > g_1$$

$g_w (> g_2^I)$ is a weighted average of $g_1$ and $g_2$.

For case (i), in which $r$ remains constant, the various growth paths are illustrated in Figure 4.1; all, with the exception of $g_2^I$, converging on the value $s_1r$.

Turning to case (ii), suppose that the labour force in the Centre is growing permanently at the rate $n_1$ and, moreover, that $n_1 < s_1r'$, where $r'$ is the value taken by the world uniform rate of profits at some finite time $t$. (It is assumed that $n_2 \geqslant s_1r'$, for all $t$.) At some point, the constraint on labour supply in the Centre can be assumed to force up the real wage there which, in turn, may lead to mechanisms (to be discussed in Chapter 6) which reduce the world rate of profits.[4] If so, $g_w$ will converge, possibly along a fluctuating path, to $s_1 r^*$, where $r^* = n_1/s_1$. In this case, Figure 4.1 can be taken to represent the various growth paths 'normalized' with respect to $s_1 r^*$.

If international investment began in some particular period when Centre and Periphery were already engaged in free goods trade and in global steady growth at the rate $n_1$, then the investment regime will be 'temporary' in the sense that after some finite time, $g_w$ will have returned to a value very close to $n_1$. In the meantime, the switch in resources to the world's more profitable economy (where there is no labour constraint) will have allowed world growth to exceed the rate $n_1$. From this perspective, international investment is seen to be a disequilibrium phenomenon, just as net intersectoral investment flows in a closed economy reflect departures from steady growth.

### 4.4 The transformation of Peripheral capitalism
We now consider a particular aspect of enclave and indigenous development in more detail. From Equation (4.8), it can be seen that, as $\alpha \to 1$, all of the profits which are generated in country 2 are either reinvested or remitted to country 1. This means that capitalist consumption as a proportion of income in country 2 tends to zero, both outside the enclave and within it. The first part of this conclusion, concerning the indigenous capitalists, follows easily: as $\alpha \to 1$, the proportion of indigenous to total capital falls to zero. Thus, *in relative terms*, indigenous capitalists are eliminated and, with them, indigenous capitalist consumption. (In absolute terms, of course, indigenous capital is actually increasing at the positive rate $g_2$ – provided $s_2 > 0$. But the social and economic significance of this capital becomes less and less over time, and infinitesimal in the final state.)

The second part of our conclusion, that the enclave develops into a mere production–investment machine, is harder to imagine and difficult to accept. The conclusion can, however, be avoided by a simple reinterpretation of the model. The logic of the model remains intact if, instead of requiring that unretained profits, $F_1$, are physically remitted to country 1, we require merely that they are remitted to 1-capitalists. If 1-capitalists remained permanently domiciled in country 1 then, of course, the geographical and social specifications of the direction of remittances would coincide. But the growth of an enclave employing 1-capital can be assumed to attract also part of the 1-capitalist class (broadly defined to include managers, agents, etc.). Indeed, former indigenous capitalists (or, perhaps, landowners) would, in all probability, be co-opted into the enclave to act as agents for foreign capital and, so, become part of this class, sharing in the profit incomes that are generated. This way of specifying the model is explicitly adopted in the next chapter.

If the enclave is regarded as an offshoot of the economy of country 1, then capitalist consumption within the enclave may rise faster than national income in country 2: the rate of growth of 'remittances', from Equation (4.8), is

$$(F^{t+1}/F^t) - 1 = (\alpha^{t+1}K_2^{t+1}/\alpha^t K_2^t) - 1 = g_2^e \qquad (4.21)$$

Thus 'remittances' grow at the same rate as the enclave in general (and so faster than $g_2$). If a constant proportion of these unretained profits are consumed within the enclave and if the ratio of capitalists to capital is constant, *per capita* consumption will also be constant.

One further implication of Equation (4.8) is that

$$F_1 \to (1 - s_1)rK_2 \text{ as } \alpha \to 1$$

At the same time, in the approach to a steady state, $\beta_2 \to 0$. It follows, of necessity, that after some finite time, $F_1 > B_2$; that is, the 'debt-servicing' on accumulated investments will exceed the continuing capital inflows. Even if only a portion of $F_1$ is actually returned to country 1, at some period the Periphery's net financial inflow will become negative.

### 4.5   Workers' savings

It has so far been assumed that all savings come out of profits. Although this assumption will be retained in succeeding chapters the implications of positive savings by workers will be briefly examined in this section. In the operation of the Pasinetti process in a closed economy, the existence of workers' savings has no bearing on the outcome. Exactly the same is true of the international Pasinetti process. This can readily be demonstrated by a simple adaptation of Pasinetti's own argument (1962, pp. 270–2) in which, throughout, $I$ is replaced by $I_i + B_i$ (reflecting the change from the closed-economy equilibrium condition, $I = S$, to the open-economy condition of Equation (4.5), $I_i = S_i - B_i$). The intuitive explanation of this conclusion (Pasinetti, 1974, pp. 127–8) is that, in the long run, the profits received by each class come to bear the same proportion to the savings generated by that class. Thus, letting $P$ be profits; $W$, wages; and denoting workers by $w$ and capitalists by $c$,

$$\frac{P}{S} = \frac{P_c}{S_c} = \frac{P_w}{S_w}$$

Then, from Equation (4.5),

$$\frac{P}{I+B} = \frac{1}{s_c} \cdot \frac{P_c}{P_c} = \frac{P_w}{s_W(P_W + W)} \tag{4.22}$$

whence, from the first equality,

$$I = s_c P - B$$
which, dividing through by $K$, yields

$$g = s_c r - \beta$$

Thus, provided $s$ in the previous sections is understood as the capitalist savings ratio, the growth equation for country 1, Equation (4.9), is unaffected by workers' savings. For country 2, workers' savings in that country are similarly irrelevant, but neither is Equation (4.10) affected by workers' savings in country 1. From the second equality of Equation (4.22), we get

$$s_c P_w = s_w(P_w + W)$$

That is, total workers' savings are equal to what capitalists would have saved had the profits of workers gone to them. Total savings generated in country 1, therefore equals $s_c(P_w + P_c) = s_c r K$ so that, again, so long as s is interpreted as $s_c$ our previous analysis requires no modification.

Workers' savings do, of course, affect the distribution of income and the distribution of property. If workers' savings are invested directly abroad then workers in country 1 become part-owners of the enclave capital. If workers' savings are simply lent to 1-capitalists to invest as they please, then the interest (profits) on those savings are paid, in part, out of the earnings of enclave capital. To

the extent that workers accumulate capital they become active parti-
cipants in the development of capitalism, even on a world scale.

### 4.6   Taxation and international transfers

Up to now, the analysis has been conducted on the basis of private
capitalist relations and, given the scale of government activity in
both domestic and international economic affairs, is in obvious need
of qualification. Government intervention takes a wide variety of
forms and they cannot all be considered here. What we shall do is to
consider the effects of government tax raising, expenditure and
international transfers (such as foreign aid). The introduction of
government activity introduces the possibility of feedbacks into the
Eigen–Pasinetti dynamics. In Eigen's more complicated selection
models, the $z_i$ of Equation (4.1) are not independent of one another
with the consequence that total domination by one species may
become unattainable. In the present context, taxation and government productive expenditure will be shown to have the same effect.[5]
The main problem of interpreting conclusions is that in a long-run
model the nature and extent of intervention can hardly be assumed
constant, yet, in the interests of simplicity, that is what we shall have
to assume about tax rates and other coefficients. The conclusions
may, nevertheless, be of value provided they are interpreted merely
as indicating directions and rates of movement.

Suppose that in each country the government earns profits from
its own productive activity and, in addition, raises revenue, $T$, from
a proportionate tax on profits earned in the private sector:

$$T_i = \theta_i r_i \left( K_i - G_i \right) \tag{4.23.i}$$

where $G_i$ is the value of public-sector capital and $r_i$ is now to be
interpreted as the rate of profits *before* tax payments. (It is assumed,
for simplicity, that both public and private sectors earn the same
pre-tax rates of profits. This assumption does not affect the general
nature of the argument.) In the long run the governments' budgets
will need to be balanced, expenditures out of revenues being productive investment, $I_G$, social consumption, $C_G$, and foreign transfers,
$R$ (which may, of course, be positive or negative). Thus,

$$T_i + r_i G_i = I_{Gi} + C_{Gi} + R_i = \lambda_i (r_i G_i + T_i - R_i) + C_{Gi} + R_i \tag{4.24.i}$$

where $\lambda_i$ is government $i$'s propensity for productive accumulation out of revenue available for domestic expenditures. The interesting case is, presumably, that in which aid flows from country 1 to country 2, for which we may write

$$R_1 = -R_2 = R > 0 \tag{4.25}$$

The rest of the analysis merely requires some straightforward modifications to the earlier discussion, starting with the injections-with-drawals Equation(4.3.i) which now becomes

$$I_i + I_{Gi} + C_{Gi} + E_i + F_i = S_i + M_i + T_i + r_i G_i \tag{4.26.i}$$

where $I_i$ now stands for private investment. (Note that the transfer is not a separate withdrawal for country 1, being included in $T_1 + r_1 G_1$, nor a separate injection for country 2, being included in net government expenditure.) The external balance equation becomes

$$E_i + F_i = M_i + B_i + R_i \tag{4.27.i}$$

Equations (4.26.i) and (4.27.i) together give

$$I_i + I_{Gi} = S_i + T_i + rG_i - C_{Gi} - R_i - B_i \tag{4.28.i}$$

Taking each country separately, we obtain from Equations (4.24.i), Equations (4.25) and (4.28.i)

$$I_1 + I_{G1} = S_1 + \lambda_1(T_1 + r_1 G_1 - R) - B_1 \tag{4.29.1}$$

and

$$I_2 + I_{G2} = S_2 + \lambda_2(T_2 + r_2 G_2 + R) + B_2 \tag{4.29.2}$$

(remember that $B_1 = -B_2$).

In the presence of profits taxes there is no longer any necessity for $r_1 = r_2$. Free international investment will lead instead to the equalization of returns on private investment, net of taxes. Denoting this equalized rate by $\hat{r}$, then

$$\hat{r} = (1 - \theta_1)r_1 = (1 - \theta_2)r_2 \tag{4.30}$$

from which it follows that

$$S_i = \overline{s}_1(1 - \theta_i)r_i(K_i - G_i) = \overline{s}_i\,\hat{r}(1 - \gamma_i)K_i \qquad (4.31.i)$$

where $\lambda_i = G_i/K_i$ is the public-sector share of total capital, and $\overline{s}_i$ is weighted by national ownership shares. Similarly,

$$\lambda_i(T_i + r_iG_i \pm R) = \lambda_i[(\theta_i/1 - \theta_i)\cdot\hat{r}K_i + \hat{r}G_i \pm R] \qquad (4.32.i)$$

Substituting Equations (4.31.i) and (4.32.i) into Equation (4.29.i) and dividing through by $K_i$ gives, for each country

$$g_1 = [s_1(1 - \gamma_1) + \lambda_1(\theta_1/1 - \theta_1) + \lambda_1\gamma_1]\hat{r} - \lambda_1\rho_1 - \beta_1 \qquad (4.33.1)$$
and

$$g_2 = [\overline{s}_2(1 - \gamma_2) + \lambda_2(\theta_2/1 - \theta_2) + \lambda_2\gamma_2]\hat{r} + \lambda_2\rho_2 + \beta_2 \qquad (4.33.2)$$

in which $\rho_i = R/K_i$.

The first conclusion that can be drawn from this analysis is that the process of denationalization of the peripheral economy through the influx of foreign capital is now subject to a lower limit. Corresponding to Equation (4.13), in the present case we have

$$\alpha^{t+1}/\alpha^t = [1 + s_1\hat{r}^t + (\beta_2^t/\alpha^t)]/(1 + g_2^t)$$

Provided $\lambda_2 > 0$ and either $\rho_2 > 0$ or $0 < \theta_2 < 1$, then it is impossible for $\alpha^t$ to reach unity.

As for the enclave and indigenous rates of growth in the Periphery, these can be obtained by writing out expressions for $\alpha^t K^t$ and $(1 - \alpha^t)K^t$, as in Equation (4.13) and using the procedure of Equation (4.18). For the enclave,

$$g_2^e = s_1\hat{r} + \beta_2/\alpha$$

This will be smaller the greater the tax rate in the Periphery, but higher Centre taxes may induce a faster outflow of capital. For the indigenous sector,

$$g_2^I = s_2\hat{r} + [\lambda_2(\theta_2/1 - \theta_2)\hat{r} + (\lambda_2 - s_2)\gamma_2\hat{r} + \lambda_2\rho_2]/(1 - \alpha)$$

Care must be taken in interpreting both these equations. They cannot be directly compared to Equations (4.18) and (4.19) since, in general, the pre-tax profits rate in the presence of taxes will not be the same as the profits rate without taxes. If, in order to facilitate a comparison, we assume these rates to be the same then a sufficient condition for government intervention to increase the growth rate of the indigenous sector is that $\lambda_2 > s_2$, i.e., the government has a greater propensity to accumulate than the private sector. The growth process is strengthened if $\rho_2 > 0$ and also becomes stronger as $\alpha$ rises, a reflection of the fact that profits earned in the enclave form part of the tax base.[6]

In practice, the distinction between enclave and domestic investments of 'foreign aid' implied here may be too sharp. No doubt a substantial proportion of such investments are directed towards providing infrastructure and support for enclave producers. To the extent that transfers are thus tied, only in terms of ownership can it be considered indigenous. In terms of the returns it generates, a substantial portion of it may benefit foreign investors.

### 4.7 Monopoly capitalism
Modern writings on dependency tend to stress the role of large transnational corporations which are able to exercise considerable monopoly power.[7] Since our model is one of long-run competitive capitalism, is it of limited relevance as a description of the modern phase of global development?

First, we must be clear what we mean by 'long-run', since we have, in effect, *two* 'long runs' in this analysis. On the one hand, long-run may refer to the entire process of convergence to a global steady state, in which case it is a *very* long run. On the other, it may refer to the period necessary for the convergence of rates of profits which, by comparison, is a much, much shorter long run! In fact, of course, we will never have precise convergence of profits rates because of the continuous disturbances that are occurring in the short run. And, even in the absence of such disturbances, the process of convergence would be retarded by the barriers to entry that protect monopoly positions. But the (very) long-run dynamics of the analysis will not be much affected if the barriers to entry are not so powerful as to prevent a tendency to profit rate equalization in a sufficiently shorter 'long-run'. Unless barriers to entry are overwhelming, short-run monopoly positions may be consistent with long-run competition.[8]

This is not to deny, of course, the considerable importance of unequal bargaining power in determining the course of development. Nevertheless, the principal bias is towards Central capital, taken as a whole, rather than between larger and smaller firms irrespective of location and nationality. The consequence of Central monopoly power is simply to exacerbate the processes discussed in this chapter.

## 4.8   Conclusions and interpretation

The framework of the present chapter will be extended in the following by appending to it the Sraffa–Leontief production model. This will permit an analysis of the terms of trade, levels of consumption, the effects of technological change, and so on. Nevertheless, even at the present level of aggregation and abstraction a number of important conclusions concerning the dynamics of development has already been deduced. It may be useful to summarize these conclusions:

1. The model of unimpaired global accumulation is consistent with a form of capitalist development in the Periphery. The rate of growth in country 2, as a whole, can be higher than the rate of growth in country 1.
2. The form of capitalist development is, however, very uneven, with rapid growth in the investment enclave and low growth (or stagnation if $s_2 = 0$) in the rest of the Peripheral economy. It should, however, be recalled that the enclave includes portfolio capital and is thus defined in terms of capital ownership rather than of control.
3. In consequence, the enclave grows at the expense of indigenous capital and the Periphery becomes increasingly dominated by foreign-owned capital.
4. Repayments of foreign debt grow more rapidly than the Periphery as a whole and, after some time, will exceed the inflow of new foreign capital.

In brief then, capitalist development in the Periphery is not only possible; it may also be very rapid. But it is also extremely lop-sided and accompanied by growing foreign indebtedness. The indigenous capitalist class is displaced by the growth of a new class of capitalists with its base in the enclave and its allegiance to the corporate head offices of the global Centre. The social, cultural and political implications of this transformation have been thoroughly documented in the literature on underdevelopment.

These conclusions have been derived from a long-run model which describes the path of capitalist evolution from some initial state to a terminal state. The final outcome of the Eigen–Pasinetti process is reached asymptotically. The historical time needed for these tendencies to attain something approaching complete dominance by one group of capitalists may be enormous. But the properties of the end state are not especially interesting in and of themselves. Their interest lies entirely in indicating the direction of movement of the world economy, and its component parts, in the intermediate phases of evolution, which may well have some reflection in real historical processes.

In the simple model without feedbacks the critical parameters are the savings propensities. It must be conceded that the $s_i$ themselves are likely to be averages of personal ratios and, within a country, there may be a considerable spread of savings propensities. However, reinterpreting the process at the level of individual capitalists is neither necessary nor especially helpful. The lifespan of nations is (generally) considerably longer than the life of individual or institutional capitalists. So long as the distribution in one nation lies unambiguously above that of the other, that nation will eventually dominate, even if a similar process of domination is going on among its native capitalists. If this is so, the outcome is only dependent on the ranking of average propensities and not on their precise values. Should the ranking change then, for some time, the direction of the process may change but not its nature.

These conclusions may not be comforting for those countries which are unable to generate sufficient domestic private savings to finance investment programmes. If foreign dominance is a matter for national concern then it may be possible to retard the Pasinetti process through the deliberate creation of feedbacks. In the case of purely domestic tax-expenditure arrangements feedbacks arise because governments typically tax profits earned within their territorial jurisdiction irrespective of who owns the assets. A large foreign enclave thus provides a large tax base which can be used to finance domestic investment. The dynamics are also modified where governments partake of foreign aid transfers. If these have a genuine grant component then the assets financed by that component belong to the recipient nations. In neither of these cases is the outcome a consequence of raising the withdrawals ratio above the private savings ratio. With government activity, the long-run outcome is not determined by the ranking of withdrawals propensities alone.

Although, in principle, the Periphery does have the ability to modify the course of dependent development through the productive accumulation of tax revenues, in practice, the possibilities of raising such revenues must naturally be seen against the background of poverty in the indigenous sector and of political and cultural alliances in the enclave.

Although the analysis of this chapter has been conducted in the context of a two-country world it may be worth pointing out that it is equally applicable to a world of many national economies characterized by different savings propensities. In the absence of public accumulation the process of simple self-organization continues to hold – that group of capitalists with the highest savings propensity will eventually dominate all others provided, of course, that the ranking of propensities remains constant. As in the two-country case, the process of complete domination will be thwarted by government accumulation. Indeed, any nation which undertakes public accumulation will be represented in the final outcome.[9]

## Notes

1. The adaptation of the biological theories of selection to economic phenomena is relatively common in theories of technical progress; see, for example, Metcalfe (1984). For a specific application of the self-organization principle, see Silverberg, Dosi and Orsenigo (1988).
2. A more general expression of Eigen's equation involves 'feedback' between the $z_i$, in which case Equation (4.2) no longer holds, in general. Feedbacks are discussed in 4.6.
3. Analysis of the effects of technical progress is postponed to Chapter 9.
4. These mechanisms are not exhaustive. Others may occur which do not require a fall in the rate of profits. (See 6.5.) Symmetrical mechanisms occur where natural resource constraints in the Periphery generate increasing rents.
5. In Chapter 5 it is shown that incomplete dominance may also occur where indigenous capitalists in a dual Peripheral economy gradually adopt the savings propensity of Centre capitalists as a result of entry into the 'advanced' sector.
6. Of course, the relation between indigenous sector and enclave growth can be improved further if the burden of taxation falls disproportionately on the latter.
7. See, for example, Sunkel (1973) and Villamil (1979).
8. See, for example, Sylos-Labini (1962) and Clifton (1977).
9. For a full analysis of this case, see Mainwaring (1990).

# 5 Production, consumption and the terms of trade

## 5.1 Background and assumptions

The analysis of Chapter 4 was concerned entirely with value aggregates. From this chapter on we shall adapt the two-commodity Sraffa–Leontief model to the analysis of international investment. We begin on the assumption that wages in both global regions remain constant over time (case (i) of Chapter 4). In part, this is an initial, simplifying assumption, permitting the introduction of certain tools of analysis while avoiding the complications which arise out of changes in wages and, as a consequence, of the terms of trade. But it is also, arguably, a more relevant description of the earlier experience of overseas investment by the relatively industrialized countries, investment stimulated in part by the opportunities of exploiting new sources of raw materials and in part by the difference in wages. Once we allow rising wage costs to threaten Central profitability, there occurs a qualitative change in the nature of global capitalism, discussion of which is postponed to Chapter 6.

In Chapter 2 some scepticism was expressed about whether the standard trade-theoretic approaches provide historically valid analyses of international trade. A similar methodological unease prevails in relation to those theories of international investment that proceed by employing the technique of comparative statics (or dynamics) or by explicitly considering the transition from one regime to another within a context which would not be recognizable to a historian of international economic relations. If capitalism inherited from the mercantile period a world accustomed to the international movement of goods, so did the liberal epoch inherit from the colonial a world accustomed to the foreign ownership of productive assets. Those theories which depict a transition from a no-investment regime to a with-investment regime as taking place wholly within the framework of liberal capitalism may be useful for considering changes in the intensity of investment flows in the modern world (for which reason a conventional 'gains-from-investment' analysis will be presented in Chapter 7). But they do not seem to be of direct relevance in understanding development and underdevelopment as processes taking place in historical time. Thus Chapters 5 and 6 attempt a more evolutionary view of global accumulation by examining the development of a liberal capitalist system in which the pattern of productive specialization and the existence of foreign investments are taken as part of the inheritance of that system.

Although some of the basic assumptions of this chapter have already been alluded to, it is as well to make them explicit before proceeding.

### Technology

The technology is of the Sraffa–Leontief single-products type employed in the analysis of Chapters 1 and 2. There is no technical progress (the effects of which are considered in Chapter 9).

### Commodity specialization

Each country is completely specialized in one commodity which it trades with the other, without having to incur transport costs or overcome artificial barriers (tariffs and other trade restrictions). This pattern of specialization is taken as given throughout. The assumption implies that the two countries are of whatever relative magnitudes are necessary in order to satisfy condition (2.7).

### Wages

In each country, real wage rates, expressed as a quantity of the commodity *numéraire*, are exogenously determined by sociological factors. In particular, it is supposed initially that Peripheral wages are kept close to some conventionally defined subsistence level by a pool of surplus labour which is taken to exist in a non-capitalist mode. (A different division of the Peripheral economy is analysed from 5.5 onwards.) Since the uniform wage rate in the Centre is higher than that in the Periphery, investment flows from the high-wage to the low-wage country (implying that if international investment were suddenly restricted the rate of profits in 1 would fall relative to that in 2). Setting wages in terms of a *numéraire* is not entirely satisfactory but it makes for expositional simplicity and is unlikely to affect the conclusions in any significant way.

*Profits remittances*

In the last chapter it was assumed that overseas profits not saved were repatriated and entirely consumed. In 3.4, however, it was argued that, logically, it would make no difference whether the consumption occurred within country 1 or within the enclave. In other words, so far as 1-capitalist consumption is concerned, the enclave can be regarded as a geographical extension of country 1. In this chapter we shall follow this approach explicitly. This merely requires some care in the specification of the external balance equation: actual remittances, $F$, now exclude that part of unsaved enclave profits which are expended on consumption within the enclave. In what follows, then, 1-capitalist consumption refers to the consumption *of* 1-capitalists and thus includes consumption within the enclave; 2-capitalist consumption refers to the consumption of indigenous 2-capitalists.

On the basis of these assumptions we shall now attempt to determine the levels of consumption per worker in each country in the presence of fully mobile capital.

## 5.2   The consumption frontier

Let commodity $i$ be that which is produced and exported by country $i$ ($i = 1,2$). (Note that the assumption of complete specialization allows us to drop the general use of the $Z = I$, II superscripts of Chapters 1 and 2.) Each commodity is used in its own production and in the production of the other commodity so that, with obvious modifications to the notation of Chapter 2, the process price equations may be written as follows:

$$p = (1 + r)(p_1 a_{11} + a_{21}) + w_1 l_1 \tag{5.1}$$
$$1 = (1 + r)(p_1 a_{12} + a_{22}) + w_2 l_2 \tag{5.2}$$

Equations (5.1) and (5.2) contain two unknowns, $p$ and $r$, so that the price system is wholly determinate. Since the terms of trade depend only on the exogenously given wage rates and the fixed technical coefficients, they are constant throughout the analysis of this chapter.

The physical relationships between sectors may be summarized as follows. For the outputs of country 1,

$$X_1 = (1 + g_1)a_{11}X_1 + (1 + g_2)a_{12}X_2 + C_{11} + C_{1e} + C_{12} \tag{5.3}$$

where $X_i$ is the gross output of sector $i$; $g_i$ is the annual rate of growth of sector i; $C_{11}$ the consumption of commodity 1 by workers and 1-capitalists resident in country 1; $C_{1e}$ the consumption of 1 by 1-capitalists resident in the enclave; and $C_{12}$ consumption of 1 by workers and indigenous capitalists in country 2. Equation (5.3) says that the annual gross output of commodity 1 just provides for the replacement and net investment requirements of the two sectors/countries plus the global consumption of commodity 1. The corresponding equation for the outputs of commodity 2 is

$$X_2 = (1 + g_1)a_{21}X_1 + (1 + g_2)a_{22}X_2 + C_{21} + C_{2e} + C_{22} \qquad (5.4)$$

The relationships between output and employment in the two countries are given by

$$L_i = l_iX_i \qquad\qquad (5.5.\text{i})$$

where the $L_i$ are the total employed workforces in country $i$ (and are such as to satisfy Equation (2.1)). There is no international migration of wage-earners in the model but we have already admitted the possibility of 1-capitalists migrating to the enclave.

The external balance condition, Equations (4.4.i), is

$$E_i + F_i = M_i + B_i$$

(where $E$ is exports; $M$, imports; $F$, foreign remittances; and $B$, capital inflow). To make explicit allowance for capitalist consumption within the enclave, remittances are now written as

$$F_1 = U_1 - C_e = U_1 - (pC_{1e} + C_{2e}) \qquad (5.6)$$

where $U_1$ denotes the total unretained earnings on enclave capital, and $C_e$ is the *value* of enclave consumption. Then, recalling that $F_1 = -F_2$ and $B_1 = -B_2$, Equations (4.4.i) may be expanded and rearranged as

$$E_1 = M_1 + B_1 - U_1 + pC_{1e} + C_{2e} \qquad (5.7)$$
$$E_2 = M_2 - B_1 + U_1 - pC_{1e} - C_{2e} \qquad (5.8)$$

Equation (5.7) may be further expanded. Exports are given by

$$E_1 = p[C_{12} + C_{1e} + (1 + g_2)a_{12}X_2] \tag{5.9}$$

and imports by

$$M_1 = C_{21} + (1 + g_1)a_{21}X_1 \tag{5.10}$$

so that Equation (5.7) can be written in full as

$$p[C_{12} + C_{1e} + (1 + g_2)a_{12}X_2] = C_{21} + (1 + g_1)a_{21}X_1 + B_1 - U_1 + pC_{1e} + C_{2e} \tag{5.11}$$

Now, multiplying Equation (5.3) through by $p$ and re-ordering the terms on the right-hand side gives

$$pX_1 = p[C_{12} + C_{1e} + (1 + g_2)a_{12}X_2] + p(1 + g_1)a_{11}X_1 + pC_{11} \tag{5.12}$$

The first term on the right-hand side of Equation (5.12) is identical to the expression on the left-hand side of Equation (5.11), for which may be substituted the expression on the right-hand side of that equation to give

$$pX_1 = p(1 + g_1)a_{11}X_1 + (1 + g_1)a_{21}X_1 + p(C_{11} + C_{1e}) + C_{21} + C_{2e} + B_1 - U_1 \tag{5.13}$$

Equation (5.13) is simply an expression for gross domestic product, $pX_1$, in terms of expenditures. The value of the capital stock in country 1 is

$$K_1 = (pa_{11} + a_{21})X_1 \tag{5.14}$$

which allows Equation (5.13) to be rewritten as

$$pX_1 = (1 + g_1)K_1 + C^I + C_e + B_1 - U_1 \tag{5.15.1}$$

where $C^I$ is the value of domestic consumption, that is, consumption *within* country 1 (capitalist consumption plus worker consumption). The sum

$$C_1 = C^I + C_e$$

therefore represents the value of consumption of all 1-natives wherever their domicile.

Defining

$$\beta_i = B_1/K_i \qquad (5.16.i)$$
$$u_i = U_1/K_i \qquad (5.17.i)$$

allows Equation (5.15) to be rearranged as

$$C_1 = pX_1 - (1 + g_1 + \beta_1 - u_1)K_1 \qquad (5.18)$$

which, dividing through by $L_1$, can be expressed in 'per (employed) worker' terms (indicated by lower-case symbols), as

$$c_1 = px_1 - (1 + g_1 + \beta_1 - u_1)k_1 \qquad (5.19)$$

By use of Equation (4.9), namely

$$g_1 = s_1 r - \beta_1$$

Equation (5.19) can alternatively be written as

$$c_1 = px_1 - (1 + s_1 r - u_1)k_1 \qquad (5.20.1)$$

Turning now to Equation (5.1), the price equation for commodity/country 1; rearranging to solve for $w_1 l_1$ and multiplying throughout by $X_1$, yields

$$w_1 l_1 X_1 = pX_1 - (1 + r)(pa_{11} + a_{21})X_1 \qquad (5.21)$$

Dividing through by $L_1$ gives, by virtue of Equation (5.5.1)

$$w_1 = px_1 - (1 + r)k_1 \qquad (5.22.1)$$

Finally, solving both Equations (5.20.1) and (5.22.1) for $px_1$ and equating gives

$$c_1 = w_1 + [r - (s_1 r - u_1)]k_1 \qquad (5.23.1)$$

The similarity of the forms of Equations (5.20.1) and (5.22.1) may be noted. The relationship between $c_1$ and $(s_1 r - u_1)$ is of exactly the same form as the 'relationship' between $w_1$ and $r$. A degree of

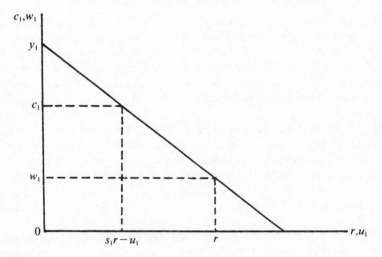

*Figure 5.1*

caution is, however, required in interpreting this similarity, for the equations are *not* an open-economy generalization of the dual relations that are found in standard capital theory (as applied in Chapter 1 to the $w-r$ and $c-g$ frontiers). In the latter context, the $w = w(r)$ relation is a reduced form of the price equations in which prices have been eliminated. Thus, though prices normally change with variations in the rate of profits, these changes are fully taken into account in determining the relation between $w$ and $r$. This is not the case with Equation (5.22.1) which explicitly includes the price ratio $p$ (not only in the $px_1$ term, but also in the value-of-capital term, $k_1$). Given prices, Equations (5.20.1), (5.22.1) and (5.23.1) may be represented by the same straight line (Figure 5.1). (They are effectively the same as the $(w-r)_i$ 'trade-offs' of Chapter 2.) But whereas variations of $c_1$ and $(s_1 r - u_1)$ are possible along this line (due to changes in $u_1$), there is no question of variation of $w_1$ and $r$ along a given line. Were $r$ to change (a possibility admitted in subsequent chapters), the price ratio would also change, and with it the slope and vertical intercept of Equation (5.22.1).

One further cautionary note on the identity of Equations (5.20.1) and (5.22.1) may be in order. In standard capital theory, the relations $w = w(r)$ and $c = c(g)$ are duals so long as the vector of wage goods is proportional to the vector of all consumption commodities (which means that workers and capitalists consume in the same proportions). This composite-commodity assumption is necessary if $w$ and $c$ are to refer to different amounts of the same variable in the presence of relative price changes. In the present case, however, there can be no variation of $w$ along a given line and there is no need to assume proportionality of capitalist and worker consumption vectors.

The vertical intercept of Equation (5.23.1) is equal to net *domestic* product per worker (p.w.), $y_1$, which in turn is equal to gross domestic output p.w. less replacement capital p.w., on the one hand, and to the wage plus domestic profits p.w., on the other:

$$y_1 = px_1 - k_1 = w_1 + rk_1 \tag{5.24.1}$$

Note, however, that net *national* income exceeds net domestic product by the amount of foreign remittances. Similarly, the maximum level of $c_1$ (which includes consumption abroad by 1-capitalists) exceeds $y_1$ by the amount of unretained foreign profits p.w. (whether these are remitted or not):

$$c_1(\text{max}) = y_1 + u_1k_1 \tag{5.25.1}$$

Henceforth, we shall refer to Equation (5.23.1) as the *consumption frontier* (for country 1 plus enclave capitalists[1]).

The above reasoning can be applied *mutatis mutandis* to country 2, to yield the following:

$$X_2 = (1 + g_2)K_2 + C^{II} - C_e - B_2 + U_1 \tag{5.15.2}$$
$$c_2 = x_2 - (1 + \bar{s}_2r + u_2)k_2 \tag{5.20.2}$$
$$w_2 = x_2 - (1 + r)k_2 \tag{5.22.2}$$

(the cautionary notes on 'duality' apply equally to country 2), and

$$c_2 = w_2 + [r - (\bar{s}_2r + u_2)]k_2 \tag{5.23.2}$$

the consumption frontier for country 2 (excluding enclave capitalists[2]). Net domestic product p.w. is given by the vertical intercept of Equation (5.23.2)

$$y_2 = x_2 - k_2 = w_2 + rk_2 \tag{5.24.2}$$

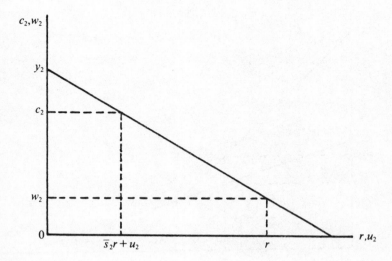

*Figure 5.2*

but maximum indigenous consumption p.w. falls short of $y_2$ because the latter includes the unretained earnings of enclave capitalists. Thus,

$$c_2(\max) = y_2 - u_2 k_2 \qquad (5.25.2)$$

The consumption frontier for country 2 is drawn in Figure 5.2 while the relationship between the frontiers for the two countries is shown in Figure 5.3 (for the case in which $k_1 > k_2$, as reflected in the slopes of the frontiers).

**5.3   The volume of investment flow**
Given the assumptions of this chapter, the positions of the consumption frontiers remain fixed throughout the accumulation process but the location on these frontiers of the points $[c_i, (\bar{s}_i r \pm u_i)]$ will change in a manner to be examined in the next section. There is, however, no variation in the wage rates (by assumption) nor, therefore, in the uniform rate of profits which, together with the terms of trade, is wholly determined by the two Equations (5.1) and (5.2). Given $r$, the growth rates $g_1$ and $g_2$ are obtained from Equations (4.9) and (4.10) and, since $p$ is constant, are also equal to the growth rates of output

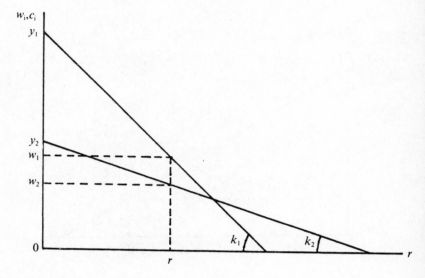

*Figure 5.3*

and employment in the two sectors. We know that these rates rise over time (both converging on $s_1 r$) as a consequence of changes in the $\beta_i$ and $\alpha$, but it is not possible to say which is greater. It has already been observed (in Chapter 1.6) that when the world growth rate is rising it will normally be the case that one sector will have to grow faster than the other to satisfy increasing investment demands. But this is a matter of technology and we are unable to say *a priori* which the faster growing sector will be.

Throughout this process, the uniformity of the rate of profits is maintained by a critical flow of capital: $B^t_1 (= \beta^t_i K^t_i)$, per period. It has been stated that $\beta^t_i \to 0$ as $t \to \infty$, but very little has actually been said about the nature of the flow or why it diminishes (relative to global capital) over time. In fact, the flow is a manifestation, in an international context, of what is sometimes referred to (usually in the context of a closed economy) as the process of 'gravitation' of prices to their 'natural' values. This process is implicitly an adjustment mechanism for equilibrating supplies and demands. With constant returns, the natural or long-run prices (and rate of profits) are determined wholly on the cost (supply) side. This has been the case in the preceding section where there has been no reference to demand. If, however, the relative demands that would obtain at some set of natural prices are not equal to the actual supply proportions, those prices cannot be sustained. The relative price of the good in excess demand will be higher than its natural price and the rate of profits earned in its production will be higher than the rate earned on the other good.[3]

Gravitation implies the elimination of the deviations of actual from natural values as a consequence of the redistribution of investment away from the industry producing the 'over-supplied' good at a low rate of profits toward the industry where the return is higher. If the process is stable (which is assumed to be the case[4]) supplies are brought into line with demands at natural prices which reflect the constant costs of production at the uniform rate of profits.

In a closed economy with a uniform savings propensity, the redistribution of investment following some disturbance may be a once-and-for-all matter. In the present case, however, in no period are the investment resources generated by savings in the Periphery sufficient to keep the growth of good 2 output in line with its demand for consumption, net investment and intermediate needs. As a result $\beta_1$ is positive in each period. This very fact, however, means that the proportion of capital in the Periphery which is owned by capitalists with a high savings propensity rises over time towards unity. Average savings propensities in the two regions are thus moving closer and closer together and the world economy in the limit will have uniform savings behaviour.

So long as natural values are constant, the implication of this is that $\beta_1$ will tend to zero. For once the savings propensities in Centre and Periphery are equal, balanced growth of outputs can be achieved without net transfers of capital between the two regions: investments become geographically self-financing. To put the matter just a little more formally, continued $\beta_1 > 0$ would involve a contradiction. For with the same rate of net domestic savings in each country, $s_1r$, equal to the constant world growth rate, from Equation (4.16) the Periphery would be growing faster than the Centre and prices would need to be continuously changing. (This argument would have to be qualified if the aggregate income elasticities of demand were not equal to unity. For then continuing capital transfers would be needed to prevent the price of the good with elastic demand from rising over time. If, as one might presume, it is good-1 demand which is elastic, this actually implies an acceleration in the decline of $\beta_1$ to zero followed by a reversal in the direction of the investment flow as the Centre becomes inherently more profitable than the Periphery. This complication will be ignored henceforth by continuing with the assumption of a balanced growth of demands at natural prices.)

In the present context we may regard the 'actual' price ratio as that which would emerge at the end of period $t$ were $B_1{}^t = 0$ (creating a divergence of the rates of profits), and the 'global natural' price ratio as that which is sustained by international investment, sufficient to equalize the rates of profits and hence consistent with Equations (5.1) and (5.2). Then what the argument boils down to is that the volume of investment needed to maintain the natural values depends on the misalignment of actual supplies and the demands that would exist at the natural price. Specifically, it depends on how much extra supply of the good in excess demand is needed to remove the excess. This, of course, depends on the elasticity of relative *final* demands with respect to relative price (with a fixed coefficients technology, relative intermediate demands are derived directly from relative final demands) which is assumed to be given. In the framework of the model it is good 2 which should be understood as being in potential excess demand. In the long run this potential excess demand falls with the continuing investment flow into the Periphery, vanishing as $\alpha$ approaches unity.

### 5.4 Consumption over time

We now consider in detail the implications for consumption of the convergence of the global economy to a distant steady state. For this purpose we can refer to Figures 5.1 and 5.2, paying particular attention to the $u_i$ variables. Unretained enclave earnings in period $t$ are given by

$$U_1{}^t = (1 - s_1)r\alpha^t K^t{}_2 \tag{5.26}$$

Dividing through (5.26) by $K_i$ gives

$$u_1{}^t = (1 - s_1)r\alpha^t K_2{}^t / K_1{}^t \tag{5.27}$$

and

$$u_2{}^t = (1 - s_1)r\alpha^t \tag{5.28}$$

Consider what happens as $\alpha^t \to 1$.

For country 1, the outcome is clear for the case in which $g_2 > g_1$, for then the direct effect of $\alpha^t$ on $u_1^t$ is reinforced by the effect of the differential growth rates of the capital stocks. It follows that $u_1^t$ rises over time. The same is true, if rather less obviously, in the case in which $g_2 < g_1$; from Equation (5.27) we get

$$u_1^{t+1} - u_1^t = r(1 - s_1)\left[\frac{\alpha^{t+1}K_2^{t+1}}{K_1^{t+1}} - \frac{\alpha^t K_2^t}{K_1^t}\right]$$

Using Equation (4.13), we can substitute for the term $\alpha^{t+1}K_2^{t+1}$ to give

$$u_1^{t+1} - u_1^t = r(1 - s_1)\left[\frac{\alpha^t K_2^t + s_1 r\alpha^t K_2^t + \beta_2^t K_2^t}{(1 + g_1^t)K_1^t} - \frac{\alpha^t K_2^t}{K_1^t}\right]$$

On further manipulation, the term in brackets becomes

$$(s_1 r\alpha^t + \beta_2^t - g_1^t\alpha^t)K_2^t/(1 + g_1^t)K_1^t$$

which can be shown to be positive by expanding $g_1^t$ according to Equation (4.9) to give

$$(s_1 r\alpha^t + \beta_1^t - s_1 r\alpha^t + \beta_2^t) = \beta_1^t + \beta_2^t > 0$$

We thus, finally, have

$$u_1^{t+1} - u_1^t = r(1 - s_1)(\beta_1^t + \beta_2^t) > 0 \qquad (5.29)$$

Turning to Figure 5.1, the implications of growing $u_1$ over time are clear. As the term $(s_1 r - u_1)$ gets smaller, consumption p.w. rises. There is, however, a limit to this process. As can be seen from Equation (5.29), as the global economy approaches a steady state, with $\beta_i \to 0$, the *growth* of unretained earnings *relative* to $K_1$ also approaches zero. (The absolute volume of unretained earnings continues to grow, of course, as $g_2^e \to g = s_1 r > 0$.) The lower limit to the term $(s_1 r - u_1)$ is given by Equation (5.27.1) in which $\alpha^t = 1$:

$$s_1 r - u_1^t = s_1 r + (s_1 - 1)r K_2^t/K_1^t$$

which may be positive or negative. If negative, this means that p.w.

consumption exceeds the vertical intercept $y_1$ in Figure 5.1. This possibility arises from the divergence between maximum consumption and country-1 net domestic product, when $u_1 > 0$, which was noted in Equation (5.25.1).

For country 2, it is clear from Equation (5.28) that as $\alpha'$ increases so also does $u_2'$. Since $\bar{s}_2'$ also increases with $\alpha'$, this implies a period-by-period decrease in consumption p.w. (Figure 5.2). In the limit, when $\alpha = 1$ and $\bar{s}_2 = s_1$, we have

$$\bar{s}_2 r + u_2 = s_1 r + (1 - s_1)r = r \tag{5.30}$$

In other words, consumption p.w. falls to the level of the fixed wage. This is hardly surprising in view of the fact that $\alpha = 1$ implies the elimination of domestic capitalists.

In Chapter 4 it was shown that the Pasinetti process would be restrained if the Periphery government participated in accumulation using either transfer receipts or tax revenues raised partly on foreign capital. The consumption frontier derived from the assumptions of that analysis is of exactly the same form as Equation (5.23.2).[5] Its position may well differ, however, since the imposition of profits taxes will normally alter the terms of trade. (A higher $\theta_2$, given $\theta_1$, will shift the terms in favour of the Periphery and so move its frontier outward.) Since the sources of government revenue persist to the limit and since part of that revenue is used for social consumption (if $\lambda_2 < 1$), then $c_2$ now converges to a value higher than the wage rate.

### 5.5   Dualism in the Peripheral export sector

Up to now the analysis has been conducted using a very simple representation of the Peripheral economy. The exportable commodity 2 is produced by a single technique available equally to indigenous and foreign capitalists. Wages are kept close to subsistence by a large excess supply of labour. Labour that is not employed implicitly pursues a marginalized existence, perhaps a subsistence mode outside the mainstream of the externally oriented sector. Within the latter, the only division is one of ownership, splitting the enclave away from indigenously owned productive assets. This representation is consistent with orthodox dual-economy approaches. In the rest of this chapter we modify this slightly by allowing the 'backward' part of the economy to sell some part of its production on the world market. In other words, the dualism is extended to the Peripheral export sector, which thus has 'advanced' and 'backward' subsectors, both producing the same product though with different techniques and offering different levels of remuneration to workers. Sufficient labour, excess to the needs of both sectors, continues to prevent 'backward' wages rising above sociologically determined levels.

There has been some debate in the dependency literature as to whether, and in what sense, a backward sector can be regarded as capitalistic. Whereas, for example, Frank (1967) believes that the existence of commodity markets is sufficient for capitalism, Laclau (1971), citing the authority of Marx, argues that a free labour market is a necessary condition. In our analysis it certainly is necessary that real wages in the backward sector are uniform. Whether this requires a competitive labour market is another matter. It could be consistent with a degree of labour servility if, nevertheless, the rewards to labour in such semi-feudal conditions were a matter of traditional consensus (and biological underpinning). What is also necessary is that, taken as a whole, labour should be free to move from the backward to the advanced sector. But again this only requires that there exists a sufficient quantity of labour that is surplus to the requirements of the backward sector. (It may, perhaps, be easier to think of the Periphery as a 'triple' economy, having a domestic subsistence or informal sector, a backward export sector and an advanced export sector.)

The proprietorial class in the backward sector is assumed to be profit-maximizing. The only remarkable characteristic of this class is that, as compared to those in the advanced sector, its members have a lower propensity to save. This could be thought of as a consequence of feudal habits (having, in that respect, something in common with the behaviour of that feudal relic identified by the classical economists as the 'landlord' class). But it could just as easily arise out of a savings function, common to all those whose incomes derive from the surplus product, in which the average propensity to save is less than the marginal propensity. One could, for example, imagine an individual savings function of the form

$$S = zrK - \bar{z}$$

(where z and $\bar{z}$ are constants). If the ratio of capital to capitalists in each sector is constant (equal to unity, say), this would imply an aggregate savings propensity

$$s = z - (\bar{z}/r)$$

If, as we shall argue shortly, the rate of profits in the advanced sector is higher than that in the backward, the former will be associated with a higher savings ratio. A specific function such as this does, however, create unhelpful complications since saving rates would have to change whenever the rate of profits of a particular sector changes (as, for example, between no-investment and with-investment regimes). Since the important determinant of the dynamic properties of the model is the ranking of savings ratios rather than their precise magnitudes, in the interests of simplicity we continue to assume that the ratios are fixed. This discussion is nevertheless of interest because of its relevance to the debate between the proponents of the dependency perspective and those of the 'modernization' paradigm (Valenzuela and Valenzuela, 1979). The point is that in this model it is possible to ascribe the 'backwardness' of the backward sector merely to low incomes rather than primitive attitudes.

At this point it is natural to ask what relationship the backward/advanced distinction has to the indigenous/enclave distinction? As it was used in previous chapters, the latter distinction referred only to ownership and not to technology or social relations. But, clearly, the backward and advanced sectors are defined precisely in these terms. If the advanced sector is what it says it is then, presumably, it will employ a different probably more capital-intensive technique. Moreover, it may be supposed that wages there, although held down by the earnings of labour in the backward sector, exceed those earnings by some margin.[6]

It follows that, unless the higher wages of the advanced sector were to exactly offset the greater productivity of the superior technology, the rate of profits in that sector will exceed the rate earned in the backward sector. (If the 'backward rate' exceeded the 'advanced rate' then foreign capitalists would confine their investments to the backward sector where, it is reasonable to assume, they would be paying lower wages.) Note that, in this case, the free movement of capital between the two sectors will not serve to equalize the rates of profits on the two co-existing techniques. One technique is unambiguously inferior to the other and if there were free capital markets within the Periphery what would normally be expected to happen is the rapid adoption by *all* capitalists of the superior technique. Peripheral dualism therefore implies a degree of capital market imperfection. We need not stop to speculate on the nature of the imperfections, though a minimum efficient scale of production, and hence of investment, in the advanced sector may be a contributory factor. At any rate, the implication is that the indigenous entrepreneurs in the backward sector will, as a general rule, be obliged to accept a lower rate of profits than capitalists in the advanced sector.

Capital market imperfection does not, however, mean that all indigenous capitalists would be excluded from adopting advanced techniques so that, in principle, the advanced sector could include not only enclave capital but domestic capital as well. If, however, we suppose that those indigenous capitalists who become incorporated into the advanced sector were to adapt to a higher savings ratio then the outcome of the Pasinetti process will require some modification.[7]

### 5.6  The Pasinetti process with dual savings behaviour

If indigenous capitalists who gain entry into the advanced sector adopt 'advanced' habits with respect to thrift, in other words, a savings ratio $s_a = s_1$, then one might expect those capitalists to be represented in the final outcome of the Pasinetti process, thus avoiding the total elimination of indigenous Peripheral capitalism. This, indeed, turns out to be the case, as we shall now see.

Let $K_a$ and $K_b$ be the values of the capital stocks in the advanced and backward sectors. $K_e$, enclave capital (owned by 1-capitalists) is a fraction, $\epsilon$, of advanced capital, and advanced capital is, itself, a fraction $\mu$ of all Peripheral capital, $K_2$. Thus,

$$\epsilon = K_e/K_a,$$
$$\mu = K_a/K_2$$

and so

$$\alpha = \epsilon\mu = K_e/K_2$$

In any period $t + 1$, the components of advanced capital (by ownership) are given (remembering that $s_a = s_1$) by

$$\epsilon^{t+1}K_a{}^{t+1} = \epsilon^t K_a{}^t + s_a r_a{}^t \epsilon^t K_a{}^t + B_1{}^{t+1} \tag{5.31}$$

and

$$(1-\epsilon)^{t+1}K_a{}^{t+1} = (1-\epsilon)^t K_a{}^t(1 + s_a r_a) + v s_b r_b{}^t K_b{}^t \tag{5.32}$$

where $v$ is the rate of 'seepage' of savings from the backward to the advanced sector. The term

$$v s_b r_b{}^t K_b{}^t = V^t$$

thus represents that part of backward-sector savings (out of profits of the preceding period) which is added to the current-period capital of the advanced sector. Writing

$$V^t / K_a{}^t = \psi^t$$

and

$$B_1{}^{t+1}/K_a{}^t = \beta_2{}^t/\mu^t$$

(by virtue of Equation (4.11) and the definition of $\mu$), Equations (5.31) and (5.32) can be rearranged as

$$\frac{\epsilon^{t+1}}{\epsilon^t} = \frac{1 + s_a r_a{}^t + (\beta_2{}^t/\epsilon^t\mu^t)}{1 + g_a{}^t} \tag{5.33}$$

and

$$\frac{(1-\epsilon)^{t+1}}{(1-\epsilon)^t} = \frac{1 + s_a r_a{}^t + \psi^t/(1-\epsilon)^t}{1 + g_a{}^t} \tag{5.34}$$

(where $1 + g_a{}^t = K_a{}^{t+1}/K_a{}^t$). From this it follows that

$$\frac{\epsilon^{t+1}}{(1-\epsilon)^{t+1}} \gtrless \frac{\epsilon^t}{(1-\epsilon)^t} \text{ as } \frac{\beta_2{}^t/\mu^t}{\psi^t} \gtrless \frac{\epsilon^t}{(1-\epsilon)^t} \tag{5.35}$$

The ratio $\epsilon^t/(1-\epsilon)^t$ represents the present division of the advanced sector between foreign and domestic ownership. Relation (5.35) says simply that this will increase if it is exceeded by the ratio of current additions to $K_a$ coming from overseas ($\beta_2'/\mu'$) to additions coming from the backward sector. It may be noted that the ploughing back of profits made within the advanced sector has no bearing on this matter since the rate of refinancing, $s_a r_a$, is the same for both groups already established there.

How does the ownership ratio $\epsilon/(1-\epsilon)$ behave over time? Consider first how the advanced sector may become initiated. Two possibilities are: (i) that it developed during a period of colonial accumulation, during which time it was wholly externally owned; and (ii) that the advanced technique was introduced by 1-capitalists as a consequence of a transition to an investment regime occurring within the epoch of liberal world capitalism. (The possibility of an advanced sector initiated by Peripheral capitalists seems less plausible and will be ignored.) In either case the initial ownership ratio (that is, at decolonization or at the beginning of the transition) is infinite. Once indigenous capitalists enter the advanced sector, it falls to a finite value. At this point, however, the advanced sector grows more rapidly than the backward and thus, if $v$ is constant, the contribution coming from backward-sector seepage, represented by $\psi$, declines rapidly, approaching zero in the limit. Because of this the ownership ratio may once again rise. It does not, however, follow that it will return to infinity for, as we approach the limiting state when the world economy is growing at the uniform rate $s_a r$, $\beta_2$ will also approach zero, so that the ownership proportions become frozen, perpetuated by equal rates of refinancing.

This means that domestic capitalists are represented in the final state, the relative size of their representation depending on how soon and how quickly they can convert backward into advanced capital and so establish a base from which they can refinance advanced-sector investments. The sooner the process of conversion is completed, the higher will be their representation. An important aspect of capital market imperfections is that they help confine domestic capital to the relatively unprofitable and sluggish part of the economy.

## 5.7 Consumption

The division of the Periphery necessitates obvious modifications to the system of prices. Now that two processes (*a* and *b*) exist side by side to produce commodity 2, the full system is

$$p = (1 + r)(pa_{11} + a_{21}) + w_1 l_1 \tag{5.36}$$

$$1 = (1 + r)(pa_{12} + a_{22}) + w_a l_a \tag{5.37}$$

$$1 = (1 + r_b)(pb_{12} + b_{22}) + w_b l_b \tag{5.38}$$

where $r_b$ is less than $r$. Equations (5.36)–(5.38) are three equations in three unknowns ($p$, $r$ and $r_b$) and are wholly determinate. Moreover, it is possible to solve for prices using the first two equations alone: Equation (5.38) is necessary only to determine $r_b$.

The consumption frontier of the Peripheral economy with a dual export sector can be derived by some straightforward modifications to the algebra of 5.2. Corresponding to Equations (5.3), (5.4) and (5.5.2) are

$$X_1 = (1 + g_1)a_{11}X_1 + (1 + g_a)a_{12}X_a + (1 + g_b)b_{12}X_b + C_{11} + C_{1e} + C_{12}$$

$$X_2 = X_a + X_b = (1 + g_1)a_{21}X_1 + (1 + g_a)a_{22}X_a + (1 + g_b)b_{22}X_b + C_{21} + C_{2e} + C_{22}$$

and,

$$L_2 = l_a X_a + l_b X_b = \hat{l}_2 X_2$$

where $\hat{l}_2$ is the output-weighted average of sectoral labour coefficients. We define also the following weighted averages (in which the enclave is included in the advanced sector):

$$\hat{r}_2 = r_a \mu + r_b(1 - \mu) \tag{5.39}$$

$$\hat{g}_2 = g_a \mu + g_b(1 - \mu)$$

$$\hat{w}_2 = (w_a l_a X_a + w_b l_b X_b)/\hat{l}_2 X_2$$

$$\hat{s}_2 = [s_a r_a \mu + s_b r_b(1 - \mu)]/\hat{r}_2 \tag{5.40}$$

(the weights being sectoral capital stocks for $\hat{r}_2$ and $\hat{g}_2$, employment for $\hat{w}_2$ and profits for $\hat{s}_2$). By the logic of 5.2 these relations yield the Peripheral consumption frontier (corresponding to Equation (5.23.2)),

$$c_2 = \hat{w}_2 + [\hat{r}_2 - (\hat{s}_2 \hat{r}_2 + u_2)]k_2 \tag{5.41}$$

and net domestic product,

$$y_2 = x_2 - k_2 = \hat{w}_2 + \hat{r}_2 k_2 \tag{5.42}$$

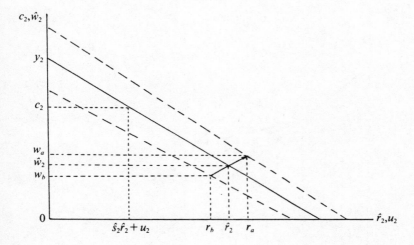

*Figure 5.4*

Equation (5.41) does, of course, represent an 'average' consumption frontier of the two sectors. Assuming that the advanced sector is more capital intensive as well as more productive, the configuration of the individual and average frontiers is as shown in Figure 5.4. Over time, the average frontier shifts outwards as the advanced sector grows relative to the backward, so pushing up the average wage rate and rate of profits.

To determine the time path of consumption p.w. with investment we need simply to adapt the argument of 5.4, beginning with Equation (5.28) which is now

$$u_2{}' = (1 - s_a)r_a\alpha^t \tag{5.43}$$

Also, from (5.39) and (5.40),

$$\hat{s}_2{}'\hat{r}_2{}' = s_a r_a \mu^t + s_b r_b (1 - \mu)^t \tag{5.44}$$

so that, adding (5.43) and (5.44)

$$u_2{}' + \hat{s}_2{}'\hat{r}_2{}' = \alpha^t r_a + s_a r_a (\mu - \alpha)^t + s_b r_b (1 - \mu)^t \tag{5.45}$$

Over time, the advanced sector grows at the expense of the back-

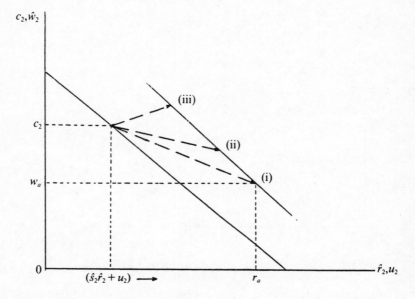

*Figure 5.5*

ward and its share tends to unity. If the complete imperfection of inter-sectoral capital markets deprives Peripheral capitalists of the opportunity to enter the advanced sector, then $\alpha \to 1$, also. With all its elements positively related to $\alpha$, the term $(\hat{s}_2 \hat{r}_2 + u_2)$ rises over time, in this case reaching the limit $r_a$, as in Equation (5.30). Thus, as the frontier moves outwards, consumption p.w. falls to the level of the advanced wage rate (outcome (i) in Figure 5.5). If, on the other hand, indigenous capitalists do become incorporated in the advanced sector, $\alpha$ tends to a limit $\alpha^* < 1$, and (5.45) correspondingly tends to

$$r_a[\alpha^*(1 - s_a) + s_a] < r_a$$

Because domestic capitalists continue to have economic significance so too does domestic capitalist consumption, $c_2 - w_a$ (outcome (ii)). Indeed, there is nothing in these dynamics to prevent consumption p.w. *rising* over time (outcome (iii)). It really depends on the extent of indigenous incorporation into the advanced sector and the advanced–backward wage differential.

We finish this section with a brief remark on employment trends in the external sector. With constant prices and technology, employment growth is equal to capital growth and is thus greater in the higher-wage, but lower-labour-intensity advanced sub-sector. The proportion of higher-wage workers in export employment approaches unity over time. The growth rate of export employment thus rises continuously to the limit $s_a r_a$. What happens to the proportion of higher-wage earners amongst all earners (including those who exist outside of formal employment) depends, of course, on the overall rate of growth of the potential working population.

### 5.8 Conclusion

The analysis of this and the preceding chapter has sought to trace out the evolution of some important variables in a world of free investment. If wage rates in both countries are constant then in a Sraffa–Leontief world the terms of trade are also constant. In the absence of disturbances or modifications to the basic model the evolution of global capitalism is characterized by the following:

1. a simple Pasinetti process in which effectively all of the Periphery's capital comes to be owned by the Centre;
2. rising growth rates in both countries, both approaching the steady state $s_1 r$;
3. a volume of investment flow tending, as a proportion of world capital, to zero as investments in the two countries become self-financing; and
4. the elimination of indigenous capitalist consumption in the Periphery in line with the disappearance of indigenous capitalists.

Once the basic model is modified to allow for the possibility that the Peripheral export sector has a dual character and that indigenous capitalists can seep into the advanced sector and adopt advanced savings behaviour, conclusions 1 and 4 are no longer valid. The Pasinetti process is now impeded and Peripheral capitalists will be represented in the final outcome.

Further modifications will be introduced in succeeding chapters. In the following chapter, full employment will be allowed to drive up wages in the Centre stimulating important responses in the Periphery, and in Chapter 9 account will be taken of the effects of technical progress.

Whilst these modifications will give extra insights, the simple and stark picture which has emerged so far still represents underlying forces of considerable economic and political significance.

## Notes

1.  The inclusion of enclave capitalist consumption with that of country 1 residents is a matter of choice. If the equation $U_1 = F_1 + C_e$ were substituted into Equation (5.15), the resulting consumption frontier would be

    $$c^1 = w_1 + [r - (s_1 r - f_1)]k_1$$

    which relates consumption p.w. *within* country 1 to $(s_1 r - f_1)$ where $f_1 = F_1/K_1$. The diagrammatic apparatus developed here and used in subsequent chapters can easily be applied to this frontier.

2.  Enclave consumption can be included with the rest of country 2 consumption to yield a frontier

    $$c^{11} = w_2 + [r - (\bar{s}_2 r + f_2)]k_2$$

    where $c^{11}$ is p.w. consumption *within* country 2.

3.  The boldness of this assertion is a consequence of the simplicity of the model: specifically, that there are only two goods using single-products techniques. The statement does not generalize to higher-dimensional cases because of the interdependence of the production structure. See, for example, Steedman (1984).

4.  Again, this is plausible in the two-commodity case; much less so in others.

5.  The derivation is straightforward. First, transfer receipts, $R_2$, are deducted from the right-hand side of Equation (5.15.2). $C^{11}$, domestic consumption, now includes social consumption financed out of government revenues. Further transformation *via* Equation (5.23.2) gives

    $$c_2 = w_2 + \{r - (1 - \theta_2)[\bar{s}_2(1 - \gamma_2) + \lambda_2 \theta_2/(1 - \theta_2) + \lambda_2 \gamma_2]r_2 - u_2 + \rho_2(1 - \lambda_2)\}k_2$$

    In the long run private indigenous capitalists are eliminated and $\bar{s}_2 \rightarrow s_1$ as $\alpha \rightarrow (1 - \gamma^*_2) < 1$, where $\gamma^*$ is the terminal share of the public sector. Correspondingly, $u_2 \rightarrow (1 - s_1)(1 - \theta_2)(1 - \gamma^*_2)r_2$.

6.  See, for example, Lewis (1954, p. 150).

7.  The adaptation could be the result of higher profit incomes or it could arise from the sort of 'demonstration effect' discussed by Singer (1950).

# 6 Resource constraints

## 6.1 Introduction

It has been assumed up till now that wage rates in both regions are exogenously fixed. In the Periphery this is justified on the grounds that the existence and magnitude of a 'reserve army' of labour are sufficient to keep supply perfectly elastic. Despite the fact that, under conditions so far assumed, the Peripheral growth rate is rising over time (see Figure 4.1), we shall continue to suppose that the growth of population will be such as to maintain a ceiling on wages, even in the very long run.

The Centre, too, experiences a rising growth rate but the assumption of an indefinitely fixed wage rate there is much harder to accept. Once growth hits a full-employment barrier the model, as it has been developed so far, will need modification. One very important reaction to Central full employment could be an inducement to labour-saving technical progress in manufacturing. Discussion of technical progress is, however, postponed till Chapter 9. In this chapter, two other possible reactions are considered. One we shall refer to as the 'Emmanuel effect' in which rising real wages in the Centre necessitate a change in the terms of trade. The other is the relocation to the Periphery of part of good-1 production (which it would be natural to interpret as 'manufacturing'), thus changing the nature of foreign investments.

It has also been assumed so far that the production of good 2, naturally interpreted as 'primary products' or 'materials', has not been constrained by the availability of natural resources. Were such a constraint to operate then a positive rent would have to be paid for the use of these resources. The rent would be expected to rise if scarcity increased with growth, and this too would affect the terms of trade. Since there is a high degree of symmetry between the effects of the two resource constraints – labour in the Centre, natural resources in the Periphery – we shall treat the latter only briefly, in 6.5. Until then the assumption of zero rents will be maintained.

As a prelude to the analysis it will be useful to recall the discussion in the previous chapter on the determinants of the volume of investment flow, as represented by the $\beta_i$. Under the assumptions of that chapter it was argued that the $\beta_i$ would tend toward zero as the $g_i$ gradually approached uniformity at the steady rate $s_1r$. The magnitude of the investment flow is determined by the extent of misalignment of 'actual' supplies and 'natural' demands corresponding to the natural global price ratio. In that case the misalignment was generated by the inadequacy of Peripheral domestically generated savings in financing the necessary expansion of 2-production. Because of the chronic nature of that inadequacy the investment flow which results is an infinitely enduring phenomenon. However, the $\beta_i$ can also vary in response to more immediate factors which create a potential misalignment of supplies and demands. This will be the case, for example, when the wage rate in the Centre is allowed to vary, for each value of $w_1$ will be associated with a different global price ratio.

Before proceeding it is necessary to insert a terminological note. In conventional terms the 'short run' refers to a situation in which natural values (including a uniform rate of profits) have not (yet) been attained; the 'long run' to a situation in which they do prevail. Since the chronic inadequacy of Peripheral savings continually undermines the conventional long-period position, we previously referred to the Pasinetti process as a 'very' long-run adjustment. Because of the confusion that is liable to be caused by referring to certain processes as 'long-run' when even longer ones are present, from now on these three positions will be called short, medium and long, respectively.

## 6.2 The Emmanuel effect

To approach the problem, suppose that the rate of growth of the labour force in the Centre is fixed exogenously at $n_1$. (For the time being labour-saving technical progress is excluded.) Then, if $n_1 < s_1r$, the process of accumulation that has been previously described, with $g_1$ rising over time towards a limit $s_1r$, will sooner or later come up against a full employment barrier and the assumption of a fixed real wage will have to be dropped. For the immediate consequence of incipient excess demand for labour is that $w_1$ rises. With $w_2$ remaining constant we then have precisely that situation envisaged by Emmanuel (1972) of an increasing difference between Central and Peripheral wages and a consequent deterioration in the terms of trade of the Periphery. If the Periphery has a dual export sector, the terms of trade depend only on the ratio of Central wages to wages in

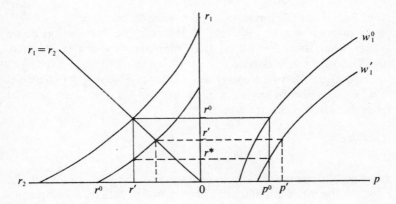

*Figure 6.1*

the advanced part of that sector. (See the discussion in 5.7, relating to Equations (5.36)–(5.38).) Thus, in the following discussion the ratio of wage rates is defined as $\omega = w_1/w_a$, where $w_a$ is constant.

The Emmanuel effect and its implications are illustrated in Figure 6.1. Each curve in the left-hand quadrant shows the potential relationship between the rates of profit in the two countries for a given value of $w_1$ (and hence $\omega$). Each $r_1(p)$ function in the right-hand quadrant is similarly drawn for given $\omega$. These relationships are derived from Equations (5.1) and (5.2) slightly modified to allow the $r_i$ to differ. As a result the two equations contain three unknowns and so possess a degree of freedom which allows any one variable to be expressed as a function of any other. They may therefore be solved to give

$$p = \frac{[1-(1+r_2)a_{22}]l_1\omega + l_2a_{21}(1+r_1)}{[1-(1+r_1)a_{11}]l_2 + l_1\omega a_{12}(1+r_2)} \tag{6.1}$$

from which it follows that

$$dp/d(r_1/r_2) > 0 \tag{6.2}$$

For any value of $p$ a rise in $w_1$ reduces $r_1$ (see Equation (5.1)), shifting down the $r_1(p)$ curve. Similarly, global profitability is reduced by the increase in global primary factor income so that the $r_1 - r_2$ frontier in the left-hand quadrant contracts towards the origin. As may be seen from Equation (5.2) (or, in the dual-economy case, Equation (5.37)), at the original prices $p^0$ the rate of profits in the Periphery is $r^0$, no matter what the value of $w_1$, thus enabling us to fix the relative positions of the new curves.

Comparing the two Central wage rates in Figure 6.1 (where $w_1^1 > w_1^0$) yields the following inequalities (which are easily derived from the basic price equations):

$$dp/d\omega > 0 \tag{6.3}$$
$$dr/d\omega < 0 \qquad (r = r_1 = r_2) \tag{6.4}$$

The first of these is the Emmanuel effect and the second refers to the effect on the internationally uniform rate of profits. Following from the previous discussion, is it possible to say what the effect of a wage increase will be on $\beta_i$?

Refer to Figure 6.1 and suppose (momentarily) that following the increase in $w_1$ relative prices remained at $p^0$. This would only be possible if the rates of profits diverged: $r_1$ would need to fall to $r_1^*$ whereas $r_2$ would, as just noted, remain the same ($= r^0$). In this situation prices would be sustained at $p^0$ only if supplies were equal to demands at these prices. On the other hand, for the new natural prices $p'$ to be attained (implying a lower relative demand for good 1) the output ratio of 1:2 would have to fall. In the short run, supplies appropriate to $p^0$-demands could be sustained by continuing the existing flow of foreign investment. But even if this were to happen, over time the output ratio would adjust as a consequence of the reduction in $g_1$ accompanying the fall in $r_1$. In the course of this adjustment, $r_1$ would converge asymptotically to $r'$ and $p$ to $p'$. If the flow of investment were free to respond directly to the new circumstances, however, the same result would be brought about much more quickly simply by an increased volume of outflow. Assuming such freedom, to the above inequalities can be added one more:

$$d\beta_1/d\omega > 0 \tag{6.5}$$

From Equation (4.9), Relations (6.4) and (6.5) immediately imply a reduction in $g_1$. Thus, in general terms, the mechanism by which the shortage of labour is relieved appears straightforward: due to a combination of falling global profitability and an increased outflow of foreign investment, the rate of growth of the Centre's capital stock is reduced and brought into line with $n_1$.

Unfortunately, things are not quite as simple as they seem. It was noted in 4.3 that when prices are changing (as is the case here) the rate of growth of physical capital (call it $\gamma$) is not the same as the rate of growth of value capital, $g$ (in general). Equation (4.9) is valid in value terms but one cannot be certain that a reduction in $g_1$ implies a reduction in $\gamma_1$. When $p$ is rising a capital stock valued in terms of good 2 may rise in value even as its quantity falls. Although this possibility cannot be ruled out, henceforth we shall assume that quantity responses to changes in $\omega$ outweigh any contrary price variations. In particular, it is assumed that $d\gamma_i/dg_i > 0$. With a given technique, the rate of growth of physical capital is, of course, equal to the rate of growth of employment. On these assumptions the Emmanuel effect will succeed in equalizing $\gamma_1$ and $n_1$.

It may be mentioned in passing that while Relation (6.5) is consistent with the classical view that the main stimulus to overseas investment is downward pressure on the Centre's rate of profits (exerted in this case by wages rather than rents), it is not consistent with the theory proposed by J. A. Hobson (1902). In Hobson's view overseas investment acts as a 'vent' for over-saving (the obverse of underconsumption) in the Centre due to the bias in income distribution in favour of high-saving capitalists. From Hobson's standpoint an increase in the Centre's rate of profits at the expense of wages would generate larger outflows of capital whereas from the classical position a higher rate of profits helps retain domestic savings. The inconsistency between the two perspectives disappears if Hobson's theory is confined to the short run with excess capacity of capital equipment.[1]

The Emmanuel effect might be expected to stimulate a number of counteracting responses which cushion its further consequences without altogether eliminating them. Some of these will be considered in greater detail subsequently, but one must be dealt with straight away. In response to the increasing Central wage rate capitalists may opt for a different technique, one which was previously available but not previously profitable. It is not only capitalists involved in producing good 1 who may be induced to adopt a different method of production, for the change in relative prices may also make a different combination of inputs desirable in the production of good 2. If this happens then the new technique (that is, a combination of methods for producing the two goods) will necessarily have a higher rate of profits than the discarded one at the new

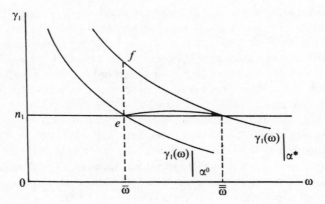

*Figure 6.2*

value of $\omega$. The global $\omega$–$r$ relation for each technique is downward-sloping. (This follows from Relation (6.4).) The $\omega$–$r$ frontier, the outer boundary of the individual relations is thus, also, downward-sloping. The price ratio for adjacent techniques is equal at their switchpoint.[2] Thus, whether or not there is a change of technique, the rate of profits must fall and the price ratio must rise. (The extent to which the price ratio needs to rise will also depend on the elasticity of relative demands. A small rise may choke off sufficient demand for good 1 to ease the pressure of excess demand for labour in the Centre.)

The Emmanuel effect is not a once-and-for-all response to collision with the full-employment barrier. Once labour supply is exhausted, the effect needs to operate continuously to maintain full-employment growth of output. To see this, let $v = L_1/N_1$ be the rate of employment and $\bar{v}$ be the 'full employment' rate beyond which $\omega$ rises. If the Emmanuel effect is no longer necessary then $\gamma_1 = n_1$ at $\bar{v}$ and $\omega$ is constant. This position is shown by point $e$ in Figure 6.2. Here the 'quantitative' growth rate

$$\gamma_i = G(\omega, \alpha) \qquad G_\omega < 0, G_\alpha > 0 \tag{6.6}$$

is drawn for a given, initial value of $\alpha = \alpha^0$. The wage ratio cannot, however, remain at the value $\bar{\omega}$ indefinitely. For constant $\omega$ implies constant $p$, but only because $\beta_1 > 0$ keeps global supplies and demands in line. This is the situation described by the Pasinetti process: $\beta_1 > 0$ implies rising $\alpha$, falling $\beta_1$ and a rising growth rate $g_1$. (Moreover, with constant $p$, $g_1 = \gamma_1$ of necessity.) As $\alpha$ rises, the $\gamma_1(\omega)$ curve in Figure 6.2 shifts upwards. Then if $\omega$ were to remain at $\bar{\omega}$, employment growth $\gamma_1$ would exceed labour supply growth and the economy would shift from point $e$ toward point $f$. But this, of course, implies $v > \bar{v}$ and hence rising wages and terms of trade. The Emmanuel effect is again put into operation until growth is sufficiently dampened once more.

Only in the limit, when $\alpha$ has reached its maximum and $\beta_1 = 0$ is the contradiction absent. In approaching this state $v$ is greater than $\bar{v}$ but converges towards it, while $\omega$ is rising towards some maximum value $\bar{\bar{\omega}}$, as indicated by the arrow. The other side of the coin is a global rate of profits converging to the value $n_1/s_1$, bringing the uniform world growth rate into line with $n_1$.

## 6.3 Fluctuating growth

In what follows we consider the behaviour of the system in continuous time. This raises the possibility of inconsistency with the preceding discrete-time analysis. The mixing of continuous and discrete-time analysis may be found in Goodwin and Punzo (1987) where it is implicitly justified on the grounds that the periods can be made very small.[3] They fail to point out, however, that in the circulating capital model (which they employ) this means that all capital is used up in a very short period of time. This can be avoided by replacing the uniform unitary depreciation coefficient by coefficients (not necessarily uniform) of less than unity (or, for infinitely durable capital, of zero).[4] With infinitesimally small periods all rates (depreciation, profits and growth) should be interpreted as instantaneous ones. The qualitative nature of all the relationships relevant to the present discussion (for example, between wage rates, rates of profits and prices) would be unaffected by such a modification.

There is another problem which also needs consideration before proceeding. Variability of real wages and, as a consequence of rates of profit, growth and investment flows, is self-evidently a departure from (conventional) long-period analysis, doing considerable violence to the assumptions on which that analysis is based. If, for example, the growth rate now fluctuates over time then the system is effectively undergoing an infinite series of transitions from one state to another. But if the available analyses of relatively simple transitions (say, from one steady state to another) are sketchy, those of fluctuating growth in multi-sector models are wholly inadequate. There are at least two issues: one is feasibility in a purely physical sense; the other concerns the existence of realistic and appropriate market reactions to changing situations.[5] In the discussion of the transition from one steady state to another in Chapter 2 it was assumed that sufficient flexibility in consumption existed to facilitate the switch. This, or some other form of accommodation (inventories, perhaps) will be needed here. Whether there are realistic expectations mechanisms and behaviour patterns that could generate change in historical time of the sort generated here in logical time, is largely a matter of faith.

The cyclical implications of the Emmanuel effect are considered initially by confining attention to the medium run, that is, by supposing, on the one hand, that $\gamma_1$ is independent of the long-run stage of global development as indicated by $\alpha$ and, on the other, that overseas investment is sufficiently fluid to maintain a globally uniform rate of profits.[6] This will, of course, lead to a contradiction when viewed from the long-run perspective and the contradiction will have to be resolved subsequently.

Suppose that instead of there being a precisely defined point of full employment beyond which real wages rise, wage behaviour is determined by a real Phillip's curve of the general form

$$\frac{\dot{\omega}}{\omega} = \frac{\dot{w}_1}{w_1} = \mu(L_1/N_1) = \mu(v) \qquad \mu_v > 0 \tag{6.7}$$

The proportionate rate of change of $v$ is

$$\frac{\dot{v}}{v} = \frac{\dot{L}_1}{L_1} - \frac{\dot{N}_1}{N_1} = G(\omega) - n_1 \qquad G_\omega < 0 \tag{6.8}$$

Equations (6.7) and (6.8) are a pair of simple non-linear differential equations. From Equation (6.7) we may postulate some $v = \bar{v}$ for which $\mu(\bar{v}) = 0$ and $\dot{\omega} \gtrless 0$ as $v \gtrless \bar{v}$. Similarly, from Equation (6.8) we suppose there exists some $\omega = \bar{\omega}$ for which $G(\bar{\omega}) = n_1$ and $\dot{v} \gtrless 0$ as $\omega \lessgtr \bar{w}$. The general behaviour of the system is illustrated in Figure 6.3.

The diagram clearly implies some sort of cyclical trajectory around the only non-trivial critical point, $(\bar{v}, \bar{\omega})$. The precise nature of the cycles is easy to see once it is recognized that Equations (6.7)

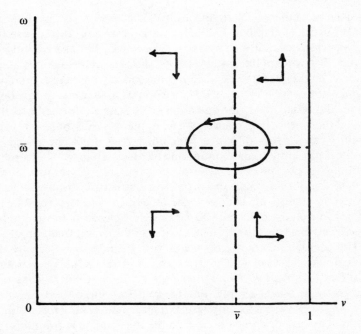

*Figure 6.3*

and (6.8) are equations of the predator–prey type made familiar to economists through the work of Goodwin (1967). This can be made more explicit by taking linear approximations to the $\mu(v)$ and $G(\omega)$ functions to yield

$$\dot{\omega} = (-\theta + \delta v)\omega$$
$$\dot{v} = (\xi - n_1 - \eta\omega)v$$

As is well known (Hirsch and Smale, 1974, Chap. 12), in the predator–prey model, each path in the phase diagram is a closed orbit and there is an infinite number of such orbits each nested within another. The particular orbit which obtains depends on the initial conditions of the model. If, in an extreme case, the system begins at $(\bar{v}, \bar{\omega})$ it will continue on a non-fluctuating growth path.

Theoretically, the model described by Equations (6.7) and (6.8) is unsatisfactory since the cycles associated with predator–prey equations are structurally unstable: a small change in the structure of the model leads either to the fading away of the cycle or the break-down of the system (Velupillai, 1979). This could prove problematic in the present case because the system may be jolted by a change in technique. If switchpoints occurred at discrete intervals, technical change might lead to a sudden economizing on labour and we should not be able to write $\dot{L}_1/L_1 = G(\omega)$ as a continuous function. If, on the other hand, the spectrum of techniques formed a continuum then, since the choice of technique depends only on $\omega$ we could write $\dot{L}_1/L_1 = G^*(\omega)$, a function representing the effects of both output growth and continuous technical change. This modification does not, however, change the predator–prey nature of the system and leaves intact the problem of structural instability with respect to other disturbances to the model. In fact, structural instability can only be overcome by adding new elements to the model, specifically making $\dot{\omega}/\omega$ a function of $\omega$ and/or $\dot{v}/v$ a function of $v$.

The average values of this medium-run model are given by the critical values $\bar{v}$ and $\bar{\omega}$. The introduction of a Phillip's curve may thus be thought of as a way of endogenizing the Central wage rate and fixing its average value. But, as we have seen, once the mechanism is placed within its long-term context, maintaining trend values $\bar{v}$ and $\bar{\omega}$ involves a contradiction. In the long run, $\omega$ is continuously pulled up as a result of 'over-full' employment, its average value converging to a rate $\bar{\bar{\omega}}$. This follows from the long-run version of Equation (6.8):

$$\dot{v}/v = G(\omega,\alpha) - n_1$$

The proportionate rate of growth of $\alpha$ at time $t$ is a function of the capital inflow $\beta_2(\beta_1)$ which itself is directly related to $\omega$. But since $\alpha$ is a share rising to a limit $\alpha^*$, its growth rate must become constrained as $t \rightarrow \infty$. We can thus add a third equation

$$\dot{\alpha}/\alpha = A(\omega,\alpha(t))$$

to complete the long-run system. It is easy to see that this system has a fixed point $(\alpha^*, \bar{v}, \bar{\bar{\omega}})$ though its dynamics are more complicated than those of the medium-run model and we make no attempt to examine them in detail. It may, however, be noted that the fixed point does not possess local stability from which it might, perhaps, be inferred that $v$ and $\omega$ continue to cycle as $\alpha \rightarrow \alpha^*$.[7]

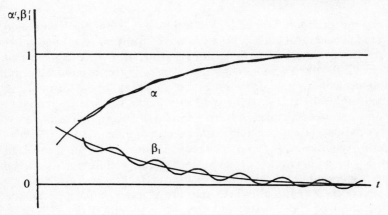

*Figure 6.4*

Thus inflationary–deflationary phases in the Centre may be reflected in fluctuations of sustained amplitude in the flow of overseas investment. Even when $\alpha \approx \alpha^*$, $\beta_1$ will continue to cycle around a near-zero trend so that there will still be fluctuations in the *stock* of foreign-owned capital even if variations in the Centre's *share* have faded away. These time paths are illustrated in Figure 6.4. As compared with the smooth operation of the Pasinetti process previously portrayed, in the present case the Centre's accumulation of Peripheral capital goes in spurts induced by periodic wage pressure at home.

### 6.4 Overseas investment in manufacturing

Thus far, the inter-regional pattern of specialization has been taken as given and immutable. Geographical factors are major determinants of the production locations of primary goods, but much less so for manufactured goods, whose technology can be replicated with relative ease in any part of the world. Since it would be natural to interpret good 1 as a manufactured good, the question then arises as to the implications of a full-employment barrier in a world of relatively footloose manufacturing firms.

If the manufacturing technology could be replicated anywhere at no cost at all, the entire analysis up to now would involve a major inconsistency. For good 1 producers would relocate production in the Periphery where wages are lower and would continue to do so until wages in the two regions had become equalized. The reason why this does not happen is that technology is not costlessly replicated. There is, of course, the existence of transport costs and other trade impediments which we are ignoring. But there is a host of other difficulties which range from operating in a culturally and linguistically foreign environment to obtaining labour of the right skills and quality. Since these difficulties can only be overcome at some cost (for example, of training and education), the 'technology' in a broader sense is actually different: manufacturing in the Periphery requires more inputs per unit than it does in the Centre. In order to compensate for these costs a wage differential will be necessary and it may need to be substantial.

Nevertheless, the ability to relocate places a constraint on the operation of the Emmanuel effect. As wage rates diverge, there comes a point at which foreign locations become equiprofitable with domestic locations. At that point (assuming that relocation is not subject to increasing costs), the flow of foreign investment into manufacturing will be such as to maintain the critical difference between wage rates. That being so, this type of inflation-induced investment is qualitatively different from that which generates additional growth of primary production. In the latter case, the extra supply of primary goods necessitated a deterioration in the Periphery's terms of trade. But expansion of manufacturing output at constant returns and globally uniform costs can be accomplished without any changes in relative prices.

To analyse this type of investment we begin at the point at which the balance of locational advantage is so fine at the existing wage differential that an infinitesimal increase of $w_1$ will trigger a flow of manufacturing investment. (Discussion of possible cyclical behaviour is postponed until later.) If wage increases are effectively avoided by this means, the rate of profits also remains the same. Given a perfectly elastic supply of labour to the Peripheral advanced sector (to undergo the necessary training) expansion can take place there without generating wage increases.[8] The Periphery thus provides the global capitalist economy with a 'reserve army of labour'. Tightness in one regional labour market is overcome by switching production to the region where the labour market is slack. In that way, world profitability can be maintained, and so too can the average world growth rate. However, the relocation of production necessarily affects the distribution of growth between the Centre and the enclave. The additional flow of investment means an increase in $\beta_1$ and a corresponding fall in $g_1$, which has its counterpart in a rise in $g_e^2$ (and hence in both $g_a$ and $\hat{g}_2$). In this, as in the previous case, then, a full-employment barrier in the Centre generates faster growth in the Periphery. Thus $\alpha$ will rise faster than it otherwise would have.

The only change required to the model of Chapter 5 is to supplement the price equations with an equation representing the production of good 1 in the Periphery:

$$p = (1 + r)(pe_{11} + e_{21}) + w_a l_{a1} \tag{6.9}$$

Even though the underlying technology may be the same in the two regions, in a more general sense $e_{i1} \geqslant a_{i1}$ and $l_{a1} \geqslant l_1$ (with a strong inequality holding for at least one of the coefficients), because of the additional cost of operating in a foreign environment. This revision of the earlier model has obvious implications for our original assumption concerning the pattern of international specialization. But although the initial pattern has now broken down, the direction of commodity flows is unaffected. The Centre has only good 1 to offer the Periphery and will want only primary products in return. The only modification introduced by the possibility of locating manufacturing production in the Periphery is that the region can now supply itself with some of the goods it would formerly have imported.

The analysis of this section began at the point at which the Central wage rate was such that any further increase would trigger an outflow of manufacturing investment. How should the approach be generalized? Conceptually, one could imagine the accumulation process taking place in three stages. In the first stage, the reserve army of labour in the Centre is of sufficient proportions that real wages may effectively be taken as constant, as in the discussions of Chapter 5. But as the reserves of labour become exhausted by the rising growth rate, Phillips-type wage pressure begins and puts in train the Emmanuel effect. Finally, the wage rises to a threshold value at which overseas manufacturing investment becomes profitable. The important difference between the second and third stages, as described so far, is that the Emmanuel effect depresses the Peripheral terms of trade, whereas induced manufacturing investment leaves them unaffected.

The third stage can easily be modified to allow for the possibility of cyclical behaviour of the type already discussed in 6.3 and described in the medium run by Equations (6.7) and (6.8). The important difference with the previous case, however, is that because the terms of trade are unaffected the medium-run cycles around a centre $(\bar{v}, \bar{\omega})$ do not contradict the long-run characterization of the accumulation process. Constant terms of trade are consistent with constant $\omega$. In terms of growth rates and investment flows, manufacturing investment gives Centre capitalists an extra option: sufficient investment can always take place to ensure no further upward pressure on $g_1$ and hence no further excess demand for labour. Thus, the previous chain of reasoning $(\dot{\alpha} > 0 \Rightarrow \beta_1 < 0 \Rightarrow \dot{g}_1 > 0)$ is no longer valid. Contrary to Figure 6.4, even if $\alpha$ has reached unity, $\beta_1 > 0$ may hold on average, a continuous outflow of capital being necessary to keep trend Centre wages at their threshold level. Whether structurally unstable cycles will survive a transition from one stage to another and, if so, how, is a matter on which we offer no speculation.

It has been assumed so far that whatever the volume of manufacturing investment needed to prevent further growth in the wage differential, it can be accommodated by an elastic supply of higher-cost inputs within the Periphery. Suppose, however, that there is a limit to the rate at which skilled labour can be trained and other obstacles overcome, so that the supply curve of additional higher-cost inputs rises after some point, quickly becoming very inelastic. If that is so, then a higher wage differential may be needed to sustain an increasing flow of manufacturing investment. The option of investing in manufacturing production rather than primary products would then exercise a degree of restraint on the Central wage but would not succeed entirely in halting its growth. Thus, the second stage, the Emmanuel effect, is not entirely eliminated and neither is the deterioration in the Peripheral terms of trade. If the Emmanuel effect and the 'relocation effect' operate side-by-side the analysis of this section is subject to a trivial modification.

## 6.5 Summary and extension to natural resources

This chapter has so far been concerned with two reactions to a full-employment barrier in the Centre. In the first, the Emmanuel effect, Central wage growth induces a faster outflow of investment than would occur otherwise, leading to a decline in the Periphery's terms of trade. If real wage behaviour in the Centre is determined by a Phillips-type relationship with the rate of employment, perpetual cycles may obtain which are transmitted to other key variables of the model. The Emmanuel effect does not, however, prevent the trend wage rate from rising, since it needs to act continuously to keep the Centre's growth rate in line with the growth of its labour force. Only the limit when $\alpha = \alpha^*$ and $g_1 = g_2 = s_1 r = n_1$ does the Emmanuel effect become exhausted.

The second reaction, which occurs once the wage differential has reached a particular magnitude, is to locate part of good 1 production in the Periphery. This induced form of investment does not affect the terms of trade and if the flow is perfectly elastic the Central wage is prevented from rising further. This means that a higher aggregate world growth rate can be sustained, the Periphery providing a reserve army of labour not only for primary products but also, now, for manufacturing. But if, because of various obstacles, the flow of manufacturing investment is not perfectly elastic, the relocation effect may only be partial and will, therefore, not substitute for the Emmanuel effect but will simply accompany a weakened form of that effect.

There is a certain resemblance between the story just told and what Molana and Vines (1989) refer to as the original 'North–South' model, that of Ricardo. In the case of Ricardo, however, it was natural resources, or more precisely land, that posed a constraint on accumulation in the Centre (i.e., 'England'). Rising rents forced down the rate of profits, threatening convergence to a stationary state.[9] This, in Ricardo's opinion, could be averted by exploiting the 'reserve acres of land' in the Periphery (i.e., 'Portugal') through international trade. In the present story the constraint is labour and it is investment rather than trade, which already exists, which relieves the pressure on the Centre. In the absence of a release valve the world growth rate would be forced to adjust to the rate of growth of population in the Centre. In this respect there is perhaps a stronger correspondence to the model of Findlay (1980). But starting with a specialized trading world, Findlay offers no mechanism for relieving the Central labour constraint. Although Burgstaller and Saavedra-Rivano's (1984) extension of Findlay allows for perfect capital movements, they too have complete specialization so that the terms-of-trade effect of Central wage growth cannot be neutralized by the partial relocation of manufacturing production.

The switch of concern away from a Central resource constraint to a Central labour constraint was precisely because the growth of world trade which Ricardo advocated helped successfully avert the stationary state. From a global perspective, however, the success could only be temporary. For it is now the Periphery which is the (net) provider of primary products and shortages of natural resources have come to manifest themselves dramatically in recent decades. A re-focusing on the resource constraint, this time in the Periphery, is found in the papers by Vines (1984) and Molana and Vines in which the assumption of Peripheral resource scarcity is coupled with exogeneity of real wages in both regions.[10] In the rest of this section we consider briefly how a natural resource constraint can be incorporated into the present model.

For this purpose it is necessary to reformulate the process of production in the Periphery and the corresponding price–distribution relationship. (For simplicity's sake the export sector will be assumed homogeneous.) This can be done by supposing that the price of materials contains an element for the payment of extensive rent, in which case Equation (5.2), which contains no such payment, can be taken as the price equation corresponding to the marginal grade at time $t$, $z^t$, of natural resource. Superior grades, $\zeta = 1, \ldots, z^t - 1$, are recognized by the fact that the combined value of capital and labour used in production is less than that at the margin. As is well-known,[11] the ranking of grades is not, in general, independent of prices, an analytical complication which is avoided here by assuming that commodity and labour input coefficients maintain constant proportions from grade to grade. The ranking is thus fixed over time and extends to the potentially infinite number of grades not in current use: $z^t + 1$, $z^t + 2$, ..., etc. Thus

$$\rho(\zeta) > \rho(\zeta + 1) \text{ for all } \zeta = 1, \ldots, \infty$$

where $\rho(\zeta)$ is rent per unit of resource grade $\zeta$.

Suppose that as a result of the balance of new discoveries and extensions of existing sources, on the one hand, and of depletions, on the other, the availability of each grade grows at the uniform rate, $h$. Then if a rent already exists on some grade, $\gamma_2 > h$ implies a continual extension of the margin, from $z^t$ to $z^{t+1}$ ($= z^t + 1$), etc. This gives rise to a symmetrical response to the Emmanuel effect: the increasing marginal cost of production simultaneously increases the relative price of good 2 and reduces the global rate of profits and, hence, the world average rate of accumulation. The reduced attractiveness of the Periphery as a location for investment retards the

Pasinetti process. (This is necessary to reduce the relative supply of good 2 in accordance with its higher price.) Thus, corresponding to Relations (6.3)–(6.5), we have

$$dp/d\rho(1) < 0$$
$$dr/d\rho(1) < 0 \text{ and}$$
$$d\beta_2/d\rho(1) < 0$$

The first and second of these inequalities might reasonably be called the 'Ricardo effect' which, as in the case of the Emmanuel effect, needs to be a continuous response. For if it were to cease, the restraints on growth would be released and $\rho(\zeta)$, like $w_1$, would rise without limit. Assuming that $h$ cannot be manipulated by economically induced technical progress or search for new sources, the implication of the global Ricardo effect could be every bit as dramatic as in the original classical story of convergence to a stationary state.

If the Ricardo effect operates in isolation ($w_1$ is constant), rent will rise, possibly along a cyclical path, as $g_w \to h$, a rate which could be very low or even negative. If the Ricardo and Emmanuel effects operate together the limit growth rate will be determined by the lower of $h$ and $n_1$. If $n_1 < h$, natural resources would return to their previous status of a 'free good'; whereas if $n_1 > h$, Centre wages would fall back to some socio-subsistence level and might eventually call forth a Malthusian adjustment to population growth rates.

In the course of the Ricardo effect the terms of trade move in the Periphery's favour. When the two effects operate simultaneously the net impact on the terms of trade is unclear. Further confusion will be caused by the stimulation of natural resource exploitation in the Centre which could occur at a sufficiently high value of $\rho$. For a while there may be sufficient immediate reserves in the Centre to bring a halt to the deterioration in its terms of trade, but once rent there begins to rise the Ricardo effect is restored albeit less intensely. Again it is plausible to assume that rising rents induce a search for effective increases in resource supply, consideration of which is postponed to Chapter 9.

### 6.6 Conclusions
A result of introducing resource constraints is that we can develop a set of possible chronologies of investment regimes, each regime

characterized by a combination of conditions of production of each good. Take good 1. Initially it is produced entirely in the Centre under conditions of constant (over time) costs. When the Centre's reserve army of labour becomes exhausted, costs of production rise over time. Finally, when Centre wages reach a point at which it becomes profitable to diversify the nature of foreign investment, the production of good 1 is initiated in the Periphery. Good 2 is subject to three symmetrical stages, though here the third stage is overseas investment discouraging rather than promoting. According to the precise timing of the three stages for each good, various permutations are possible, each describing a particular chronology of regimes.

It is, in theory, possible to extend the chronology backwards. As we have seeen, complete specialization is only possible if the economies of the trading partners are of compatible sizes, a condition summarized by the inequalities (2.7). One could imagine an initial, perhaps 'Ricardian', stage in which the Periphery were unable to provide all the primary goods needed by the Centre and the latter, consequently, were forced to produce both products. Low resource costs in the Periphery would generate very high returns to investment, leading to rapid growth and movement in the direction of the regime with which we began in Chapter 5: full specialization.

In describing how patterns of global specialization may evolve over historical time this approach avoids the need to invoke the 'cross-section' value analysis criticized by J. H. Williams (see 2.1), or, more typical of this literature, to assume a particular unchanging pattern of specialization. It goes without saying that the patterns implied by such chronologies are extremely simplistic. Of course it is true that the Centre has always produced primary products and that manufacturing has a very long history in much of the Periphery. With greater disaggregation and (especially relevant for primary products) the inclusion of transport costs, and a host of other factors, it would be possible to reflect reality more accurately. To take just one example, with a disaggregated Periphery it would be possible using the processes described in this chapter to develop an endogenous explanation of the formation of the newly industrialized countries (NICs) of South East Asia and Latin America. For the relocation of manufacturing takes place first in those economies whose conditions are most favourable to Centre capitalists (which will have much to do with the practices of the states concerned). A rapid seepage of indigenous capital into the manufacturing sector would then allow the creation of a strong manufacturing-based economy with high domestic participation. The process might be expected to spread as wage pressures begin to build in the NICs themselves (and in this manner the division of the world between Centre and Periphery itself becomes endogenized). On the other hand, learning-by-doing on the part of domestic capitalists together with cultural learning-by-accumulating on the part of foreign capitalists could prolong the NICs favoured position for a considerable time.[12]

Even as the model stands the simple patterns outlined above are defensible abstractions which are unlikely to prove wildly misleading.

## Notes

1   This is implicit in models which represent the Centre in Kalecki-Steindl terms, such as Taylor (1983) and Dutt (1989, Chapter 8).

2.  For a fuller discussion of the choice of techniques and the nature of switch-points, see Mainwaring (1984, Chapter 8).

3.  See, for example, their page 21, where the mix first occurs and the following approximation is found: $(p^{t+1} - p^t)/p^t \simeq \dot{p}/p$.

4.  Treating durable capital by exogenously fixing the lifespans of equipment is open to objection, but no more so than is the circulating capital model which, in fact, is a special case of this approach.

5.  In my view, Goodwin (1986) and Goodwin and Punzo (1987) do not properly address these latter issues.

6.  Maintaining uniform $r$ over the cycles is for ease of exposition. Some cyclical divergence of rates could be accommodated. In a variant of this model incorporating labour migration in Chapter 10, divergences of $r_i$ are taken into account.

7.  It is very easy to see that the Jacobian of the linearized system at the fixed point has zero trace, since $A_\alpha(\alpha^*) = 0$. Note that when $\alpha = \alpha^*$ the system is restored to the previous two-dimensional form so that disturbances would again give rise to Goodwin-type cycles.

8.  The temptation to introduce a wage differential within the advanced sector, between workers in manufacturing and primary production, is resisted in the interests of simplicity. Its implications are, however, straightforward.

9.  For a formal account, see Pasinetti (1960).

10. Molana and Vines, following Kaldor (1976), are primarily concerned with the impact of land productivity growth in the Periphery. (See also Chapter 9.) Their dynamics depend crucially on their formulation of Central consumer preferences.

11. See, for example, Mainwaring (1984, Chapter 12).

12. Cf. Chenery and Keesing (1981): 'There appears to be a strong element of learning by doing, which underlies the concentration of manufactured exports in a small number of countries. Once countries have acquired this ability, it seems to offset rising wages for a considerable period and makes it possible to retain their shares of markets in which they would otherwise be losing their comparative advantage. This accumulative aspect of export performance and

the increasing number of successful competitors may make it increasingly difficult for newcomers to get established in the sectors in which they have a comparative advantage.' (p. 111)

# 7 Consumption gains from foreign investment

## 7.1 Choosing regimes

The models of global capitalist accumulation presented so far have been purely descriptive. Although the time-path of consumption p.w. has been charted, no welfare evaluations were attempted. Indeed, if the processes so described were inevitable, welfare evaluations would be irrelevant. But the processes are not inevitable. Nation states in the post-colonial period have the option (in principle, at least) of withdrawing from, or intensifying, some or all capitalist international relations. When alternatives are available it is obviously of some importance to assess the welfare implications of switching from one to another. In this chapter we consider explicitly the alternatives of perfectly free overseas investment in the Periphery and complete investment autarky. From this the welfare implications of varying the degree of autarky may be inferred. No explicit consideration is given to the possibility of withdrawing from international trade (see Chapter 2).

An analysis of a world economy with free international investment has already been undertaken. The analysis of a no-investment regime is straightforward. But a simple comparison of these regimes is insufficient to yield conclusions concerning welfare because an alternative regime cannot be reached except by going through a process of transition, which might take some time to accomplish and which has associated with it welfare costs or benefits which need to be taken into consideration. Nevertheless, as in the case of trade in goods alone, a simple comparison of alternative paths is a useful first step. For this purpose it will be assumed that wage rates are the same in both regimes and that Peripheral rents are zero. The implications for consumption of the existence of resource constraints are considered in 7.3. This is followed by a complete evaluation of the consumption gains from a transition between regimes.

## 7.2 Comparing alternatives

Where there is no overseas investment, the price equations (5.1) and (5.2) must be modified to allow for the fact that profit rates in the

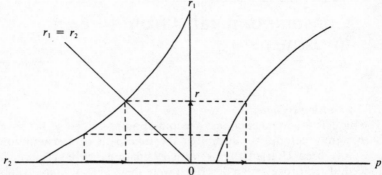

*Figure 7.1*

two countries differ (specifically, $r_2 > r_1$). In this case the price–distribution relationships are as depicted in Figure 6.1, of which a simplified version (appropriate to a single value of ω) is reproduced as Figure 7.1.

Although, in the no-investment regime, a restriction on one of the rates of profits is necessary to determine the terms of trade and the remaining rate, this need not concern us here. So long as $r_2 > r_1$, the equalization of returns as a consequence of foreign investment results in an increase in $p$, which from country 2's point of view amounts to a deterioration in the terms of trade (indicated by the arrows in Figure 7.1).

Consider now the implications for the consumption frontiers in each country of such a change (remembering that no consideration of the transition is being attempted here). Restrictions implied by the no-investment regime are

$$\beta_i = u_i = 0 \text{ and } r_2 > r_1$$

whereas with investment,

$$\beta_i > 0, u_i > 0 \text{ and } r_2 = r_1 = r$$

We consider in turn the cases of a homogeneous Peripheral export sector and a dualized sector.

*Homogeneous periphery*
From the point of view of country 1, the improvement in the terms of trade leads directly to an appreciation in the value of capital p.w.:

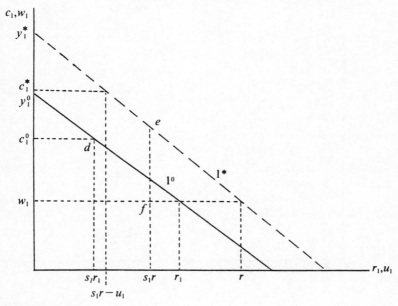

*Figure 7.2*

$\mathrm{d}k_1/\mathrm{d}p > 0$ (from Equation (5.14)) and hence (since $r_1$ also increases) to an increase in both the slope and vertical intercept of the consumption frontier:

$$c_1 = w_1 + r_1 k_1 - (s_1 r_1 - u_1)k_1$$

The new frontier is shown as the dashed line in Figure 7.2. Note that whereas in a closed economy an increase in the rate of profits is necessarily accompanied by a fall in the wage rate (assuming labour to be the only source of primary income), in the present case country 1 is able to maintain a fixed wage when the rate of profits rises. It can do this because the terms of trade are shifted in its favour.

The no-investment level of consumption p.w., $c_1^0$, is found by reading off the point on the inner frontier corresponding to $s_1 r_1$. The with-investment level $c_1^*$ is read off frontier $1^*$ at a point corresponding to $s_1 r_1 - u_1$. The difference may be analysed in two stages. First, there is a move from $d$ to $e$ simply as a consequence of the higher rate of profits. This necessarily implies a higher level of consumption p.w.[1] Second, there is the effect of unretained earnings,

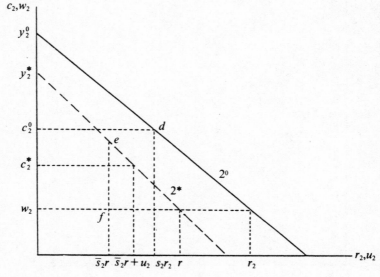

*Figure 7.3*

$u_1$, which also acts to maintain a higher level of consumption p.w. Thus, in comparing the two regimes for country 1, we may conclude that the level of consumption p.w. is higher with foreign investment than it is without.

Turning now to country 2, it can be seen from Figure 7.3 that these conclusions are reversed. The no-investment level of consumption p.w., $c_2^0$, corresponds to the point $s_2r_2$ on frontier $2^0$; the with-investment level, $c_2^*$, to the point $\bar{s}_2r + u_2$ on frontier $2^*$. (The with-investment frontier is steeper because the change in the terms of trade leads to a revaluation of the capital stock p.w. in terms of the *numéraire*.) Again, the change may be analysed in two stages. First, there is the move from $d$ to $e$ which necessarily reduces the level of consumption p.w.[2] To this is then added the effect of the unretained enclave earnings of 1-capitalists: $u_2$. The shift in the consumption frontier ceases once the regional rates of profits are equalized. Thereafter, consumption p.w. continues to slide downwards (*along* frontier $2^*$), in accordance with the Pasinetti process until it reaches $w_2$.

To summarize briefly, we see that consumption p.w. in the high-wage country is higher than it would have been without foreign investment. Remembering that wages are fixed by assumption, this increased consumption is appropriated entirely by capitalists. In the low-wage country the opposite prevails, with the domestic capitalist class suffering lower levels of consumption p.w.


### Dual Periphery

The dual economy assumptions confuse the comparison of alternative regimes by increasing the number of possible outcomes. There are two sources of ambiguity resulting from the switch from autarky to free trade in assets: one is the direction of the effect on the average rate of profits, $\hat{r}_2$, defined by Equation (5.39); the other is the direction in which the consumption frontier shifts.

Consider first the average rate of profits. If an advanced sector does not exist in the absence of foreign investment, then $\hat{r}_2 = r_b$. For given terms of trade, $r_b$ is determined directly by Equation (5.38) and it follows immediately that

$$dr_b/dp < 0$$

so that the introduction of foreign investment, which leads to a deterioration in the terms of trade (an increase in $p$), causes a reduction in the profitability of the backward sector. But it also creates an advanced sector with a higher (and possibly much higher) rate of profits. The with-investment average rate may, therefore, be greater or less than the autarky rate. And as investment continues and the advanced sector becomes relatively more important, so the average rate rises (see Figure 5.4).

Next, consider the slope and vertical intercept of the with-investment frontier. The slope is given by total capital p.w., $k_2$, and the intercept by net domestic product p.w. What can be said with some confidence is that the slope will be greater. This follows from the change in the terms of trade which increases the value of capital p.w. in both sectors, and the presumption that the advanced sector is more capital-intensive than the backward. But, precisely because the backward sector is likely to be using more labour per unit of output than the advanced sector, the relative growth of the latter means that $x_2$, average output per unit of labour, will be greater with investment. Thus, looking at the first part of Equation (5.42),

$$y_2 = x_2 - k_2 = \hat{w}_2 + \hat{r}_2 k_2$$

since both $k_2$ and $x_2$ rise together it is not possible to say whether $y_2$ will be greater or smaller (or stay the same). Neither is the second half of this equation of any help in settling this matter: $\hat{w}_2$ is necessarily greater if the advanced sector pays higher wages, but the term $\hat{r}_2 k_2$ may be greater or less depending on what happens to the rate of profits. If $\hat{r}_2$ rises with investment then $y_2$ is necessarily greater.

We are thus forced to consider two possibilities: one in which the vertical intercept of the consumption frontier is no larger with investment than it is without; and one in which it is larger. With the latter outcome, the possibility that the no- and with-investment frontiers intersect cannot be ruled out, but it is avoided here in the interests of clarity. In either event, what happens to p.w. consumption depends very much on the extent to which workers in the advanced sector are paid more than those in the backward. To see how important this is, the cases in which wage rates are uniform and in which the advanced wage is significantly higher are considered separately.

The case of an inward-moving frontier with uniform wages needs no further investigation since this was the case discussed in the preceding section. If, as one might expect, however, the advanced-sector wage is higher than that in the backward sector the conclusion that p.w. consumption is less with investment no longer follows of necessity. An outcome with higher p.w. consumption is illustrated in Figure 7.4. It comes about not only because extremely high wages in the advanced sector lead to a high average wage rate, $\hat{w}_2$, which is, of course, a component of consumption p.w., but also because a correspondingly lower rate of profits in the advanced sector can be expected to lead to a lower level of unretained earnings per unit of capital. Although this outcome is possible in principle, in practice there is a lower limit to the advanced-sector rate of profits which would permit overseas investment in the first place, namely the rate $r_1$ which would prevail in the Centre in the absence of investment. There is also a practical limit to the differential that can be sustained between the wage rates of the two Peripheral sectors.

When the consumption frontier moves outwards, the possibilities of improved consumption levels are naturally greater (Figure 7.5).

In part (i), in which there is no wage premium in the advanced sector, the effects of a higher average savings propensity and positive unretained earnings are sufficient to bring about lower p.w. consumption with investment; but this is not the case in part (ii). Apart

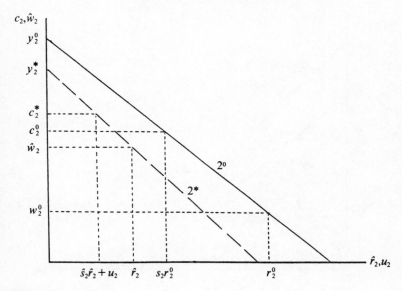

*Figure 7.4*

from the higher wage rate (which is not necessary to this outcome), it is the greater productiveness of the advanced sector which is responsible for the improvement.

The ambiguity in these outcomes is the consequence of two opposing tendencies: the deterioration in the terms of trade and the growth of the advanced sector relative to the backward. The fact that inward investment is concentrated on a more productive technique gives it two possible virtues. One is that this technique may have been unavailable without it but that, once in existence, seepage of investment from the backward to the advanced sector enhances indigenous consumption-growth possibilities. The other is that advanced-sector workers receive higher wages.

### 7.3 Implications of resource constraints
Before proceeding to an investigation of the transitional effects of regime change, we shall take advantage of the apparatus of the preceding section to consider the closely related comparative consumption consequences of changes in investment flow stimulated by resource constraints.

Both the Emmanuel effect and the Ricardo effect give rise to

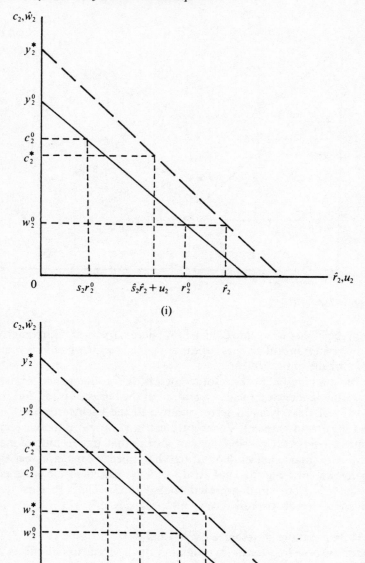

*Figure 7.5*

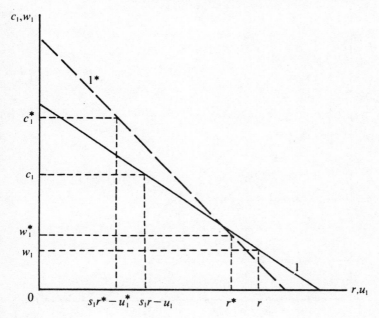

*Figure 7.6*

changes in the terms of trade and thus movements of the consumption frontiers. We shall consider only the consequences of the Emmanuel effect in any detail.

In Figure 7.6, which refers to the Centre, both frontiers relate to free investment, the one indicated by a star (together with its associated variables) referring to a later point in time and, thus, a higher wage rate. This latter frontier has a higher slope because the change in the terms of trade has increased the value of capital per worker. For the same reason, the vertical intercept, which from Equation (5.24.1) may be written as

$$px_1 - k_1 = px_1(1 - a_{11}) - a_{21}$$

is also greater. The higher wage is associated with a lower rate of profits (from Equation (6.4)). The potential squeeze on capitalist consumption p.w. is counteracted by the favourable swing in the terms of trade with the net effect being uncertain. (Uncertainty also attaches to the value of $u_1$, which falls with $r$ but rises with $\alpha$ and also

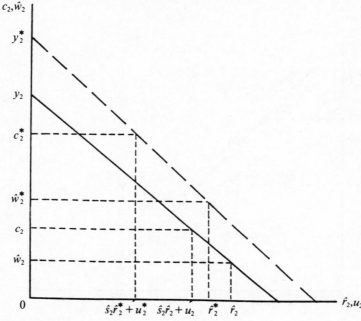

*Figure 7.7*

depends on the relative values of the two regions' capital stocks; see Equation (5.27).)

The consequence of the Emmanuel effect for the Periphery depends on whether indigenous capitalists are incorporated into the advanced sector. If not, the falling rate of profits and the deteriorating terms of trade simply aggravate the process of indigenous capitalist elimination. Figure 7.3 can easily be adapted to illustrate this by interpreting $2^0$ and $2^*$ as with-investment frontiers at earlier and later points in time. In this case we have support for Emmanuel's (1972) contention that an increase in the higher wage rate involves a redistribution of income not only from capitalists in the Centre but also from capitalists in the Periphery.

With duality in production and savings behaviour the outcome may be quite different. Under these conditions indigenous capitalists are not eliminated and consumption p.w. could rise over time. The more rapid extension of the advanced sector that is spurred by wage inflation could thus prove beneficial. Figure 7.7 shows one possible outcome (corresponding to Figure 7.5(ii)). Just as the comparison revealed a consumption gain, so here does consumption p.w. rise over time despite worsening terms of trade.

Should the rise in Central wages bring about the existence of a 1-producing sector in the Periphery, the form of the Centre's consumption frontier, Equation (5.23.1), is not affected (thanks to the cancelling of terms in the derivation). All that happens is that movement up the succession of frontiers in favour of wages is halted by the stabilization in the terms of trade. In the longer run, the effects on consumption per worker are as described in Chapter 5 (that is, $c_1$ rises over time with $u_1$). Thus by diverting an additional portion of new investments to the enclave, 1-capitalists are able to maintain their level of consumption p.w. through the flow of foreign remittances.

The *appearance* of the Peripheral consumption frontier, Equation (5.41), is also unaffected in this case, but it is subject to a slightly different interpretation in that $k_2$ is now the aggregate of capital stocks in the two commodity sectors divided by the total workforce. The immediate effect of the introduction of manufacturing investment will be insignificant given that manufacturing will be a tiny proportion of the advanced sector. But, as the share of manufacturing capital rises, it will be reflected to some degree in the way in which the average consumption frontier (weighted by the backward and advanced sectors) shifts and becomes steeper. For example, if in Equation (6.9)

$$(pe_{11} + e_{21})/l_{a1} > (pa_{12} + a_{22})/l_{a2}$$

the frontier becomes even steeper than is indicated in Figure 5.4. Thus a higher capital intensity in manufacturing would allow capitalist consumption p.w. to be higher than otherwise. It may be mentioned in passing that if manufacturing is relatively capital-intensive this will have a direct negative effect on Peripheral employment. But this is counteracted indirectly by the fact that the Periphery's growth rate is higher in this situation than if it were faced with a deterioration in its terms of trade. The net effect in this case would thus depend on the relative growth of manufacturing within the economy and the growth of the economy as a whole. If, on the other hand, manufacturing is more labour-intensive, the employment consequences of this type of induced investment (as compared to the pure Emmanuel effect) will be unambiguously positive.

The implications of the Ricardo effect can be pursued once it is recognized that the consumption frontier for the Periphery, defined as the dual of the $\hat{w}_2$-$\hat{r}_2$ trade-off, excludes rents. This is because the $\hat{w}_2$-$\hat{r}_2$ trade-off is determined by the production process at the marginal grade of natural resources. As the margin extends, the consumption frontier so defined shifts inwards (as $\hat{r}_2$ falls for a given $\hat{w}_2$) and becomes less steep (as $p$ falls). The Ricardo effect thus redistributes income p.w. from profits to rents. If the 'landlords' are unproductive (as implicitly assumed) then this kind of terms of trade gain is of very little benefit. It reduces profits, employment growth and the consumption level of capitalists. (The possibility should also be noted that 'landlords' are not all indigenous.) In the Centre the consumption frontier also moves inwards, becoming less steep; consumption p.w. falls on balance.

When the Emmanuel and Ricardo effects operate together the direction of the terms of trade and the consequences for consumption in each region are ambiguous. Many different outcomes can be generated by varying the relative strengths of the two effects.

### 7.4   Transitions and the evaluation of gains

It was shown in Chapter 2 that when the free-trade rate of profits is used to discount alternative consumption streams, the inclusive gain from trade in goods is necessarily positive. This demonstration followed that of Smith (1979) who initially arrived at the same conclusion in the case of trade in assets: '... it is clearly the case that a country able to invest or borrow abroad is less constrained than one that is unable to do so, so that to have international investment is potentially Pareto superior...'. But in a subsequent (1984) reworking of this argument (acknowledging criticism by Dixit), Smith showed that where a transition takes place from a with-trade, no-investment regime to a with-trade, with-investment regime it is no longer possible to establish unambiguously that both nations realize increases in the present values of their consumption streams. The intuitive reason for this failure is that any direct advantage to the Periphery of trade in assets may be offset by the deterioration in the terms of commodity trade that results.

Recognition of the immiserizing potential of foreign investment has stimulated a growing literature in neoclassical theory. In the context of the standard two-good Heckscher–Ohlin model, the theory assumes that each country continues to produce both goods so maintaining a one-to-one correspondence between factor prices and commodity prices. Then it follows that if the terms of trade of the capital-importing country deteriorate as a result of such imports, that country will suffer a fall in welfare.[3] A comparable conclusion deriving from an explicit growth model is found in Burgstaller and Saavedra-Rivano (1980) though its applicability is limited by the specific assumptions employed.[4] To obtain a more general intertemporal assessment of the gains from investment we shall once again follow Smith (1984). The nature of the demonstration follows closely that of Chapter 2. However, there are enough important differences between the earlier case (a switch from autarky to trade in goods) and the present (a switch from trade in goods only to trade in goods and assets) to justify developing the argument afresh.

We consider an economy which up to period 0 makes or receives no foreign investments (though it is engaged in international trade). During period 0 it undergoes a transition from this state to a regime with free international investment. To keep the exposition as simple as possible each economy is assumed to be fully specialized and rents are assumed to be zero throughout. Following the reasoning of Chapter 2 the consumption streams with and without investment are valued at prices and interest rates prevailing on the with-investment path. The price ratio and quantities on the no-investment path are indicated by a bar (for example, $\bar{p}$ and $\bar{X}$): variables expressed in value terms on the no-investment path are also indicated by a bar when evaluated in the prices of that regime (for example, $\bar{C}$ and $\bar{K}$), but by a 'hat' when evaluated in the prices of the with-investment regime (for example, $\hat{C}$ and $\hat{K}$). Variables on the with-investment path carry no special distinction. Superscripts refer to time periods until otherwise stated. Country subscripts are dropped to avoid clutter.

In terms of the prices *of their own regimes*, the values of consumption at the end of period 0 are:

$$C^0 = p^0 X^0 - (K^1 + K_e^1) \tag{7.1}$$

and

$$\bar{C}^0 = p^0 X^0 - \bar{K}^1 \tag{7.2}$$

where $p^0 X^0$ is the value of gross output of period 0 ( $= \bar{p}^0 \bar{X}^0$ since it is the same for both regimes); $K^1$, the value of that part of the following period's capital requirements of the transition-plus-investment path which is devoted to domestic production; $K_e^1$, overseas investment in the following period (added, as here, in the case of the lender; subtracted in the case of the borrower). Henceforth, $K_e^1$ is to be regarded as a stock variable. $\overline{K}^1$ is the value of the capital requirements of the following period on the no-investment path.

The right-hand side of Equation (7.2) is the value of the net output of the no-investment regime, which we shall call $\overline{Y}^0$. The result,

$$\overline{C}^0 = \overline{Y}^0$$

follows naturally from balanced trade at equilibrium terms of trade (that is, at the equilibrium prices of the investment autarky regime). At any other prices the same quantities entering international trade would not, in general, have equal values. Thus, in the prices of the with-investment regime,

$$\hat{C}^0 \neq \hat{Y}^0 (= p^0 \overline{X}^0 - \hat{K}^1)$$

Rather, since (by definition)

$$\hat{C}^0 = \hat{Y}^0 + \hat{C}^0 - \hat{Y}^0 - \overline{C}^0 + \overline{Y}^0$$

then,

$$\hat{C}^0 = p^0 \overline{X}^0 - \hat{K}^1 + (\hat{C}^0 - \overline{C}^0) - (\hat{Y}^0 - \overline{Y}^0) \tag{7.3}$$

Subtracting Equation (7.3) from Equation (7.1) (and remembering that $X^0 = \overline{X}^0$) gives the difference in consumption in period 0 in terms of the prices of the transition-plus-investment path:

$$C^0 - \hat{C}^0 = -(K^1 + K_e^1) + \hat{K}^1 - (\hat{C}^0 - \overline{C}^0) + (\hat{Y}^0 - \overline{Y}^0) \tag{7.4}$$

At the end of period 1, consumption with investment can be obtained from Equation (5.15):

$$C^1 = p^1 X^1 - K^2 - B^2 + U^1 \tag{7.5}$$

(where $K^2 = (1 + g^1)K^1$ and $B^2 = \beta^1 K^1$). In words: consumption of nationals is equal to gross domestic product, less replacement and net investment, less capital outflow, plus unretained overseas earnings. Unretained earnings in period 1 are obtained by deducting from the depreciation and profits of period-1 enclave capital whatever is needed to provide for period 2's capital beyond the provision already made by the capital inflow $B^2$. In general,

$$U^t = (1+r^t)K_e^t - K_e^{t+1} + B^{t+1}$$

From the price equation

$$p^1X^1 = (1+r^1)K^1 + w^1L^1 \tag{7.6}$$

Equation (7.5) can be rewritten as

$$C^1 = (1+r^1)K^1 + w^1L^1 - K^2 + (1+r^1)K_e^1 - K_e^2 \tag{7.7}$$

Consumption with investment autarky, valued at investment prices, is, by the same argument as previously,

$$\hat{C}^1 = p^1\bar{X}^1 - \hat{K}^2 + (\hat{C}^1 - \bar{C}^1) - (\hat{Y}^1 - \bar{Y}^1) \tag{7.8}$$

in which the first term on the right-hand side may be expressed as the inequality:[5]

$$p^1\bar{X}^1 \leqslant (1+r^1)\hat{K}^1 + w^1\bar{L}^1 \tag{7.9}$$

so that Equation (7.7) becomes:

$$\hat{C}^1 \leqslant (1+r^1)\hat{K}^1 + w^1\bar{L}^1 - \hat{K}^2 + (\hat{C}^1 - \bar{C}^1) - (\hat{Y}^1 - \bar{Y}^1) \tag{7.10}$$

Comparing Relations (7.7) and (7.10), we get

$$C^1 - \hat{C}^1 \geqslant (1+r^1)(K^1 - \hat{K}^1 + K_e^1) - K^2 - K_e^2 + \hat{K}^2 - (\hat{C}^1 - \bar{C}^1) \\ + (\hat{Y}^1 - \bar{Y}^1) + w^1(L^1 - \bar{L}^1)$$

And, in general,

$$C^t - \hat{C}^t \geqslant (1+r^t)(K^t - \hat{K}^t + K_e^t) - K^{t+1} - K_e^{t+1} + \hat{K}^{t+1} - (\hat{C}^t - \bar{C}^t) \\ + (\hat{Y}^t - \bar{Y}^t) + w^t(L^t - \bar{L}^t) \tag{7.11}$$

Relations (7.4) and (7.11) may be inserted into Equation (2.20) to obtain the present value of the difference in consumption streams up to time τ. After much cancelling this gives

$$C(\tau) \geqslant -\frac{(K^{\tau+1} + K_e^{\tau+1} - \hat{K}^{\tau+1})}{\Delta^\tau} - \sum_{t=0}^{\tau} \frac{[(\hat{C}^t - \bar{C}^t) - (\hat{Y}^t - \bar{Y}^t)]}{\Delta^\tau}$$
$$+ \sum_{t=1}^{\tau} \frac{w^t(L^t - \bar{L}^t)}{\Delta^\tau} \tag{7.12}$$

where $\Delta^\tau$ is the discount factor $(1 + r^1)(1 + r^2) \ldots (1 + r^\tau)$. Relation (7.12), which we shall express more succinctly as

$$C(\tau) \geqslant C' + C'' + C''' \tag{7.13}$$

is a general expression which can be evaluated under various assumptions. In what follows we shall focus discussion on the case in which wage rates in both countries remain constant over time (thus, for the time being, ruling out both a dual wage structure in the Periphery and full-employment wage determination in the Centre). In this case rates of profits are assumed to be equalized after some finite time and, thereafter, to remain constant. From that same moment the terms of trade in the investment regime are also constant. The free-trade no-investment world is assumed to have existed in steady growth.

To determine the sign of $C(\tau)$ for borrower and lender we consider the three terms on the right-hand side of Relation (7.13) separately and in order.

## $C'$

The sum $K^t \pm K_e^t$ is the stock of capital in the ownership of the capitalists of the country under consideration. In the case of the lender (country 1) the enclave capital is added, as in Relation (7.12), to the domestic capital; in the case of the borrower it is subtracted. If, as previously, we denote ownership by superscripts and location by subscripts, we have

$$K^{1,t} = K_1^t + K_e^t$$
$$K^{2,t} = K_2^t - K_e^t$$

so that $C'$ can be written, more generally, as

$$C' = -(K^{i,\tau+1}/\Delta^\tau) + (\hat{K}^{i,\tau+1}/\Delta^\tau) \qquad (i = 1,2) \qquad (7.14)$$

which can be evaluated as $\tau \to \infty$.

The growth paths of $K^i$ (obtained in the manner of Equations (4.19) and (4.20)) are given by

$$g^{i,t} = s_i r^t < r^{t\cdot} \text{ (for } s_i < 1)$$

Thus, in the first term of Equation (7.14), the numerator grows more slowly than the denominator as $\tau \to \infty$ so that the discounted values of the $K^i$ converge to zero over time.

The no-investment capital stocks valued in their own prices $(\bar{K}^i)$ grow at the rates

$$\bar{g}^{i,t} = s_i \bar{r}_i{}^t$$

But growth rates of autarkic capital valued in terms of with-investment prices $(\hat{K}^i)$ may diverge from the $\bar{g}^{i,t}$ during the transition period when the price ratio is settling on its equilibrium value (which corresponds to the equalized interest rate, $r$). After some finite time this equilibrium is reached and the value of capital grows at the same rate as the quantity of capital (or its value in terms of any other constant set of prices). Thus

$$\hat{g}^{i,t} = s_i \bar{r}_i{}^t$$

which then holds to infinity. In the case of the lender, $\hat{g}^{1,t} < r$ (the equalized rate) since lending raises its interest rate. The second term of Equation (7.14) thus also converges to zero as $\tau \to \infty$. The same conclusion applies to the borrower despite the fact that borrowing reduces its interest rate, given the assumption of steady-growth equilibrium of the free-trade, no-investment world economy. For then $\hat{g}^{2,t} = \hat{g}^{1,t}$, of necessity. Thus we may conclude that Equation (7.14) is zero for both countries.

$C''$

Turning to the second term in Relation (7.12), $(\hat{Y}^t - \bar{Y}^t)$ shows the extent to which investment-autarky net output is revalued according to with-investment prices, while $(\hat{C}^t - \bar{C}^t)$ shows the corresponding revaluation of consumption. If imported goods contribute any part

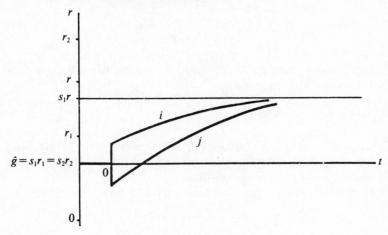

*Figure 7.8*

of consumption then the sum of these expressions changes as the terms of trade change. We know from Figure 7.1 (or Equation (6.2)) that the terms of trade move in favour of the lender and against the borrower. For the lender, since the value of domestic output rises relative to imports, $C'' > 0$; for the borrower, $C'' < 0$.

$C'''$

The final term makes allowance for wage-consumption gains or losses arising out of different growth rates of employment. Unfortunately this lends an ambiguity to the evaluation of the gains because it is not clear how the growth paths compare in the two alternatives. Compared to its no-investment rate $s_1 r_1$, growth in the Centre will be enhanced by the higher rate of profits but restrained by the outflow of capital. The Peripheral growth rate will suffer the reverse of these occurrences. Over time both rates converge to $s_1 r > s_i r_i$ but it is not possible to say whether growth during and immediately after the transition is greater or less than it would otherwise have been. (See Figure 7.8 which, for simplicity, assumes a single-period transition.) If it is greater and remains greater then $C'''$ must be positive. (Though, as was noted in Chapter 2, if the wage rate in informal employment is positive, $C'''$ should be deflated to take account of this lower opportunity cost. If the subsistence remuneration in the informal sector is the same as the formal wage rate there is no gain at all from expanded employment.) If the rate of growth is initially reduced, as on path $j$ in the diagram, then discounting will place a heavy weight on the early losses, possibly sufficient to outweigh the perpetual gains that succeed them. (There is an additional problem that, during the transition when prices are variable, the growth rates of employment, $\gamma_i$, are not the same as the rates of growth of value-capital.)

The term $C'''$ is clearly problematic. If we could put it aside and consider only the first two terms in Relation (7.13) then we should obtain a clearcut conclusion for the lender: $C^1(\tau) \geqslant 0$, a strict equality holding only in very special circumstances (essentially, no change in the terms of trade). But for the borrower no definite conclusion is possible (even ignoring $C'''$): $C^2(\tau)$ is greater than or equal to a sum of expressions one of which is zero and one negative.

Is it possible that an unambiguous conclusion for the lender can be sustained when Central wages adjust (before, during and after the transition) so as to clear the labour market? The answer is 'yes' , provided full employment is a precisely defined point. In that case we should have $L^{1,t} = \bar{L}^{1,t}$ and $C^{1'''} = 0$. Deterioration in the Periphery's terms of trade also continues to hold. (This follows from the reduction in its rate of profits with $w_2$ constant.) The only remaining issue concerns the present valuation of the $\hat{K}^i$, for now with-investment prices will be changing continuously under the influence of the Emmanuel effect. However, since $\hat{K}^{i,t} > 0$, it must be the case that $\hat{K}^{i,\tau+1} \geqslant 0$ as $\tau \to \infty$ and hence that $C' \geqslant 0$. For this case, then, we can definitely state that the lender will gain from foreign investment, but for the borrower ambiguity persists. An intuitive explanation of this outcome is provided by Smith (1984, p. 296) on the basis that the transition we have examined represents an extension of international trade from goods alone to goods plus assets: 'A move to free trade is a special kind of terms-of-trade improvement: the opening up of new forms of trade when some trade already exists is, in the absence of optimal trade (and investment) taxes, an unambiguous terms-of-trade improvement only if the terms of the existing trade do not deteriorate.'[6]

The consequences of a dual wage structure in the Periphery will be considered next. To finish this section it should be noted that, in the cases so far discussed, the time profiles of consumption are qualitatively the same as in the transition from goods autarky to goods trade: in the Centre, consumption initially falls, then rises; the reverse occurs in the Periphery. Thus the points made in Chapter 2 about

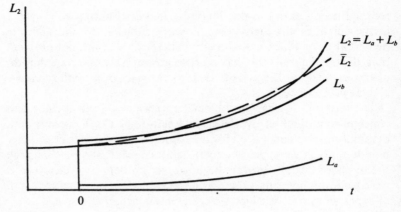

*Figure 7.9*

the appropriate choice of social discount rate apply equally here: a rate slightly lower than the with-investment interest rate puts more weight on the Centre's gains and less on the Periphery's (or more on its losses).

### 7.5    Employment and welfare with peripheral dualism

With a higher wage in the advanced sector, and thus an average wage increasing over time, the $C'''$ term in Relation (7.13) is potentially of some importance. How important depends on the relative levels of formal employment on the alternative paths. These are illustrated in Figure 7.9 (again taking a single-period transition for diagrammatic clarity).

On the assumption that the advanced sector is introduced by foreign capital then, in the absence of such capital, overall employment would have grown according to the curve $\bar{L}_2$, corresponding to the rate $s_b\bar{r}_b$,[7] where it is confined entirely to the backward sector. At the end of the transition, the backward sector's growth rate is permanently reduced, not only because of the negative terms-of-trade effect on $r_b$ but also because of the 'seepage' factor $v$. This lower growth rate, $s_b(1-v)r_b$ underlies the curve $L_b$. The employment loss is compensated for to some degree by the advanced sector, but it is not possible *a priori* to say precisely to what degree.

The lower labour intensity of the advanced sector means that for every unit of backward-sector output displaced overall employment falls. But, in order to equalize international profit rates, the price of commodity 2 must fall and for that to happen output must be expanded beyond what it would otherwise have been. Thus a significant investment in the advanced sector is needed to effect the transition and the immediate effect on employment is beneficial. Thereafter, employment could rise or fall relative to the no-investment path. The greater is the labour productivity of the advanced sector the more likely it is to fall. As a *reductio ad absurdum* if the advanced sector were fully robotized the line $L_a$ would coincide with the horizontal axis and there would be a permanent displacement effect. But so long as $l_a > 0$, the more rapid growth of the advanced sector ensures that, sooner or later, $L_2$ rises above $\bar{L}_2$ after which there will be infinitely enduring employment gains.

In principle, $C'$ and $C'''$ are subject to the same considerations as in the previous section, the argument being unaffected by a rising average savings ratio with investment.

Thus it seems that again no clearcut conclusions are available for the Periphery, though the presumption in favour of a positive gain is greater the more labour-intensive is the advanced sector, the faster is the rate of seepage of indigenous capital into that sector and the greater is the sectoral wage differential.[8] If foreign investment brings a superior technology to which domestic capitalists have access and stimulates thriftier behaviour among them then its attractions are considerably increased.[9]

## 7.6  History versus policy

It was argued in Chapter 2 that the existing pattern of global commodity specialization is, in large part, the consequence of factors inherited from the past, a past characterized more by colonial than by liberal international relations.

Colonialism does not imply the absence of capitalism nor of capitalist competition between different sections of the Centre. What it does imply is a degree of physical subordination of the Periphery to the Centre and of the imposition of capital accumulation within the former by the latter. How much, if at all, the time preference of the Peripheral populations had to play in this historical conditioning is a matter for sceptical speculation. In earlier colonial times, Peripheral accumulation appears to have derived less from consumption sacrifices out of European incomes and more from the spoils of colonial conquest. It was not a question of hoped-for mutual gains, but a simple matter of plunder and exploitation.[10]

To the extent that modern global capitalism – a system in which the Periphery, nominally at least, is an equal partner – has inherited what the colonial period left behind, how should this be reflected in theoretical terms? In this case, the frontiers $i^*$ in Figures 7.2 and 7.3 should no longer be regarded as a mid-point in the analysis (after the equalization of profits rates but before the full working out of the Pasinetti process) but, rather, as the starting point. The potential consumption boost to the 'borrower' in the early phase of development of the global economy would largely have been restored to the 'lender' in the form of plunder and tribute.

In fact, of course, the historical picture is much more complicated than this. Decolonization led to the nationalization of many assets that were previously owned in the Centre. And later extensions to the world capitalist system were undertaken on a much more voluntary basis, underlining the relevance of traditional analysis and the attempt to evaluate the consumption gains from inward investment.

Given its assumptions, one might have expected the neoclassical prescription to be quite clear: leave everything to the market. It turns out, however, to be nothing like as simple. To effect the first-best optimum requires considerable conscious and skilful manipulation on the part of government(s). Even an attempt to bring it about seems unlikely given the political reality that most governments are concerned, above all else, with their own short-term survival. The fact that additional injections of foreign investment bring about temporary consumption gains makes them a considerable political attraction especially as populations in general are unlikely to appreciate that current improvements may be at the expense of future generations. Yet from a social welfare point of view which encompasses the future, borrowing unaccompanied by redistribution could be a much inferior outcome.

To this must be added what some might regard as a major external diseconomy: the de-nationalization of the economy. The direction of the Pasinetti process is towards the increasing dominance of the world's capital by owners based in the Centre.[11] It is impossible to weigh the political and cultural implications of the loss of national control of production with the consumption gains or losses associated with it.

**Notes**

1.  Inspection shows that

$c_1{}^0 - w_1 = (y_1{}^0 - w_1)(1 - s_1)$ and
$e - f = (y_1{}^* - w_1)(1 - s_1)$

where $y$ is the vertical intercept. Since $y^* > y^0$, then $(e - f) > (c_1{}^0 - w_1)$.

2.   By inspection,

$c_2{}^0 - w_2 = (y_2{}^0 - w_2)(1 - s_2)$
$e - f = (y_2{}^* - w_2)(1 - \bar{s}_2)$

since $y_2{}^* < y_2{}^0$ by assumption, and since $\bar{s}_2$ is a weighted average of the backward and the (higher) advanced savings ratios, implying $\bar{s}_2 > s_2$, it must be that $(c_2{}^0 - w_2) > (e - f)$.

3.   See, for example, Brecher and Choudri (1982). Immiserization can also occur when investment takes place in the presence of domestic distortions. An overview (and extension) of this literature is found in Bhagwati and Brecher (1985).

4.   Quibra (1986) also offers an immiserizing result but his is strictly comparative in nature.

5.   See footnote 8, Chapter 8 for explanation of the use of the inequality.

6.   Smith actually assumes labour-market clearing in both countries but his remarks apply equally to the present case.

7.   This assumes that there is no revaluation effect in operation so that employment grows at the same rate as value capital.

8.   If we confine attention to consumption *per worker* we could connect various components of the analysis already undertaken. First, the switch of regimes shifts the consumption frontier inward or outward (Figures 7.4 and 7.5); then the advanced sector growth shifts the frontier outward (Figure 5.4) during which process consumption p.w. may rise or fall (Figure 5.5). It is conceivable that as a result of each of these effects consumption p.w. rises. Taking into account the transitional consumption boost (glossed over in the first stage) we would not need any discounting procedure to conclude that the Periphery had gained in per worker terms. But we should still be unable to say what would happen to the present value of consumption overall.

9.   The discussion implicitly assumes that superior technology is available only through foreign investment. The possibility of acquiring foreign technology through outright purchase of machinery was discussed in Chapter 3, though no allowance was made there for changes in savings behaviour.

10.   See, for example, Barratt-Brown (1974, Chapters 4 and 5). Sau (1978, p.37) estimates that in the period 1783/4–1792/3, 'India was furnishing an amount to Britain that was almost 30 per cent of the latter's total national saving transformed into capital.'

11.   The Centre, as noted in the last chapter, is not a fixed entity. Thus some of the newly-industrialised countries together with the capital-rich oil-surplus countries would form part of the contemporary Centre.

# 8 Non-equivalent exchange

## 8.1 Introduction

There is now a substantial body of literature deriving from Marxian theories of value and exploitation concerning international trade under conditions of free capitalist global accumulation. This chapter attempts a critical assessment of some of the propositions of this body of theory. Although it is something of a digression from the main theme its inclusion is justified on two counts. One is a question of balance. Previous discussion has included some critical comments on certain aspects of neoclassical theory, particularly the notion that the rate of profits in long-run equilibrium can be taken as equivalent to the social rate of time preference. Such equivalence seems to be crucial to any practical interpretation of neoclassical intertemporal welfare theorems yet it is clearly inconsistent with the classical and Marxian view of profits as representing a surplus from production, the rate of which is determined by technical and social or physiological factors. A rejection of the neoclassical construction of intertemporal preference would seem essential to the concept of exploitation, or of welfare loss through exchange (under competitive conditions), for otherwise a surplus can always be justified as recompense for sacrificing current consumption. In Marx, on the contrary, the propensity to save results from an urge to accumulate – animal spirits – whose fulfilment is their own reward. This criticism of neoclassical theory may, however, give the spurious impression that we regard the neo-Marxian theories of international exchange either as satisfactory or as consistent with the model developed in the preceding chapters. The second justification for considering this subject is opportunistic. It is that the simple Sraffa model of production and exchange used above provides an ideal framework within which to examine some of the neo-Marxian propositions.

Although the previous chapters have highlighted crucial differences between the neoclassical approach and our own, in one important respect there has been agreement: in evaluating material (as opposed to political or cultural) gains and losses it is the physical availability of goods over time that is relevant. The price evaluations that were undertaken are consistent with this because what they did, in effect, was to compare the consumption possibility frontiers under different circumstances. In some of the cruder neo-Marxian theories, on the contrary, material gains and losses are assessed by net gains and losses of labour value. It is this transfer of labour value as a result of international exchange (in the context of internationally mobile capital) that underlies the concept of 'non-equivalent exchange'. While this term is sometimes used interchangeably with 'unequal exchange', the meaning of the latter does vary from writer to writer so that, to avoid confusion, we refer throughout to non-equivalent exchange.

Non-equivalent exchange arises because of the exchange of commodities between countries at prices which deviate from the ratios of labour embodied in those commodities. Initially, the various examples of non-equivalent exchange were displayed in terms of Marxian tableaux. A welcome development has been the substitution of the system of price determination proposed by Sraffa for Marx's cumbersome and incorrect transformation procedure. It seems, however, that a central feature of the Sraffa system, namely the circularity of the production process, has been neglected. The purpose of this chapter is to show that this circularity in production has an important bearing on the direction of transfer of labour value. Indeed, it is our contention that, once the consequences of this circularity are taken fully into account, nothing can be said *a priori* about the direction of non-equivalent exchange. Thus, whether or not net value transfers imply anything about more relevant economic magnitudes, the basic proposition of the theory – that the Centre 'exploits' the Periphery by appropriating some of its surplus value – cannot be sustained on purely logical grounds.

Because of the diverse nature of the writings on this subject, a single model cannot possibly be fully representative of each contribution. Although our central proposition is demonstrated in a simple two-country, two-commodity model, the relationships between this model and some of the more important versions of neo-Marxian theory are briefly discussed in 8.4.

## 8.2 Basic assumptions

With the same production and specialization assumptions that were employed in Chapter 5, the price equations (5.1) and (5.2) can be applied directly to the present discussion. The relationships between relative prices and the equalized and non-equalized rates of profits

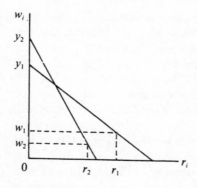 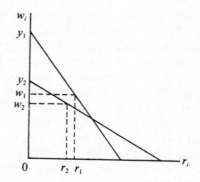

*Figure 8.1*

shown in Figures 6.1 and 7.1 are also directly relevant. The relationship between $r_1$ and $p$ shown in the right-hand quadrants of those diagrams can be derived immediately from Equation (5.1) (with $r$ replaced by $r_1$) for a given level of $w_1$. Whenever $w_1$ is fixed any change in $w_2$ or $r_2$ affects both the price ratio and $r_1$ and leads to a movement along this curve. For example, an increase in $w_2$ (with $r_2$ fixed) or an increase in $r_2$ (with $w_2$ fixed) leads to reductions in both $r_1$ and $p$ which are reflected by a movement along the curve. On the other hand if $w_1$ should vary, the curve itself will shift: an increase in $w_1$ would reduce $r_1$ at any price, so shifting the curve in the direction of the $p$-axis.

A key element in all unequal exchange theories is that free international mobility of capital leads to the international equalization of profits rates. It is precisely this mechanism operating between sectors of a closed economy which, in the presence of unequal organic compositions of capital, leads to the deviation of prices from labour values,[1] and therefore to domestic non-equivalent exchange. This process is operating here in the world economy in which processes are located in different countries.

Standard assumptions of non-equivalent exchange theories are that, in the absence of international investment, $r_1 < r_2$ and $w_1 > w_2$. A sufficient condition for these inequalities is that: (a) the capital: labour ratio (or organic composition of capital) in country 1 exceeds that in country 2, i.e., that $k_1 > k_2$; and (b) the international wage differential exceeds the international productivity differential. This can be seen by superimposing the wage frontiers (Equations (5.22)), defined at investment autarky prices, as in Figure 8.1. The vertical intercepts $y_1$ and $y_2$ are the values of net domestic product per worker and are therefore a measure of labour productivity. In Figure 8.1(i), condition (b) is satisfied but not condition (a); in (ii) condition (a) is satisfied but not condition (b). It is clear, however, in this second (and more plausible) case that if $(w_1 - w_2) > (y_1 - y_2)$ then $r_1 < r_2$. If $r_1$ is less than $r_2$ then equalization of the rates of profits leads to a deterioration in country 2's terms of trade; that is, to an increase in $p$. In the present context this should be regarded as a notional rather than an actual deterioration.

### 8.3 The transfer of labour value

So far the discussion has been conducted in terms of prices. Reference must now be made to labour values. Non-equivalent exchange refers to the transfer of surplus value from one country to another. The question which arises is whether exchange at international *prices* is less favourable for country 2 than exchange according to values. But care is needed in specifying exactly what is meant by 'exchange according to values'. For the relevant concept here is not the *total* labour embodied in the commodities exchanged but the quantity of country 1's labour embodied in a unit of 1's export commodity, etc. Remembering that each process may use imported means of production, these two concepts will not generally be the same. Thus non-equivalent exchange occurs if the amount of 1-labour exported exceeds or falls short of the amount of 2-labour imported when a unit of commodity 1 is exchanged for some amount of commodity 2.

To approach this problem we make the rather strong assumption (implicit in the literature) that units of labour in the two countries are qualitatively the same. Letting $\lambda_{ij}$ be the quantity of country-$i$ labour embodied directly and indirectly in a unit of commodity $j$ (and remembering that $l_i$ is the quantity of $i$-labour embodied directly in a unit of commodity $i$) we may write:

$$\lambda_{11} = l_1 + \lambda_{11}a_{11} + \lambda_{12}a_{21}$$
$$\lambda_{12} = \lambda_{11}a_{12} + \lambda_{12}a_{22}$$
$$\lambda_{21} = \lambda_{21}a_{11} + \lambda_{22}a_{21}$$
$$\lambda_{22} = l_2 + \lambda_{21}a_{12} + \lambda_{22}a_{22}$$

(8.1)

The first of these equations says that the amount of 1-labour embodied in commodity 1 is made up of labour used directly in production, plus the amount of 1-labour embodied in the inputs of commodities into commodity 1. Since commodity 2 is not produced in country 1 there is no direct 1-labour embodied in it; $\lambda_{12}$ (in the second equation) is therefore made up solely from the indirect labour passed on through means of production. The second and third equations can be similarly interpreted. From Equations (8.1)

$$\lambda_{ii} = (1 - a_{jj})l_i/[(1 - a_{22})(1 - a_{11}) - a_{12}a_{21}] \qquad (i,j = 1,2) \quad (8.2)$$

This allows us to define two separate labour embodied ratios:

$$\eta = \frac{\lambda_{11} + \lambda_{21}}{\lambda_{12} + \lambda_{22}} = \frac{(1 - a_{22})l_1 + l_2 a_{21}}{(1 - a_{11})l_2 + l_1 a_{12}} \tag{8.3}$$

and

$$\lambda = \frac{\lambda_{11}}{\lambda_{22}} = \frac{(1 - a_{22})l_1}{(1 - a_{11})l_2} \tag{8.4}$$

The first of these, $\eta$, is the ratio of total labour, *irrespective of origin*, embodied in units of the two commodities. Once it is recognized that production normally requires imported inputs it becomes apparent that the relevant ratio for non-equivalent exchange is $\lambda$ which refers to the amount of each country's labour that is exchanged. This distinction is not normally made even in discussions which employ a circular production system and yet it is clearly of some significance for the concept of non-equivalent exchange: $\lambda$ and $\eta$ are equal if, and only if,

$$(l_1)^2 a_{12}(1 - a_{22}) = (l_2)^2 a_{21}(1 - a_{11})$$

which is satisfied only by very particular combinations of the coefficients. (Obtaining satisfaction by putting the 'cross' coefficients $a_{12}$ and $a_{21}$ equal to equal zero is of especially limited interest because it rules out international exchange of intermediate goods.)

Weighting the $l_1$ terms in Equation (8.3) by the relative wage factor $\omega = w_1/w_2 > 1$, allows us to define the relative wage costs of the two commodities as:

$$\pi = \frac{(1 - a_{22})\omega l_1 + l_2 a_{21}}{(1 - a_{11})l_2 + \omega l_1 a_{12}} \tag{8.5}$$

from which it follows that

$$d\pi/d\omega > 0 \text{ if } (1 - a_{11})(1 - a_{22}) > a_{12}a_{21} \tag{8.6}$$

The scond inequality is the well-known Hawkins–Simon condition for a productive system, which is naturally assumed to hold. When $\omega = 1$, $\pi = \eta$. It follows from Relation (8.6) that

$$\omega > 1 \implies \pi > \eta \tag{8.7}$$

But it is not possible *a priori* to say whether $\pi > \lambda$ or $\pi \leqslant \lambda$. Comparing Equations (8.4) and (8.5) reveals that

$$\pi < \lambda \implies (1 - a_{11})a_{21} > (1 - a_{22})a_{12}(\omega l_1/l_2)^2 \tag{8.8}$$

Since the second inequality of Relation (8.8) violates neither the Hawkins–Simon condition, Relation (8.6), nor the restriction on relative capital:labour ratios, $k_1 > k_2$, it is perfectly possible that

$$\eta < \pi < \lambda$$

This particular ordering of these ratios is shown on the horizontal axis of Figure 8.2; $\eta$ and $\lambda$ have fixed, technologically determined magnitudes, but $\pi$ is dependent on the exogenously variable relative wage parameter $\omega$.

To begin, consider the broken-line curves rising from the horizontal axis of Figure 8.2. These curves relate the price ratio $p$ to the *equalized* rate of profits for various values of $\omega$ and we shall refer to them as $\omega$-curves. In a two-commodity Sraffa system with uniform rate of profits and uniform wage, it is a standard result that the price ratio $(p_1/p_2)$ rises with $r$ when the capital:labour ratio (or price composition of capital) is greater for commodity 1 than it is for commodity 2.[2] This result would apply to the global system considered here if it were the case that $w_1 = w_2$ (or $\omega = 1$). When, however, $w_1 > w_2$ it must be modified in a straightforward manner, as follows:

$$dp/dr \gtreqless 0 \text{ as } k_1/\omega \gtreqless k_2 \tag{8.9}$$

A uniform world rate of profits reaches its theoretical maximum,

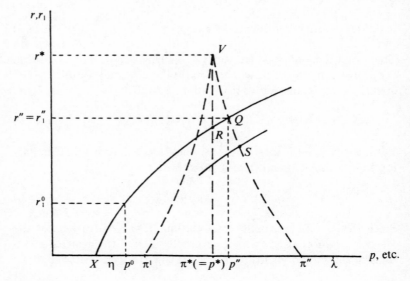

*Figure 8.2*

$r^*$, when $w_1 = w_2 = 0$. The price ratio corresponding to this value of $r$ we denote by $p^*$. This price $p^*$ holds at $r^*$ whatever the value of $\omega$, since $w_1 = w_2 = 0$. Thus the entire family of $\omega$-curves all meet at the point $(r^*, p^*) = V$, in Figure 8.2. Consider now a particular value of $\omega = \omega^* = k_1/k_2$. It follows from the inequalities in (8.9), that, no matter how much $r$ falls from its maximum $r^*$, the price ratio in this case remains constant at $p^*$. The $\omega$-curve, in this case, is the vertical line $\pi^*V$ (remembering that $\pi$ represents relative wage costs and is equal to the price ratio when $r = 0$). For $\omega = \omega' < k_1/k_2$ prices are equal to $\pi'$ (when $r = 0$) and rise to $p^*$; for $\omega = \omega'' > k_1/k_2$ prices fall from $\pi''$ to $p^*$ as $r$ increases.

The curve $XQ$ is the relationship between $p$ and the non-equalized rate of profits taken from the right-hand quadrant of Figure 6.1. Notional variations in $\omega$ can be brought about by varying $w_1$ with $w_2$ given, or by varying $w_2$ with $w_1$ given. It has already been noted that the former case involves a shift in the $XQ$ curve and to avoid this complication suppose that only $w_2$ is variable. Then, for a given value of $\omega$, the intersection of the corresponding $\omega$-curve and the $XQ$ curve defines the equilibrium equalized rate of profits and the associated price ratio. For example, if $\omega = \omega''$, the curves intersect at point $Q$ where $r''_1 = r''_2 = r''$ and $p = p''$.

The non-equalized rate of profits in country 1 (that is, the rate prevailing in the absence of free international investment) would, of course, have been lower than $r''$, say at $r_1^0$, at which the terms of trade would be $p^0$. This price may be above or below the relative value $\eta$, but the price ratio $p''$ corresponding to the equalized rates of profits is necessarily above $\eta$. This follows since, when $\omega = \omega'' > \omega^*$, the corresponding price $p''$ must be greater than $p^*$ ($= \pi^*$). Since $\omega^* = k_1/k_2 > 1$ (by assumption), there are values of $\omega$ satisfying $1 < \omega < \omega^*$, and corresponding values of $\pi$ such that $\pi < \pi^*$. We know from the inequalities in (8.7), that these values of $\pi$ exceed $\eta$. It, therefore, follows that $p'' > \eta$.

It is this result which has come to be known as non-equivalent exchange. Trade takes place at terms $p''$ which deviate from the relative value $\eta$ in a direction which is advantageous for the high-wage country and to the detriment of the low-wage country. But the view that this trade necessarily involves a transfer of surplus value from country 2 to country 1 is mistaken, for the relevant ratio in this respect is $\lambda$. If the technical conditions of production are such that $\pi'' < \lambda$ (satisfying inequalities (8.8)), then it follows that $p'' < \lambda$ which means that country 1 is engaged in a net export of surplus value, though to a lesser extent than would be the case if trade occurred without capital flows (at price $p^0$). While the equalization of the rates of profits has indeed made country 2's terms of trade poorer than they would otherwise have been, it has merely served to shift them in the direction of $\lambda$ but has not succeeded in completely closing the gap. Country 1 (the Centre) therefore remains the victim of non-equivalent exchange.

We are not saying that the Centre necessarily 'suffers' in this way; merely that this is a logical possibility. What has been shown is that there is no presumption in favour of the proposition that the Periphery necessarily transfers part of its surplus value to the Centre. To retain the proposition would require the use of additional assumptions which may be so restrictive as to leave the theory virtually empty.

## 8.4   Unequal Exchange

The implications of the result of the previous section for some of the more important versions of unequal exchange theory may now be considered.³ There are two basic distinctions we wish to focus on. The first concerns the definition of unequal exchange, as such; the second concerns assumptions about the extent of international specialization. Although the theory of unequal exchange originated with Emmanuel, it is probably true that on the first of these his version is different from succeeding ones and discussion of him will be left till last. Other major contributors tend to regard unequal exchange as identical to non-equivalent exchange (as defined above). However, some like Braun (1974), assume that commodities are 'specific' to countries; that is, that specialization is complete. This is the assumption made above and so the conclusion applies directly. On the other hand, Amin (1976; 1977), whilst in general approving of Braun,⁴ and Saigal (1973) are insistent that commodities are 'non-specific'. They argue that Periphery countries do produce the same (or similar) manufactured products as the Centre. What then happens to the conclusion if (say) both countries produce both commodities? The answer is: nothing – provided that imports are not used solely for final consumption. So long as some imported goods are used as means of production there will still be a distinction between the two ratios $\eta$ and $\lambda$. Although the difference between them may be somewhat narrower than in the previous case, the conclusion that surplus value *may* move from country 1 to country 2 remains intact.

An alternative definition of unequal exchange is proposed by Sau (1978, Chapter 3). This is peculiar in that the labour contents that are unequally transacted are 'dated labours', calculated in the manner of Sraffa (1960, Chapter VI) by weighting labour inputs by a compound profits term $(1 + r)^t$, according to the date of their expenditure. It is not clear why, in a Marxian model, labour values should be weighted by a measure of the surplus compounded over time. Indeed, ignoring the problem of circularity of production, Sau's conclusion that the higher wage country gives less dated labour than it receives is almost trivial. The further question of imported intermediate goods is sidestepped entirely by supposing that the global technology matrix is completely decomposible into 'specific' self-reproducing systems, one for each country (and thus only final goods are traded). The applicability of Sau's idiosyncratic concept to real-world trading patterns is thus rather limited.

The model of this chapter is also directly applicable to Emmanuel (1972) in as much as he, too, assumes commodities to be specific. But for him unequal exchange arises not as a consequence of equalized profit rates but as a consequence of unequal wages (in the presence of equalized profit rates). Unequal exchange is, therefore, reflected not in the deviation of prices from values but in the deviation of prices, as they are, from prices as they would have been had wages been uniform. Since Emmanuel's definition does not refer to values, only to prices, it is not affected by our result. What his basic proposition amounts to is that a widening of the wage differential (an increase in $\omega$) leads to a deterioration in country 1's terms of trade. The consequences of an increase in $\omega$ have already been analysed in Chapter 6 where the terms of trade deterioration was referred to, less emotively, as the Emmanuel effect. In terms of Figure 8.2 an increase in $\omega$, from say $\omega^*$ to $\omega''$, resulting from a fall in $w_2$ ($w_1$ constant) is reflected in a move from point $R$ to point $Q$. The same increase in $\omega$ resulting from a rise in $w_1$ ($w_2$ constant) is reflected in a shift from $R$ to $S$.

## 8.5  Conclusion

Little has been said in this chapter about why anyone should be concerned about the quantities of labour time that nations exchange with each other. If foreign trade and/or foreign investment allow both nations to improve their living standards then it is difficult to understand the relevance of non-equivalent exchanges of labour. It has already been suggested that foreign trade and investment may both fail to raise the welfare of the Periphery under certain circumstances, but these circumstances have little if any connection with the propositions which have just been examined. For some Marxists the exchange of labour appears to be a deeply moral issue not to be confused with material reality; to 'professional Marxists', wrote Joan Robinson (1966, p.vii), 'the metaphysic is precious for its own sake'.

Having for the sake of argument accepted this metaphysic, we have in this chapter attempted to address a specific question: In a two-country world in which profit rates are equalized, in which wage differences exceed productivity differences and in which the high-wage country employs the more capital-intensive technique, is it possible to say that international trade must lead to a net transfer of value from the low- to the high-wage country? A positive answer to this question would seem to be crucial to theories of non-equivalent exchange but we have tried to show that it is not possible to give an unqualified response. Our reasoning is directly analogous to that underlying the concept of 'effective protection': in circular production systems, that is, systems involving the use of intermediate goods, it is necessary to 'net out' that part of the gross (labour) value of a commodity which is contributed by imported means of production in order to obtain the true (labour) value-added in any one country. Once that is done, it is seen that a net transfer may occur in either direction.

Proponents of the unequal exchange theories may claim empirical support for their existing assumptions, but there can be no such support for the assumption that world trade in intermediate goods is insignificant. There may, of course, be patterns of trade in intermediates which are consistent with the accepted conclusions. But the onus is on the advocates of the accepted view to show what these patterns are and that they have some counterpart in reality. As it is, the concept of unequal exchange does not appear to be particularly useful in helping us to understand the process of underdevelopment.

## Notes

1. The inequality of wage rates is a further complicating factor which is of central importance for Emmanuel, but we put discussion of this aside for the moment.
2. See, for example, Mainwaring (1984, Chapter 7).
3. The following characterization of the alternative theories focuses on those features which are relevant to the present discussion. It fails to do justice both to the variety of viewpoints and to important specific features of particular models. It should be noted that both Amin and Saigal place much emphasis on the monopolistic aspects of exploitation. For a fuller account, see Evans (1988, 1989a).
4. See, for example, Braun's numerical example reproduced in Amin (1976, p.150). Whilst this example perfectly well demonstrates Emmanuel's proposition (see below) it is odd in that surplus value moves from the high- to the low-wage country (at $\omega = 0.7/0.12$, $p = 0.55$ and $\lambda = 0.583$), a circumstance which is largely attributable to the fact that $k_2 > k_1$ (2 = wheat, 1 = iron).

# 9 Technical progress

## 9.1 Introduction

Up to now our description of the global accumulation process has ignored entirely the possibility of technical progress. Yet improvements in labour productivity, the economizing on raw materials and the introduction of manufactured substitutes for primary products are bound to affect the process to a greater or lesser degree. Indeed, some economists believe that technical progress is a fundamental determinant of the pattern of global development. According to Toye (1985), for example, 'the process of technological change has for many years been the means by which global inequalities in wealth and power have been continuously recreated'. He supports this proposition by means of examples, such as the replacement of natural fibres by synthetics, the use of plastic or ceramic substitutes for non-ferrous metals, and recycling technologies, all of which reduce immediate demands for the products of third-world countries. Separate from materials-saving innovations is the introduction of 'progressively ever more labour-saving and capital-intensive' technologies which are 'highly inappropriate for the factor endowments of labour-abundant countries'.

The purpose of this chapter is to investigate the impact of such innovations on the development process as a whole on the basis of some highly simplifying assumptions. In doing so we shall run the risk of raising a target for Toye's (widely shared) criticism of the economist's approach to technical change: 'to represent technological change as an outward shift of a production possibility curve, a shift which itself is either not explained or else taken to be merely a response to changes in relative prices; to conceive of technology abstractly as an amorphous means of transforming inputs into outputs ... encourage the belief that understanding it is someone else's problem'. There is, undoubtedly, a grave danger of over-abstraction in the approach to any problem but there is a symmetrical danger in having a too narrow, concrete focus. To rely solely on the insights of economic historians, industrial archaeologists and applied scientists, who earn Toye's praises, would risk losing the 'macroeconomic' perspective which he seeks to preserve. Specific examples of technical change may provide compelling stories of harm done to underdeveloped countries but they fail to take account of feedbacks that may arise from changes in the terms of trade or from faster growth stimulated by the innovation. But to embrace these wider issues it is regrettable that other simplifications have to be made.

The rest of this chapter consists of several separate analyses of technical progress. The next section considers the consequences of globally uniform reductions in labour coefficients on the assumption that wage rates in both countries are fixed. The analysis proceeds on the basis that technical progress is both exogenous and costless. This assumption may be regarded as a serious limitation on the usefulness of the conclusions and is particularly inappropriate when considering the case of variable wages in the Centre. There it may reasonably be supposed that research and development expenditures (which are largely confined to the Centre) would be particularly directed at labour-saving innovations. 9.3 presents a simple model of wage-induced innovation and the medium- and long-run effects on system behaviour of such innovations are considered in 9.4. Next we look at the effects of materials savings, interpreted as (exogenous) reductions in the use of the Periphery's export good. Finally, and very briefly, the long-run implications of induced natural resource search are examined in 9.6.

It goes without saying that each of these analyses is incomplete. Yet the perspective each gives on the question of technical change is useful provided its partial nature is fully recognized. And it is additionally useful in helping to correct, or rather, balance the perspectives obtained from other partial approaches.


## 9.2   Global augmenting of labour

The consequences of a globally uniform reduction of labour coefficients were analysed in Chapter 1 in the case of a world without international investment. The analysis of labour-augmenting technical progress with investment can proceed very quickly using some simple adaptations of relationships derived in Chapter 1. So far as the Periphery is concerned, technical progress is assumed to be confined to the advanced sector. It was noted in 5.7 that relative prices and the internationally equalized rate of profits are independent of the production and distribution conditions in the backward sector. The importance of the backward sector is that it determines average outcomes in the Periphery – a consideration which does not require further formal analysis.

Begin with the price equations (5.1) and (5.2), replacing in the first of these equations the expression $w_1 l_1$ by the identical term $w_2(\omega l_1)$. This gives the equivalent of the closed-economy system, Equations (1.1) and (1.2), with uniform $r$ and $w$ ($= w_2$) but with $l_1$ replaced by $\omega l_1$. If this replacement is made throughout the discussion of 1.2 we obtain

$$\frac{\mathrm{d}p}{\mathrm{d}r} \gtreqless 0 \text{ and } \frac{\mathrm{d}^2 w_2}{\mathrm{d}r^2} \lesseqgtr 0 \text{ as } \frac{k_1}{\omega} \gtreqless k_2$$

where $k_1/\omega$ is the Centre's capital:labour ratio 'adjusted' as a result of deflation by the wage differential. While there may be a presumption that the Centre's unadjusted ratio is greater than that of the Periphery the same is not true of the adjusted ratio.

Individual $w_i$–$r$ trade-offs for the two countries can also be obtained as

$$w_1 = \omega w_2 = p - Rk_1 \tag{9.1}$$

and

$$w_2 = 1 - Rk_2 \tag{9.2}$$

(where $R = 1 + r$) and Equation (9.1) can be rearranged to give a $w_2$–$r$ trade-off for country 1:

$$w_2 = (p - Rk_1)/\omega \tag{9.3}$$

Then taking, for the sake of argument, the case in which $\mathrm{d}p/\mathrm{d}r > 0$, by the reasoning of Chapter 1 we get

$$k_1/\omega > -\mathrm{d}w_2/\mathrm{d}r > k_2$$

The relationship between the trade-offs, Equations (9.1)–(9.3) and the global $w_2$–$r$ frontier is shown in Figure 9.1 (which may be compared to Figure 5.3 with which it is consistent).

Recall that the effect of globally Harrod-neutral technical progress is to raise $w_2$ for a given value of $r$, whilst keeping $p$

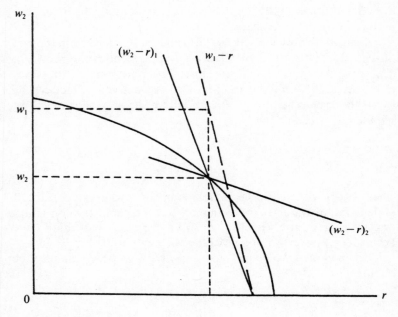

*Figure 9.1*

constant. It follows that the values of capital per worker in each country rise in proportion to the growth of labour productivity, at a given $r$, and that the $(w_2-r)_i$ trade-offs rotate vertically (hinged at their intersections with the $r$-axis) to maintain their intersection with the $w_2-r$ frontier. The $w_1-r$ trade-off rotates in a like manner. However, since it is $w_2$ that is being held constant, the entire benefit of the technical progress will be felt as an increase in the rate of profits, implying (in the case $dp/dr > 0$) an improvement in the Centre's terms of trade. Thus for the Centre, to the upward rotation of the $w_1-r$ trade-off must be added an outward shift due to the favourable effect on price (Figure 9.2(i)). Since the $w_i-r$ trade-offs double as the consumption frontiers with investment, it can be seen that the p.w. consumption effects of technical progress are magnified by the terms of trade change. For the Periphery, on the other hand, the benefits of productivity growth are partially 'crowded out' by the deterioration in the terms of trade (Figure 9.2(ii)).

This result is, however, a consequence of assuming $dp/dr > 0$ which in turn follows from $k_1/\omega > k_2$. If this inequality were reversed

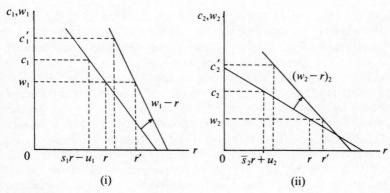

*Figure 9.2*

the terms-of-trade effect would favour the Periphery and work
against the Centre. The direction of the inequality is, of course, an
empirical matter but it may be worth recalling from Chapter 8 that a
standard assumption of unequal exchange theories is that the difference in wage rates between Centre and Periphery exceeds the difference in labour productivities. In Chapter 5 it was shown that the
vertical intercepts of the $w_i$–$r$ trade-offs define net domestic products
p.w., $y_i$. From this it can easily be deduced that when countries have
the same rate of profits.

$$y_1/y_2 \gtrless \omega \text{ as } k_1/\omega \gtrless k_2$$

it follows, somewhat ironically, that on the unequal exchange
assumption the effects of technical progress are most beneficial to
the Periphery, in terms of raising consumption p.w. It remains,
however, to consider the effects on capital and employment growth.

The world average growth rate will rise as a result of the increase
in the rate of profits. But what happens to the individual rates is less
clear. Begin, again, with the case $dp/dr > 0$. Assuming a constant
relative demand function, a sustained increase in $p$ will necessitate a
falling relative supply of good 1. This can only be brought about by
an increasing outflow of foreign investment. Capital growth in the
Periphery resulting from increased profitability is thus magnified by
additional foreign injections and so there is no doubt that $g_2$
increases (and equally no doubt that the Pasinetti process is accelerated). But for the Centre the effects work in the opposite direction

and the outcome is ambiguous (depending, among other things, on the elasticity of relative demand). When $dp/dr < 0$ the conclusions are reversed. Thus beneficial consumption effects are accompanied by restrained growth effects and *vice versa*.

It is worth noting that it is in the nature of labour-saving technical progress that the effect of a given rate of progress on the rate of profits (with given wage rates) declines over time. Although the global $w_2-r$ frontier shifts up over time, the maximum rate of profits stays the same so that $r \rightarrow r(\text{max})$ and $dr/dt$ falls as it does so.

Whatever happens to prices the impact on employment in both countries is ambiguous, though the consequences of labour saving will obviously be less severe where capital is growing more rapidly. But because the $g_i$, like $r$, are constrained, time works against employment prospects. This means that the implications for the full-employment barrier in the Centre are also unclear. Increased labour productivity would, on its own, delay impact against the barrier but the postponement could be offset, and even reversed, by faster growth. If and when the barrier is reached the incentives to raise productivity are unlikely to remain as they are. Rising wages will press Central capitalists to find ways of economizing on labour. It is to that possibility that we turn in the next section.

Consideration of regional variations in the rate of labour saving is straightforward. If $l_1$ falls faster than $l_2$ then the terms of trade are more likely to move in the Periphery's favour. The Periphery thus stands a greater chance of p.w. consumption gain. It will also benefit from faster world growth while suffering a lesser negative effect on employment growth. The reverse holds when $l_2$ falls faster. This is consistent with the general view that labour-saving technical progress is of limited benefit to the Periphery.

### 9.3   Induced labour saving in the Centre

Although research and development continue routinely in the never-ending search for cost reductions it would be reasonable to suppose that the intensity of the innovatory process increases in response to specific threats to profitability. Such a threat is posed by the full-employment barrier and we can imagine some part of technical progress being directly induced by the prospect of labour shortage in the Centre. The Emmanuel effect is incapable, by itself, of eliminating wage growth and, even if manufacturing industry is globally footloose, overseas relocation subject to increasing costs will also fail to prevent wages from rising. There is, therefore, room for a third response: technical progress aimed explicitly at reductions in labour costs. Although increases in Centre wages change the relative price of intermediate goods, it will be assumed for simplicity that induced R & D is wholly directed at obtaining savings in Central labour. To crystallize the discussion it will be supposed that the 'background' rate of technical progress is zero so that only this one form prevails. Note also that the characterization of R & D as a costless activity can no longer be sustained for then there would be nothing to prevent the innovationary effort from being infinite. Two questions which we shall attempt to answer are: will this specific form of R & D succeed in eliminating increases in Centre wage costs? and: what effect will it have on the Periphery?

In this section we shall outline a simple model of induced innovation. In Chapter 6 it was shown that Phillips-type wage behaviour in the Centre could generate perpetual cycles of $\omega$ and $v$ (the rate of employment) which would be transmitted to other key variables of the model. In the following section these dynamics are modified to incorporate the induced gains in labour productivity.

Gains in labour productivity are endogenized as follows. (While there is no risk of confusion, 1-subscripts are dropped; superscripts refer to time periods.) Consider a representative producer of good 1, whose price equation for period 0 is

$$p^0 = (1 + r^0)(p^{-1}a_{11} + a_{21}) + w^0 l^0 \qquad (9.4)$$

At the beginning of this period the firm considers devoting a proportion, $\delta$, of its capital to R & D. To avoid tedious and unnecessary complications it is assumed that the 'organic composition' in the 'development section' of the firm is the same as that in the 'production section'. The diversion of resources to R & D necessarily means a reduction in current output but, if the programme is successful, a reduction also in future labour requirements per unit of output. The proportion of resources devoted to research will therefore be determined by equating marginal expected costs and benefits. It is thus necessary to specify the firm's expectations concerning the relevant variables.

The firm knows the current price of its inputs (the vector $[p^{-1}, 1]$) and although the wage is paid at the end of the period it could be supposed that the wage contract is fixed at the beginning. It cannot know what price its output will sell for, $p^0$, nor can it know price and wage rate in the following periods. Keeping simplicity the keynote, assume that the firm expects current known prices, $p^{-1}$ and $w^0$, to continue indefinitely. Moreover, since each (small) firm acts in isolation its expectations are independent of the level of resources it devotes to R & D and therefore independent of its expectations concerning its own future output. Henceforth the time superscripts for $p$ and $w$ will be dropped.

The costs of R & D are easy to calculate. They are the loss of current output and hence (since all resources are paid for whether they are used in production or not) an equivalent loss of profits. Letting output in period 0 be unity, the cost is equal to $p\delta$, and thus rises in proportion to the research effort. Estimating the expected gains is not quite so straightforward. First the firm needs to form an expectation of the outcome of its research programme. On the basis of past experience it forms a set of predictions which are summarized by a function of the form

$$l^{t+1}/l^t = f(\delta) \qquad f(0) = 1, f(1) > 0, f'(\delta) < 0, f''(\delta) > 0 \qquad (9.5)$$

Thus more R & D resources imply greater productivity gains but with diminishing returns. As a result the expected future rate of profits is higher, the higher is $\delta$. It does not, however, follow that future profits will be higher in total since a greater diversion of current resources to R & D means less profits in this period and correspondingly less investment. The next period may well provide a higher rate of return per unit of capital but there will be less capital on which it is earned. The firm thus needs to calculate the gain in profits for each future period (in principle, to infinity), discount the stream at some appropriate rate (which would include a risk premium) and compare the result with $p\delta$. We shall, however, simplify this process greatly without losing anything essential. It is in fact improbable that a firm would discount gains to infinity; more likely, it will have a finite horizon. Since our exercise is directed at deducing some simple qualitative relationships nothing essential will be lost by taking the end of period 1 as the horizon, giving, in effect, a two-period model.

The firm then needs to calculate

$$\Delta\pi = (r^{1\prime}K^{1\prime} - r^1 K^1) \qquad (9.6)$$

where the primes refer to values which would exist following a positive research effort. The expected rates of profits in period 1 without and with improved labour productivity are

$$r = (p - wl - \mathbf{pa})/\mathbf{pa} \tag{9.7}$$

and

$$r' = (p - wl' - \mathbf{pa})/\mathbf{pa} \tag{9.8}$$

where $\mathbf{pa} = p_1 a_{11} + a_{21}$. If $\sigma$ is the ratio of net investment to profits,[1] then

$$K^1 = \mathbf{pa} + \sigma[p - wl - \mathbf{pa}] \tag{9.9}$$

and

$$K^{1'} = \mathbf{pa} + \sigma[p(1 - \delta) - wl - \mathbf{pa}] \tag{9.10}$$

where (remembering that period-0 output is unity) the terms in brackets are period-0 profits without and with R & D. Writing Equation (9.5) as

$$l' = l.f(\delta) \tag{9.11}$$

Equations (9.7)–(9.11) allow Equation (9.6) to be expanded as

$$\Delta \pi = wl[1 - f(\delta)] \cdot \left[ 1 + \sigma \frac{(p - wl - \mathbf{pa})}{\mathbf{pa}} \right] - \delta rp \frac{(p - wl.f(\delta) - \mathbf{pa})}{\mathbf{pa}} \tag{9.12}$$

(Note that the collections of terms in the two pairs of parentheses are equal, respectively, to $r$ and $r'$.) If Equation (9.12) is discounted at a rate $D - 1$ then the net gain is obtained as $(\Delta \pi / D) - p\delta$, as illustrated in Figure 9.3.

Note that all the key variables act on $\Delta \pi$ through two channels: first, their effects on period-0 profitability and hence the firm's ability to pass on resources to the next period; second, their direct effects on future profits. Consider $\delta$, for example: if a very high expenditure of resources on R & D resulted in very little saving on labour, the deflation in future profits due to lower investment might

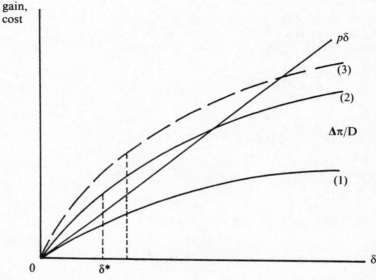

*Figure 9.3*

not be sufficiently compensated for by productivity increases; as a result, $d(\Delta\pi)/\Delta\delta < 0$. In this case, no R & D would take place. Indeed, none would take place unless the 'gain curve', $\Delta\pi/D$, cut the 'cost line', $p\delta$, as does curve (2) in Figure 9.3. Curve (1) does yield a positive gross gain but nowhere sufficient to recoup costs. If no technical progress occurs that is the end of the story and so we continue on the assumption that R & D is profitable, implying the existence of a gain curve like (2): close to the origin, $d(\Delta\pi)/d\delta > p$ but, because of diminishing returns, the curve flattens out, eventually cutting the cost line. It follows that there exists an optimal proportion, $\delta^*$, of period-0 resources directed to R & D.

How is $\delta^*$ affected by the other variables, $w$, $p$ and $l$? To avoid pages of unhelpful calculus the question will be approached intuitively. Note that $w$ and $l$ are invariably coupled in Equation (9.12) so that the no-R & D unit wage bill can be regarded as a single variable. This variable acts positively on the gain in all respects other than through its influence on the period-0 rates of profits. Price, on the other hand, works in the opposite direction: a higher $p$ increases period-0 profitability while diminishing the contribution of future productivity gains. Because of these 'two-channel' effects, the consequences of changes in $wl$ and $p$ on the gain curve are not as clear as one might wish. However, for plausible values of variables and parameters, an increase in $wl$ shifts the gain curve up, as in the move from (2) to (3).[2] In consequence, $\delta^*$ increases. Although the effect of a change in $p$ on the gain curve is also unclear, a higher price increases the cost of R & D and hence rotates the cost line upwards. When this is taken into account it turns out that $\delta^*$ falls. Assuming that the chosen value of $\delta$ does, indeed, rise with the unit wage cost, we can write

$$\delta = \delta(wl/p) = \delta(m) \qquad \delta' > 0 \tag{9.13}$$

where $m$ is thus the share of wages in product price. (Note that $w/p$ is not the same thing as a 'real wage' from the point of view of workers since good 1 may not enter or may not be representative of the wage basket. Throughout previous chapters the real wage has been denominated in terms of commodity 2. Although this, itself, is a simplifying assumption, consistency requires that it is maintained.) Despite the fact that Equation (9.13) may not hold for all feasible values of the variables and parameters, it does accord with basic intuition in suggesting that the inducement to labour-saving efforts will be greater the higher is the contribution of labour cost to the value of the product.

In the preceding discussion, $w$ and $p$ are both expected values and, by assumption, actual current values. Whether the expectations are fulfilled, so that values remain constant from one period to the next, is highly unlikely. Each firm behaves myopically and independently; but if firms in general engage in R & D both the supply of output and the demand for labour will be affected and so, therefore, will be the actual future values of $w$ and $p$.[3] Although the determination of $\delta^0$ depends on expected profits in the following period calculated on the basis of no R & D in that period, at the beginning of period 1 a fresh decision on R & D financing is undertaken, founded on a revised set of expectations. Innovations will thus normally be introduced period by period.

## 9.4 System effects of labour saving
Although Equation (9.13) has been derived from a two-period analysis it is expressed in very general terms and the same qualitative result is probable from decisions involving longer horizons. The

significance of this remark is that we now turn to continuous-time analysis in order to consider the system effects of innovation. In the model of Chapter 6 cycles occurred around a long-run growth path in which $\omega$ rises to a maximum value. However, a medium-run perspective was also possible, the medium run being defined as a period long enough to allow the equalization of the rates of profits but short enough for changes in the shares of global capital to be ignored. In that case $\omega$ and $v$ are seen to cycle perpetually around a fixed point. In this section the medium-run behaviour of the system is analysed first and the findings subsequently modified to allow for the full implications of the Pasinetti process. In what follows, $w$ and $p$ refer to actual values, while the continuous-time equivalent of Equation (9.5) is taken, in the aggregate, to be a stable function relating realized productivity gains to $\delta$.

The key variables of the analysis are $m$ and $v$ in the Centre. From the definition of $m$,

$$\frac{\dot{m}}{m} = \frac{\dot{w}}{w} + \frac{\dot{l}}{l} - \frac{\dot{p}}{p} \tag{9.14}$$

Adopting the real Phillips curve, Equation (6.7), and adapting Equation (9.5) this becomes

$$\frac{\dot{m}}{m} = \mu(v) + F(\delta) - \frac{\dot{p}}{p} \qquad F'(\delta) < 0 \tag{9.15}$$

From the definition of $v (= L/N)$,

$$\frac{\dot{v}}{v} = \frac{\dot{L}}{L} - n \tag{9.16}$$

To reconcile the preceding analysis with continuous time, **pa** can be thought of as the value of capital per unit of output used up in a very short period of time. Total employment can then be written as

$$L = l(\mathbf{pa}X)/\mathbf{pa}$$

where $X$ is aggregate output and **pa**$X$, aggregate domestic capital use in value terms, Equation (9.16) thus becomes

$$\frac{\dot{v}}{v} = F(\delta) + (sr - \beta) - \frac{\dot{\mathbf{pa}}}{\mathbf{pa}} - n \tag{9.17}$$

$sr - \beta$ is the growth rate of the domestic capital stock and $\dot{\mathbf{p}}\mathbf{a}$ measures its revaluation over time. In Chapter 6 it was assumed that any revaluation resulting from wage-cost variations would not be such as to permit an increase in the value of the stock to be accompanied by a fall in its quantity (and, therefore, a fall in output). That assumption is retained here so that the sign of $(sr - \beta) - (\dot{\mathbf{p}}\mathbf{a}/\mathbf{p}\mathbf{a})$, the growth rate of capital in real terms, will be taken to be the same as that of $(sr - \beta)$.[4] Note that in Equations (9.15) and (9.17), $F(\delta)$ can be written as a decreasing function of $m$, from Equation (9.13). It remains to consider the determinants of $g$ and $\dot{p}/p$.

The rate of profits falls with $m$, not only directly but also because higher $m$ stimulates higher $\delta$ which impinges on profitability; $\beta$, on the other hand, will rise as wage costs increase relative to $p$ (see the discussion in 6.2). Thus $sr - \beta$ is negatively related to $m$. The price ratio depends on relative supplies (the relative demand function being assumed constant), and so the proportionate rate of change of price depends on the relative rates of growth of Periphery and Centre outputs; $\dot{p}/p$ is thus an increasing function of $m$. These considerations are summarized by re-writing Equations (9.15) and (9.17) as

$$\dot{m}/m = \mu(v) + \varkappa(m) \qquad \mu_v > 0, \varkappa_m < 0 \tag{9.18}$$

and

$$\dot{v}/v = \psi(m) - \mathrm{n} \qquad \psi_m < 0 \tag{9.19}$$

This system will have a fixed point $(\bar{v}, \bar{m})$ defined by the intersection of the implicit functions

$\mu(v) + \varkappa(m) = 0$ and
$\psi(m) - n = 0$

Linearizing the system at the fixed point and writing

$$\varphi = -\varkappa'(\bar{m}) > 0. \ \upsilon = \mu'(\bar{v}) > 0 \quad \text{and } \eta = -\psi'(\bar{m}) > 0$$

Equations (9.18) and (9.19) can be approximated by

$$\dot{m} = (\theta + \upsilon v - \varphi m)m \tag{9.20}$$
$$\dot{v} = (\varepsilon - n - \eta m)v \tag{9.21}$$

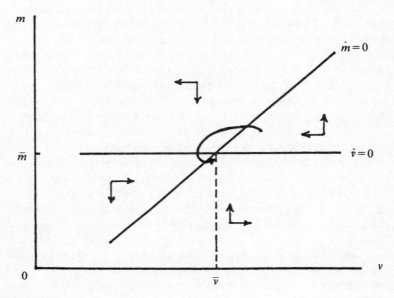

*Figure 9.4*

from which it follows that

$$\dot{m} \gtrless 0 \text{ as } m \lesseqgtr (\theta/\varphi) + (\upsilon/\varphi)v \tag{9.22}$$

and

$$\dot{v} \gtrless 0 \text{ as } m \lesseqgtr (\xi - n)/\eta \tag{9.23}$$

The general behaviour implied by Equations (9.22) and (9.23) is illustrated in Figure 9.4 and is clearly cyclical. The linearization yields the following coefficient matrix:

$$\begin{bmatrix} -\varphi & +\upsilon \\ -\eta & 0 \end{bmatrix}$$

with determinant $\upsilon\eta > 0$ and trace $-\varphi < 0$. The fixed point is thus asymptotically stable.[5]

An alternative illustration of equilibrium is presented in Figure 9.5 (a variant of Figure 6.2). Re-write Equation (9.17) as

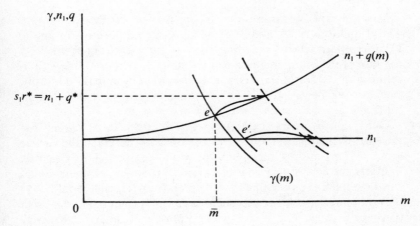

*Figure 9.5*

$$\dot{v}/v = \gamma - (n+q) \tag{9.24}$$

where $\gamma$ is the growth rate of physical capital and $q = -F(\delta)$ is the rate of enhancement of the effective labour supply through productivity gain. A fixed-point equilibrium implies

$$\gamma = n + q \tag{9.25}$$

The right-hand side of Equation (9.25) is an increasing function of $m$ and, if revaluation effects are subordinated, the left-hand side a decreasing function; $\bar{m}$ is thus defined by their intersection (point $e$). To the right of $\bar{m}$, excessive growth of the effective labour supply dampens the growth of wage costs and, in time, will reduce their level, while low output growth puts upward pressure on the price ratio. The reverse effects operate to the left of $\bar{m}$.

Although equilibrium is defined by a fixed ratio $wl/p$ it is also possible to determine the values of $w$ and $p$ separately. Considering the case in which the Periphery produces only good 2, the price equations for the two goods can be written (reverting to discrete time and the use of country subscripts) as

$$1 = (1+r)(a_{11} + a_{21}/p) + m \tag{9.26}$$

$$1 = (1+r)(pa_{12} + a_{22}) + w_2 l_2 \tag{9.27}$$

$w_2l_2$ is constant by assumption and $m$ is constant in equilibrium. Thus Equations (9.26) and (9.27) solve for unique values of $r$ and $p$. If $p$ is constant when $l_1$ is falling, then $w_1$ must be rising at precisely the same rate as the increase in productivity. Although the equilibrium global rate of profits and terms of trade remain constant, stochastic elements in the $F(\delta)$ function could trigger repeated cyclical convergence to equilibrium of $r,p$ and $\dot{w}_1/w_1$.

One might be tempted to interpret this conclusion as saying that the entire benefits of labour-saving technical progress in the Centre go to workers in the Centre, but this would be misleading. One way to assess the consequences of this form of technical progress would be to compare the outcome described above with what would have occurred in a world where such technical progress were absent (perhaps because R & D costs were prohibitively high) – effectively the medium-run model of Chapter 6. In the latter case, q = 0 and in Figure 9.5 equilibrium would be defined by the intersection of a $\gamma(m)$ function and $n_1$. The $\gamma(m)$ functions are not, however, the same in the two 'worlds'. For a given value of $m$ the rate of profits will be higher without the expense of R & D so that the $\gamma(m)$ curve for this case will be vertically above that for the case in which $\delta > 0$. Without R & D, therefore, short-run equilibrium would be at a point like $e'$.

The (comparative) effect of labour saving is thus a lower burden of wage costs in Central production. In this sense, R & D does provide a positive pay-off to Centre capitalists in aggregate. This is reflected in a real rate of growth $n_1 + q$ which obviously exceeds that which would obtain were $q = 0$. This higher growth rate must be the result of a higher rate of profits (if revaluation effects continue to be ignored). A higher rate would prevail even though $\beta_1$ were lower, for a reduction in capital outflow would reduce $p$ via its effect on relative supplies. From Equation (9.27) this necessarily implies a higher rate of profits.[6] In effect, technical progress in the Centre makes investment in the Periphery less attractive, thus endowing the latter with a superior terms of trade (and hence consumption frontier). These comparisons are, however, purely academic. They have no policy implications since Peripheral governments have little influence on the R & D activities of foreign firms.

The remaining comparisons with the model of Chapter 6 concern the dynamics of the two cases. The only essential difference in respect of the medium run is that in the earlier model (see Figure 6.3) the cycles are perpetual, the fixed point representing only an average value rather than a point of attraction. In both cases the average value of $w_1 l_1$ is constant, as are the average values of all other variables. Not surprisingly, therefore, the same modifications must be made when considering the dynamic behaviour from a long-run perspective.

In the long run, constant terms of trade would imply an increase in both countries' growth rates (see Figure 4.1), thus forcing a change to the medium-run equilibrium, including the terms of trade. The inducement to faster growth creates an excess demand for labour in the Centre, pushing up $w_1$ faster than otherwise. This is illustrated in Figure 9.5 by an outward movement of the $\gamma(m)$ curve. The path of $\gamma$ towards its limit value is shown by the arrow starting at $e$. Higher wages stimulate more R & D and productivity growth rises; the global rate of profits tends to the value $(n_1 + q^*)/s_1$. These are essentially the same dynamics as reported in 6.2, except that there $q$ was zero throughout (compare Figure 6.2). The path taken by $\gamma$ in this case is shown by the arrow beginning at $e'$.

It is the failure of the Emmanuel effect to neutralize fully the consequences of rising wages in the Centre that is responsible for additional inducements to save Central labour. If a manufacturing sector becomes established in the Periphery and its expansion is not subject to increasing costs that inducement no longer exists. Central wage pressure can always be relieved at zero cost by an increasing outflow of manufacturing investment. If, however, the growth of Peripheral manufacturing at a rate needed to prevent $w_1$ from rising can only be accommodated by incurring higher costs then there will be room for $w_1$ to rise. In this case the incentive to undertake R & D is restored.

## 9.5    Materials saving
The discussion of materials saving will follow the same pattern as that of labour. In this section we consider reductions in materials use in the absence of resource constraints. This means that rents are zero and costs are constant. Equations (5.1) and (5.2) are thus applicable as they stand. Although these equations do not adequately represent a system of production with fixed capital, for present purposes it will not be seriously misleading to refer to good 1 as 'machines' and good 2 as 'materials' when used in production (though both, of course, constitute 'capital' in its proper sense). The initial supposition might then be that innovations which save on the use of materials will

harm the Periphery. To take the matter further it will be useful to distinguish between different types of materials saving.

First, there is the substitution of manufactured alternatives for primary materials in final uses. Then there is the reduction of materials coefficients in production. This may be unaccompanied by the increased use of machines, as in the case of recycling or reduced wastage through learning. Typically, though, the use of the manufactured good will rise as that of materials falls. Examples of such partial substitution are provided by improved machines which permit the rolling of thinner steel sheets while maintaining quality, or thinner coatings of tin or zinc, or waste reduction through computerization. These different forms of materials saving will have different implications for the terms of trade and Peripheral welfare.

The first case involves a shift of the world's relative demand curve in favour of manufactures. But with no change in production coefficients or wage rates there will be no impact on the terms of trade. (Fixing wages in terms of good 1 or some other basket of goods will not affect the conclusion.) The constant returns assumption is responsible for this outcome, but even if the terms of trade do not change it is clear that the Periphery will be harmed. Even with constant returns, prices can only remain constant if supplies adjust to demands and so the levels of output and employment in the Periphery must fall compared to what they otherwise would have been. Although this implies a reduction in the flow of inward investment this can be of little comfort either to workers or indigenous capitalists. A deliberate retardation of the Pasinetti process in the presence of buoyant demand could raise welfare through an improvement in the terms of trade (by driving a wedge between profits rates). A retardation of the process enforced by declining demand is a quite different matter.

Consider next savings on materials inputs without an accompanying increase in machinery. Although the R & D process (assumed costless) is undertaken primarily in the Centre, the capitalists of that region may have overseas investments and, even if they do not, will still be interested in reducing the costs of their material inputs. Such savings will thus be manifested in reductions in both $a_{21}$ and $a_{22}$. A reduction in any input–output coefficient will push the global $w_2$–$r$ frontier outwards and hence, with given $w_i$, increase the uniform rate of profits. Bearing that in mind it is easy to see what the terms-of-trade consequences of reductions in the $a_{2i}$ will be. If $a_{21}$ alone falls it follows immediately from Equation (5.2) that $p$ must fall (to balance the increase in $r$). Similarly, if $a_{22}$ alone falls it follows from Equation (5.1) (rearranged to solve for $p$) that $p$ rises. In sum, for isolated changes:

$$dp/da_{21} > 0 \quad \text{and} \quad dp/da_{22} < 0$$

(These results continue to hold even if some of the gains are absorbed by Centre wages, so long as $r$ rises to some extent.)

Of particular interest is the fact that materials saving in the Centre improves the Peripheral terms of trade. Whether globally uniform savings have the same net effect depends on all coefficients and on $\omega$, but it is clearly a possible outcome. An improvement in the terms of trade is a sufficient but not a necessary condition for the value of Peripheral capital per unit of output, $pa_{12} + a_{22}$, to fall as a result of across-the-board savings. If that happens the consumption frontier moves outwards and the comparative effect on consumption p.w. will undoubtedly be positive. The fact remains, however, that the immediate impact of technical progress will be to reduce industrial demand for materials and in consequence the output of materials. Thus even if consumption p.w. rises the number of workers will fall. References to particular examples of technical progress tend to stress this immediate effect. But it is not the end of the story. If some of the gains are realized by higher Centre wages, increased demands by Centre workers may compensate for some of the industrial losses. And if the rate of profits rises to any degree, the rate of growth of 2-production will rise and the short-run fall in employment will be succeeded by longer-term gains.[7]

If materials saving is occasioned by the increased use of machines, these considerations require only trivial modification. Although the $a_{1i}$ coefficients rise it will still be the case that a new technique will be adopted only if it is more profitable than the old one; that is if the world $w_2$–$r$ frontier shifts outwards at the original $(w_2, r)$ combination. By the previous reasoning we can then derive the following partial effects:

$$\delta p/\delta a_{11} > 0 \quad \text{and} \quad \delta p/\delta a_{12} < 0$$

Again it is worth remarking that combined changes could, on balance, improve the Periphery's terms of trade. But the previous reservations on output and employment apply equally here.

There is no difficulty in imagining outcomes in which the Periphery loses all along the line: a net deterioration in the terms of trade; the immediate loss of output and employment; low spill-over effects from increased Centre wages; a perpetual process of innovation causing continuous reductions in demand, running ahead of the compensating growth effects. Such outcomes do not, however, follow from logical necessity. In particular, if sufficient weight is given to the longer-term effects of more rapid growth, economies in the use of materials could prove beneficial to the producer of materials. This statement does, however, refer to the Periphery in aggregate. In reality, there may be gainers and losers even within the Periphery. Faster growth brought about by the more efficient use of steel scrap will be of more benefit to countries which are not heavily dependent on exports of iron ore. A country which sees its major export product replaced entirely by plastic will find little compensation in the faster world growth that the innovation stimulates.

The discussion in this section has been at a very general level and recasting the analysis in terms of a model of durable capital (the inputs of good 1 persisting, in modified form, for several periods) would not affect the observations in any substantial way. The main additional consideration is that where the Periphery contains a manufacturing sector there now arises the possibility of profitable purchases of technologically obsolete machinery from the Centre.

## 9.6   Induced expansion of effective natural resource supply

If, because of scarcity, natural resources are no longer free, then increasing rents could induce additional efforts to relieve the scarcity. There are basically three ways in which that can be achieved: first, through savings on material usage, as discussed in the last section; second, through the more intensive exploitation of existing sources (giving rise also to intensive rents); and, third, through search for new sources. The detailed effects of these alternatives will no doubt differ, but since each has the consequence of increasing the *effective* supply of resources, the long-run implications are likely to be very similar.[8] For simplicity and brevity we shall consider only the third kind of search. The argument runs in close parallel to that of 9.4.

Suppose that resource supply grows at a rate $h = \bar{h} + h^*$, where $\bar{h}$ is autonomous and

$$h^* = h^*(\rho) \qquad h^{*\prime} > 0$$

where $\rho$ is taken as the rent per unit on the highest grade. (Thus $\rho > 0$, throughout.) Since good 2 is the standard of value and variations in the resource:output coefficient are not permitted, then $\rho$ measures the contribution of rent cost to total cost. As the burden of rents rises the intensity of exploration increases (but is subject to diminishing returns). The proportional rate of growth of rent depends on output growth relative to $h$:

$$\dot{\rho}/\rho = H[\gamma_2(\alpha,\rho) - h(\rho)] \tag{9.28}$$

Here $\gamma_2$ falls with $\rho$ (ignoring revaluation effects), directly from reduced profitability and indirectly from reduced capital inflow. Assuming no Central labour scarcity (9.28) has a long-run solution (when $\alpha$ is constant)

$$\gamma_2 = h$$

In approaching this solution (when $\alpha > 0$), $\gamma_2$, $\rho$ and $h^*$ are all rising. Figure 9.5 can be used to illustrate the process if m is replaced by $\rho$ and $n_1 + q$ by $\bar{h} + h^*$. (As in Figure 9.5 the costs of exploration are implicit in this account; without them growth possibilities would be higher.)

If there is a labour constraint in the Centre then the terms of trade will need to mediate a convergence of the world growth rate to

$$\bar{h} + h^*(\rho) = n_1 + q(m)$$

the induced components on either side of the equation helping to avoid the possibility of one of the resources becoming a free good (or 'quasi-free' in the case of labour). If real rents are subject to Phillips-type variation, the coupled dynamic sub-systems will probably generate very complex trajectories for the world economy as a whole, a consideration well beyond the scope of the present discussion.

## 9.7 Conclusion
The Centre's convergence to a stationary state, anticipated by Ricardo, has been postponed, partly by the development of interna-

tional trade and overseas investment. International economic relations allowed one Central resource constraint, land, then another, labour, to be relieved by the exploitation of surpluses in the Periphery. But even if Peripheral population can outrun world growth without any economic stimulus, as it appears to do, the same cannot be true of natural resources. Thus the exploration for new resources and improvements in materials productivity take an increasing urgency. If such improvements are inexhaustible, global capital accumulation can continue indefinitely. If a stationary state does come about it will be more likely to be because the process of accumulation is itself destroying the planet. Global externalities provide the basis for a new dismal prediction.

## Notes

1. It is easiest to assume that overseas investments are undertaken by individuals out of dividends.
2. A sufficient condition for $d(\Delta\pi)/d(wl) > 0$ is

$$1 + \sigma r > \sigma.wl/\mathbf{pa}$$

where $wl/\mathbf{pa}$ is the ratio of labour cost to capital cost.
3. More 'rational' behaviour on the part of firms is unlikely to change the qualitative nature of the outcome. Even if a firm expects $w$ and $p$ to change as a result of aggregate efforts, it still cannot afford not to participate in the R & D process.
4. For the implications of violating this assumption, see the following footnote.
5. Had we allowed 'real' capital and value capital to move in opposite directions, sufficiently large divergences could have yielded $\eta < 0$ and a negative determinant of the coefficient matrix. As a result $(\bar{v}, \bar{m})$ would be a saddlepoint.

   The phase portait of the general system, Equations (9.18) and (9.19), is likely to be much more complicated than that shown in Figure 9.4. Fuller examination might well reveal the existence of limit cycles, for example.
6. The rate of profits is $(q + \beta_1 + n_1 - \dot{\mathbf{pa}}/\mathbf{pa})/s$. It will be greater with technical progress because of $q > 0$; $\beta_1$ will be less but only because of the higher profitability.
7. In the model of Molana and Vines (1989) improvements in 'agricultural' productivity also lead to short-run immiserization of the Periphery.
8. In Mainwaring (1989b) both materials saving, via a technical progress function, and stimulated exploration of new sources are permitted. The shares of the two regions in world income and the terms of trade cycle around a fixed point. The model does not, however, include overseas investment.

# 10 Conclusions and some cautious tests

## 10.1 Summary of the main findings

Although the main findings of the book have already been summarized at the end of each chapter, it may be useful here to draw the strands together systematically. We shall be concerned mainly with conclusions arising out of the analysis of Part II but we begin with a few remarks on Part I where the analysis was directed at a world without international investment.

With zero capital mobility, complete specialization would imply that Centre and Periphery grow at the same steady rate. Unequal growth rates would, however, be the normal case where one of the regions is unable to specialize completely. Changes in parameters, such as savings rates or rates of technical progress, would also give rise to phases of unequal development. Chapters 1 and 2 were directed primarily to an evaluation of the intertemporal gains from trade. These were seen to be positive for both regions provided that the rates of discount used in the evaluation were taken to be equal to the with-trade rates of profits. A slightly lower discount rate could imply a Peripheral loss from trade. It is important to stress that an inequality of the two rates need not merely be the consequence of correctable 'distortions' but could be an inherent characteristic of capitalism. Recognizing the possibility of a loss through trade and identifying it in reality are two quite different things. Whether the Periphery, or some part of it, actually suffers from the extent of openness may be impossible to establish with any degree of certitude.

The dangers of making dogmatic policy statements were also illustrated in Chapter 3. This examined the, by now, orthodox view that countries in which real wages exceed shadow wages would benefit from imported second-hand capital equipment, whenever it is available, rather than new equipment. The initial intuition that extended maintenance is more economical where real labour costs are low was shown to fail in the presence of substitutions in inputs used for maintaining machines and also in the presence of transport costs. In this case it would surely be wise to evaluate each accumulation programme on its own merits.

Turning to Part II, the major consequence of introducing financial capital movements is that inequality of growth rates between the two regions becomes the normal state of affairs. Although the steady-state solution implies balanced growth, this state conceivably may not be reached until all of the Peripheral capital stock is owned by Centre capitalists. If this is regarded as the long-run outcome then, from the relevant medium-run perspective, the process of development is inherently uneven. To add precision to this conclusion we shall list a set of propositions which have been derived from the analysis, some of a general nature, some depending on the particular specification of the model.

We begin with the simplest case: complete specialization, exogenously fixed wages, no rents, no dualism in the Peripheral export sector, no government, no technical change. Then:

1.  The terms of trade remain constant over time.
2.  The proportion of global capital (in both value and physical terms) owned by Centre capitalists grows over time, asymptotically converging on unity. (This is the international Pasinetti process and it follows from the assumption that Centre capitalists are more aggressive in the pursuit of accumulation.)
3.  The average world growth rate rises over time. (This follows from the fact that an increasing proportion of the world's capital stock is owned by higher-saving Central capitalists.)
4.  So long as investment continues to flow from one region to the other, the capital stocks located in the two regions will normally grow (in both physical and value terms) at different rates. (This will be necessary to satisfy proportionate consumption requirements at the fixed terms of trade in the face of a rising average growth rate.)
5.  Taking the two regions as single entities there is no *a priori* reason to say that the Periphery will grow more slowly than the Centre. Thus rapid capitalist development in the Periphery is possible.
6.  Within the Periphery, however, development is extremely uneven: the enclave is the most dynamic part of the world economy (growing faster than the Centre) whereas the indigenous sector is the most sluggish.
7.  At a finite time in the Pasinetti process the outflow of remittances from the Periphery will exceed the inflow of new invest-

ment. There is thus a secular tendency for the net burden of debt to increase over time.

8. Consumption per worker in the Centre rises over time, converging to a maximum level.

9. Indigenous consumption p.w. in the Periphery falls over time, converging to the level of the fixed wage rate, as indigenous capitalists are eliminated. Nevertheless, consumption actually undertaken in the Periphery may remain high if migrant enclave capitalists consume there rather than in the Centre.

If the previous assumptions are modified by supposing that foreign investment were responsible for introducing a more profitable (higher-wage, higher-rate-of-profits) advanced export sub-sector, then:

10. Average Peripheral wages will rise over time due to the faster rate of growth of the enclave. Likewise the average rate of profits will rise over time.

If the advanced sector absorbs indigenous capitalists and induces those capitalists to adopt 'advanced' savings behaviour, then:

11. The Pasinetti process is restrained and the Central share of global capital converges to a fraction which is less than unity.

12. In consequence, indigenous capitalist consumption in the Periphery does not fall to zero and (allowing for rising average wages) it can conceivably rise over time.

If the Periphery undertakes accumulation financed from taxes on the profits of foreign-owned capital, or from transfer receipts from abroad, then:

13. The Pasinetti process is again restrained. In this case domestic capitalists are still eliminated, but not domestic capital: the public-sector share in the terminal capital stock is finite.

14. Even without an advanced sector, consumption p.w. will not fall to the level of the real wage, provided that some part of government receipts is used for social consumption.

If the world economy undergoes a transition from an investment autarky regime to one with overseas investment, or an extension of the latter, then:

15. The terms of trade of the Periphery will deteriorate.
16. The Centre will suffer a transitional reduction in consumption p.w. but because of the outward shift of its consumption frontier it will have higher consumption p.w. with foreign investment.
17. The Periphery gains in consumption p.w. during the transition, but if its export sector is homogeneous the inward shift of its consumption frontier generates an eventual and permanent reduction in consumption p.w.
18. Where the Periphery has an advanced sub-sector, the consumption frontier may move inwards or outwards and consumption p.w. may rise or fall.
19. Because of the positive terms-of-trade effect, the Centre's 'inclusive' gain from overseas investment (i.e., counting the transitional and permanent effects together) will be positive, provided gains and losses are discounted at a rate equal to or less than the with-investment rate of profits.
20. Because of the deterioration in its terms of trade, the Periphery's gain may be negative, even if consumption benefits are discounted at the with-investment rate of profits. (This conclusion is consistent with standard immiserizing results.)

If Central wages are allowed to rise in response to employment pressure, then:

21. The global growth rate converges to a steady value equal to the rate of growth of the Central workforce.
22. During the process of convergence, Central wages continue to rise (to a ceiling) provided that the initial pattern of complete specialization is maintained.
23. As a result the terms of trade shift in favour of the Centre. (This is the 'Emmanuel effect'.)
24. If the wage response is of the 'real' Phillips-curve variety, convergence may be perpetually cyclical, in which case so would be the flow of foreign investment.

If Centre wages rise to a point at which manufacturing is equiprofitable in both regions, then:

25. A flow of investment into Peripheral manufacturing (whether direct or portfolio) will restrain Central wage growth and stabilise the terms of trade. (Wages and the terms of trade will remain constant only if the supply of complementary inputs into Peripheral manufacturing is perfectly elastic.)

26. Looking at the Periphery in disaggregated terms, those countries which first receive manufacturing investments will be those whose costs to investors (which may be cultural as well as physical) are least. (This suggests the basis of a theory of the endogenous formation of newly industrialized countries and of endogenous changes in the global division between Centre and Periphery.)

If resource constraints appear in the Periphery, then:

27. This will press the terms of trade in the Periphery's favour.

28. Resources will be sought in the Centre leading to further blurring of the pattern of specialization.

If technological change takes the form of exogenous reductions in labour production coefficients, or exogenous reductions in the inputs of primary products, whether or not accompanied by increases in the inputs of manufactures, then:

29. It is not possible, in general, to say in which direction the terms of trade will move. Nor is it possible to say for certain what will happen to consumption p.w. or growth rates of capital and employment in the two regions.

Where, however, technical progress leads to manufactures being substituted for primary products in final demand, then:

30. Output and employment in the Periphery must fall. (Similar outcomes would arise from a change in tastes in favour of manufactures or as a result of a higher income elasticity of demand for manufactures.)

If technical progress is induced in the Centre by incipient shortages of Central labour, then:

31. It must be the case that the wage pressure cannot be fully relieved by investment in Peripheral manufacturing.

32. World growth now converges to a rate equal to the effective rate of growth of the Central workforce (i.e., the rate adjusted to include productivity gain).

33. The Central wage rate rises at a rate equal to the rate of growth of labour productivity, that rate itself rising and converging to a maximum. The convergence may be oscillatory.

34. The trend terms of trade remain constant over time.

35. As compared to a world in which this form of technical progress were absent: the burden of Centre wage costs (as a ratio of product price) is lower; the rate of profits is higher; and the terms of trade are more favourable to the Periphery. Consumption p.w. in the Periphery is consequently higher, but the Periphery attracts less capital inflow.

If Peripheral resource constraints induce search for resources or for resource-saving methods, then (in the absence of the labour constraint):

36. Global growth converges to a rate equal to the rate of effective expansion of resources.

Finally, if both constraints are operative, then:

37. Induced technical change will encourage convergence of world growth, the growth of effective Central labour supply and the growth of effective resources to the same steady rate.

Some of these propositions may be capable of verification; others, for example, those involving hypothetical comparisons, clearly are not. Nevertheless, they do, taken as a whole, convey a reasonably distinctive historical story whose overall consistency with actual events (or at least the stylized versions of those events) could be put to the test. The story is one of evolution through stages of the global division of labour, accompanied by a gradual expansion of the Centre in a territorial sense. The stages may be presented somewhat schematically, as follows:

1. A Ricardian stage in which a mainly agricultural Centre (in reality, Great Britain and Northern Europe) faces resource constraints and the prospect of a stationary state. Neither interna-

tional trade nor international investment is sufficiently well developed to delay significantly this prospect.
2. A freeing of overseas trade and investment allowing the Central resource constraint to be eased, then eliminated. The production of agricultural goods for the Centre then becomes increasingly dominated by the Periphery (Southern Europe and the Americas). The Centre exploits its comparative advantage in manufacturing. Thus the traditional world division of labour which still forms the basis of most Centre–Periphery models becomes established.
3. Because of rapid industrial growth, the Centre's reserves of surplus labour dry up and manufacturing investments spill over into the Periphery giving rise to the development of newly industrialized countries.
4. Depletion of the Periphery's resources likewise spreads the search for and exploitation of materials sources more evenly across the globe.

Stages 3 and 4 are not necessarily in order. Experience after the Second World War suggests that they have gone roughly hand-in-hand. The outcome is that neither Centre nor Periphery is now fully specialized even if their respective emphases remain in the traditional direction.

This may appear to suggest that the patterns of production and trade in the latest stage are consistent with those of the Heckscher–Ohlin model, but such an inference would not be valid. The two important primary factors of production in the above story are labour and natural resources. The constraints imposed by the availability of these factors control the evolutionary process. Capital, which does not itself impose a constraint, at least in the medium and long runs, is nevertheless an essential element in the story. Without it there would be no accumulation and no evolution. It is now well-established (Steedman and Metcalfe, 1977) that the introduction of produced means of production (the only correct way to characterize capital) into the two-primary-factor Heckscher–Ohlin model undermines the validity of its conclusions. The constraints, moreover, operate within one or other region at some or other stage. In the last stage the world economy as a whole is still not labour-constrained since a permanent reserve army remains in the Periphery. At no time does the Periphery have Heckscher–Ohlin characteristics. A more convincing description of the evolutionary process is provided by a version of Marxian theory in which the Periphery provides an enduring reserve army of labour for world capitalism. But even this is subject to Ricardian qualifications given the importance of global resource constraints.

## 10.2 Glimpses of reality

It appears that few, if any, long-run Centre–Periphery models have been subject to empirical confirmation, except insofar as they have been purposely constructed to explain certain empirically based beliefs (such as the belief in the secular decline in the Periphery's terms of trade).[1] This section is not aimed at anything quite as ambitious as a proper statistical test of any of the above propositions. Its purpose is simply to see whether the overall thrust of the arguments can be considered to be reasonably consistent with the somewhat stylized, but generally agreed facts from major episodes of global accumulation. The two episodes which we shall consider are the relatively undisturbed periods from the mid-nineteenth century up to the First World War and from the end of the Second World War up to the mid-1970s when events became dominated by the aftermath of the oil crisis.

*High imperialism: 1860–1913*
To apply a Centre–Periphery model to this period it is first necessary to define the two regions in a geographical sense. In this earlier phase of global capitalism the Centre was a much smaller entity than it is now. If the international credit position of a nation is taken as a reflection of its status, then the Centre was confined to a few countries in northern Europe, most importantly the United Kingdom.

The main creditor–debtor countries are shown in Table 10.1, compiled by Brinley Thomas (1967) from United Nations (1949) data. As he explains, the position of France and Germany in this table is somewhat exaggerated.

Unlike those from the UK, foreign investments from these countries were mainly government-inspired loans to foreign governments, much of them ill-fated. 'The state-controlled lending activities of France and Germany in the forty years before the First World War, although considerable in scale, had a negligible effect on the growth of the international economy. The dominant influence was the flow of long-term capital from Great Britain.' Most of that flow

Table 10.1   Main creditor and debtor nations, 1913

|  | Gross credits $100m | % |  | Gross debts $100m | % |
|---|---|---|---|---|---|
| UK | 18.0 | 40.9 | Europe | 12.0 | 27.3 |
| France | 9.0 | 20.4 | Latin America | 8.5 | 19.3 |
| Germany | 5.8 | 13.2 | USA | 6.8 | 15.5 |
| Belgium, Holland, |  |  | Canada | 3.7 | 8.4 |
| Switzerland | 5.5 | 12.5 | Asia | 6.0 | 13.6 |
| USA | 3.5 | 8.0 | Africa | 4.7 | 10.7 |
| Other | 2.2 | 5.0 | Oceania | 2.3 | 5.2 |
|  | 44.0 | 100.0 |  | 44.0 | 100.0 |

was directed to the rest of what Thomas calls the 'Atlantic Economy': 63.6 per cent of British overseas investment in publicly issued securities in 1913 was accounted for by Canada and Newfoundland, USA, Latin America and South Africa (Feis, 1930). Thus, at the risk of over-simplification, the Centre of the world economy in this period can be identified with the UK, while conditions in the Americas had an important influence on the character of the Periphery in aggregate.

Application of the model for this period comes up against an immediate obstacle. Without doubt an important part of the interplay within the Atlantic economy was contributed by movements of labour. Migration of people and migration of capital generally went hand in hand (at least to North America). The model, as developed in preceding chapters assumed no migration of workers. The adaptation, however, is straightforward. Suppose that the Centre were endowed with surplus labour. Large parts of the Periphery were able to absorb this labour with little difficulty. Indeed, lack of labour would have been a major factor limiting the development of resources in those parts. With globally surplus and freely mobile labour, real wages over the long run could be taken as given in both regions, as in the basic model of Chapter 5. The rest of the long-run analysis, conducted in per (employed) worker terms remains largely intact.

The fact is, however, that real wages in the UK were generally rising over this period (see Figure 10.1, below). This is not necessarily inconsistent with plentiful labour so long as the improvement in workers' living standards can be attributed to exogenous (social and

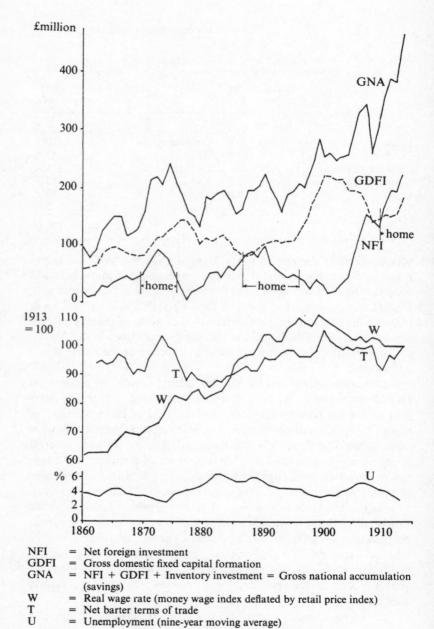

NFI     = Net foreign investment
GDFI    = Gross domestic fixed capital formation
GNA     = NFI + GDFI + Inventory investment = Gross national accumulation
          (savings)
W       = Real wage rate (money wage index deflated by retail price index)
T       = Net barter terms of trade
U       = Unemployment (nine-year moving average)

*Source* Feinstein (1972) (T extended back using Imlah 1988)

*Figure 10.1*

cultural) factors. The long-run properties of the surplus-labour model with rising wage rates are essentially the same as those of the full-employment model of Chapter 6. (Fluctuations in wage rates are considered below.)

Minor attention also needs to be paid to the treatment of Peripheral savings with migration. Entrepreneurs and would-be entrepreneurs would now be included among permanent migrants and their habits of thrift would be those of the Centre. Thus, in the so-called 'areas of recent settlement', like North America, savings rates and hence growth rates might well be higher than in older settled regions or regions with large indigenous populations, like Latin America. The former would therefore be likely to attain Centre status more quickly than the latter.

The implications of overseas investment for global growth are not affected by these considerations. Whether or not investment is accompanied by migrants it raises the proportion of global profits subject to higher savings and would thus raise the global growth rate if wages were constant (proposition 3) but need not do so if wages were rising. It is also still the case that the Centre's stock of overseas assets (the enclave) grows faster than that of its domestic capital (proposition 6). Trends in these stocks are illustrated in Table 10.2. It can be seen that throughout the period, the decadal growth rate of foreign assets was consistently higher than that of domestic capital. In 1860, foreign assets accounted for 16.4 per cent of the UK's total stock; by 1913 the proportion had risen to 36 per cent. The growth rate of the combined stock does not, however, display an upward trend.

Table 10.3 shows flows of net foreign investment and net property income from abroad. Proposition 7, which says that the outflow of remittances from the Periphery will, at some point, overtake the continued inflow of investment, is strikingly illustrated by the table. The proposition is itself based on another which says that the rate of growth of remittances is equal to that of the stock of enclave capital. Between 1870 and 1913, overseas investment earnings in current prices grew by a factor of 5.7 (Imlah, 1958); overseas assets by 5.5 (Feinstein and Pollard, 1988). Proposition 8, that consumption p.w. in the Centre rises, also derives from a more basic proposition, namely that the contribution of remittances to GNP increases. From the opening to the closing decade of the period the ratio of net property income from abroad to GNP rose from 1.8 per cent to 5.9 per cent.

*Table 10.2   Gross domestic capital stock and overseas assets, UK, 1860–1913 (£ million at 1900 prices)*

| | GDK | | OA | | GDK+OA | OA ÷ (GDK+OA) |
| | £m | % decade growth | £m | % decade growth | % decade growth | |
|---|---|---|---|---|---|---|
| 1860 | 2390 | | 470 | | | 0.164 |
| | | 26.8 | | 66.0 | 33.2 | |
| 1870 | 3030 | | 780 | | | 0.205 |
| | | 28.7 | | 59.0 | 34.9 | |
| 1880 | 3900 | | 1240 | | | 0.241 |
| | | 17.9 | | 80.6 | 29.2 | |
| 1890 | 4600 | | 2040 | | | 0.307 |
| | | 22.2 | | 25.0 | 23.0 | |
| 1900 | 5620 | | 2550 | | | 0.312 |
| | | 24.2 | | 38.0 | 28.5 | |
| 1910 | 6980 | | 3520 | | | 0.335 |
| 1913 | 7290 | | 4140 | | | 0.362 |

GDK = Gross domestic fixed capital stock; OA = Accumulated overseas assets
*Source:* Feinstein and Pollard (1988, Table xxi).

*Table 10.3   UK net foreign investment and net property income from abroad 1861–910 (£m at 1900 prices)*

| Decades | NFI | NPIA | NPIA/GNP(%) |
|---|---|---|---|
| 1861–70 | 40.7 | 17.3 | 1.8 |
| 1871–80 | 51.6 | 36.0 | 3.0 |
| 1881–90 | 83.8 | 62.5 | 4.9 |
| 1891–1900 | 56.3 | 96.0 | 5.6 |
| 1901–10 | 105.4 | 123.1 | 5.9 |

*Source:* Edelstein (1982, Tables 2.2 and 2.4), derived from Imlah (1958) and Feinstein (1972).

A final long-run observation concerns the terms of trade. Proposition 23 says that if real wages rise faster in the Centre than in the Periphery then the Centre's terms improve. Although the trend over the period does indeed show an improvement (Figure 10.1) we cannot really be too confident about its causes without knowing how average wage costs in the Periphery behaved and without knowing how technical progress in this period affected relative costs of production in the two regions.

*Table 10.4    UK emigration and unemployment, 1874–1913 (% rates of change from decade to overlapping decade)*

|  | Migration from UK to USA | UK unemployment | UK home investment |
|---|---|---|---|
| 1874–83 | + 104.0 | + 50.0 | + 12.8 |
| 1879–88 | + 74.4 | + 44.4 | − 4.8 |
| 1884–93 | − 18.7 | − 4.6 | + 6.2 |
| 1889–98 | − 37.9 | − 29.0 | + 24.3 |
| 1894–1903 | − 29.8 | − 11.4 | + 26.3 |
| 1899–1908 | + 41.4 | + 10.3 | + 10.1 |
| 1904–13 | + 4.7 | + 9.3 | − 5.5 |

*Source:* Thomas (1954).

Debates among economic historians concerned with this period have focused less on long-run trends, about which there appears to be general agreement, and more on fluctuations about the trends. A particular issue has been the explanation of the Kuznet's cycles or 'long swings' of approximately twenty years in home and overseas investment. An important feature of these cycles, first established by Cairncross (1953), is that fluctuations in home investment are inverse to those in foreign investment. In Cairncross's own explanation of this phenomenon, the terms of trade are given the major causal role. Thomas (1958) has criticized this explanation, preferring to view the inverse relationship in the context of an Atlantic economy made up of creditor and debtor nations making separate claims on a single pool of savings. If the savings are determined largely by exogenous mechanisms, then high rates of accumulation within the UK would necessarily coincide with low rates elsewhere. A cyclical mechanism is still needed and this is located in trans-Atlantic movements of labour.

The long swings in home and foreign investment are clearly visible in the series plotted in Figure 10.1. So far as migration is concerned, Thomas (1958) shows that peaks and troughs in European overseas migration coincide with peaks and troughs in UK foreign investment. There is also a clear relationship between UK emigration and UK unemployment: Table 10.4.

Can these cycles be made consistent with our model once it is adapted to allow for international labour mobility? Chapter 6 proposed a simple predator–prey mechanism for explaining cycles in

Centre wages and employment rate ($v$) in a regime of near-full employment. With labour and capital both perfectly mobile, global wages should remain tied to some (possibly rising) conventional subsistence levels. It would though be more realistic to suppose that labour mobility is less than perfect, at least in the short to medium run. Although over the long run emigration would keep Centre labour supply close to demand, over lesser periods shortages would be manifested to some degree in wage increases and to some degree in a reduction in the rate of emigration; excesses of labour would give rise to falling wages and accelerated emigration. Thus, in addition to the Phillips curve (all variables below refer to the Centre),

$$\dot{w}/w = \mu(v) \qquad \mu_v > 0 \tag{10.1}$$

we can also posit an emigration function

$$\dot{e}/e = \varepsilon(v) \qquad \varepsilon_v < 0 \tag{10.2}$$

where $e$ is the rate of emigration (the flow of migrants as a percentage of the workforce).

Is it reasonable to suppose that capital is perfectly mobile over the cycle? Evidence on UK and overseas rates of return on long-term securities for 1870–1913 (Edelstein, 1982, Chapter 6) shows significant divergences between rates for periods of long-swing duration. Thus a degree of imperfection in capital mobility must also be accepted (giving the present cycles a 'short-run' character). The magnitude of the investment flow might be expected to depend on this profit rate differential which, in turn, depends on wages in the two regions and the terms of trade. The latter will be such as to equate global supplies and demands. An increased outflow of workers and capital from the Centre into Peripheral primary production will therefore lead to an improvement in the Centre's terms of trade. However, since this is occurring at a time when wages are decelerating it must be the case that the improvement is absorbed by an increasing domestic rate of return. To model this interaction fully requires specification of a Peripheral wage adjustment equation. We shall, however, keep matters simple by supposing that production in parts of the Periphery is constrained by the availability of workers so that migration induces a corresponding flow of capital.[2] This outflow will reduce the stock of physical capital available in the Centre. Denoting that loss (as a proportion of the existing stock) by $b$, then

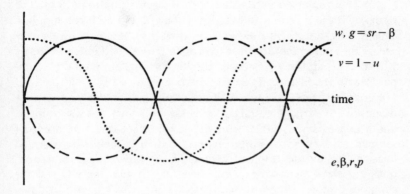

*Figure 10.2*

$$b = b(e) \qquad b_e > 0$$

Although the problem of capital revaluation arises here, it is assumed that $d\beta/db > 0$. The implication is that $\beta$ is high when $w$ is low. This does not contradict (6.5), $d\beta/dw > 0$, because that inequality referred to the case in which rates of profits were uniform.[3]

The rate of growth of the Centre's workforce is equal to the natural rate $n^*$ less the rate of emigration:

$$n = n^* - e$$

so that (neglecting technical progress)

$$\dot{v}/v = \gamma(g) - n = \gamma[sr(e,w)] - b(e) - n^* + e \qquad (10.3)$$

where $r$ depends on $e$ via the latter's effect on the terms of trade.

Equations (10.1)–(10.3) constitute a three-variable predator–prey system. It can easily be partitioned into a $v$–$w$ cycle with an anti-clockwise trajectory (as in Figure 6.3) and a $v$–$e$ cycle with a clockwise trajectory.[4] The relationship between the various cycles is shown schematically in Figure 10.2. (Note that each variable has its own vertical scale so that nothing should be inferred about relative amplitudes; moreover the upper turning point of the $w$-cycle need not coincide exactly with the lower turning point of the $e$-cycle.) The correspondence of the $e$ and $\beta$ cycles follows directly from Equation

(10.2); their inverse relationship with $w$ from Equation (10.1). The terms of trade $p$ should follow $\beta$, via the effects on global supplies. This means that $r$ also follows $\beta$. If, however, the fluctuations in $sr$ are modest compared to those in $\beta$, then $(sr - \beta)$ will move inversely with $\beta$. This stylized version of the long swings may now be compared with the historical record shown in Figure 10.1.

Capital exports in Figure 10.1 are equivalent to our $\beta K$, whereas domestic investment equals $gK$. These will vary inversely if the amplitude of $sr$ is relatively small. In that case one would expect savings to vary with capital exports but in a much less marked fashion. In fact the graph of savings (gross national accumulation) does not show clear long-swing variation, though there is just the slightest hint of sympathy with capital exports. Variation of real wages about their rising trend displays peaks coinciding with troughs in capital exports, as expected from Figure 10.2. Emigration, as reported by Thomas, fluctuates directly with foreign investment, again as in Figure 10.2 where both follow unemployment ($u$) with approximately a quarter-cycle lag. In fact, peaks in the smoothed unemployment series in Figure 10.1 do precede those in capital exports (though rates of change of unemployment and emigration reported in Table 10.4 appear to have greater simultaneity). Turning to the rate of profits, the stylized scheme predicts, somewhat paradoxically perhaps, that this is at its highest when capital exports are greatest. Edelstein's data (1982, pp. 147–8) show 'the following periodisation of home and overseas domination: 1870–1876, home (weak); 1877–86, overseas; 1887–96, home; 1897–1909, overseas; 1910–13, home'. These phases are marked in Figure 10.1; periods of home domination are seen to coincide with peaks in capital export. (During the domestic investment boom of 1900, home rates of return were actually negative.)

The final question concerns the terms of trade. It was Cairncross's view that a shift of the terms of trade away from the UK caused increasing capital outflow. This argument is difficult to sustain in the face of the evidence shown in Figure 10.1. It runs counter to the causation implied in our model (and in most other modern theories) in which foreign investment brings about declining import prices by increasing the supply of overseas products. On that basis one would expect the terms of trade to have moved in the UK's favour during periods of high capital export. This was certainly true during the peak of 1872 and also up to the peak of 1890 but thereafter the relationship broke down. Thomas (1967), however, is not so easily discouraged:

> In each upswing we note an initial phase during which the terms of trade move against Britain and there is a moderate revival in capital exports; then the terms of trade turn in favour of Britain and it is in this second phase that the rate of capital outflow is greatest. It is significant that the absorption of capital by overseas countries was at its height during years when the terms of trade were moving against them ... On this reading ... one is led to regard movements in the net barter terms of trade as a *consequence* of the fundamental forces at work rather than a causal factor ... (Original italics.)

Although Thomas's interpretation supports our hypothesis it has to be admitted that it is somewhat strained when viewing the period 1890–1913 as a whole. A certain degree of reconciliation could be provided by taking account of a higher income elasticity of demand for manufactures together with a shift in the balance of overseas investment towards manufacturing. The latter would mean that an expansion of foreign lending would no longer imply a reduction in the price of primary products. Taking these possibilities on board, it is really only the sharp peak in the terms of trade around 1900 that remains troublesome.

Quite clearly the explanation of long swings summarized by Equations (10.1)–(10.3) is over-simple and incomplete. In particular, it glosses over the role of distributional variations in the Periphery and of improvements in technology. Moreover, no distinction is made between 'productive' investments and 'population-sensitive' investments (housing, urban infrastructure, etc.) which plays a key part in Thomas's explanation. Even so, there is enough consistency between actual long-swing experience and the cycles generated by the model to suggest that further refinements might be worth pursuing. Such elaborations might, for example, yield a more convincing explanation of movements in the terms of trade.

## 1950–74

The USA, once the major Peripheral economy, is now the dominant Central economy. While its status and that of many other industrialized economies is indisputable, reaching a firm definition of Centre and Periphery in the present world economy is not easy. How, for example, should the capital-rich, oil-exporting countries be classified? Similarly, where should the newly industrialized countries be put? If the NICs are part of the Centre when did they become so? These questions are largely avoided by terminating the period at 1974. This eliminates the need to disentangle secular and stochastic elements in the oil shocks and their aftermath (the recycling of OPEC surpluses and the debt crisis which followed). And before 1974 the NICs can more confidently be left as part of the Periphery. Centre and Periphery over this period will thus be taken as synonymous with the UN's categories of Developed Market Economies (DMEs) and Less Developed Countries (LDCs). Even settling on such standard definitions it is not at all straightforward to obtain consistent series of data for these geographical aggregations over a long period of time. In the following, therefore, we attempt only to note major trends in relative growth patterns, aggregate capital flows and types of investment. Another particular difficulty in interpreting developments after the Second World War concerns the magnitude of official flows of long-term capital. Over the period 1950–74 these were considerably greater than private flows and they will have had a major impact on the way the Periphery has evolved.

Table 10.5 reports annual average rates of growth of GDP for the DMEs and LDCs with the post-1974 period included for comparison. The first thing to note is that LDC growth was consistently faster than that of DMEs up to and including the period 1975–79. If GDP growth reflects capital stock growth, then proposition 5, above – that the Periphery, in aggregate, could be the faster-growing region – is consistent with this. However, LDC growth has been extremely uneven, East Asia being its most dynamic sub-region. In terms of living standards, LDC performance has been undermined by fast-growing populations. Growth of GDP per capita has generally lagged behind that of the DMEs.

Part of LDC growth performance may be attributable to the high level of official development assistance during this period (Table 10.6). Private capital flows were lower on average but growing much faster so that by 1970–74 they exceeded official movements. The figures for private investments in Table 10.6 include reinvested earnings. Thus they are not equivalent to $B_1(= \beta_2 K_2)$ but to $(\beta_2 + s_1 \alpha r)K_2$ which (provided $s_1 > s_2$) will be greater than the rate of growth of $K_2$ itself (see Equation (4.10)). What is clearly the case from the data presented here is that private capital flows to LDCs grew much more rapidly than GDP in those countries.

Gross domestic savings (GDS = $\bar{s}_2 r K_2$) should rise as a proportion

Table 10.5  Annual average rates of growth of $GDP (and $GDP per capita),* 1950–84 (per cent)

| | 1950–60 | | 60–69 | | 70–74 | 75–79† | | 80–84 | |
|---|---|---|---|---|---|---|---|---|---|
| DMEs | 4.0 | (2.7) | 5.2 | (4.2) | 4.3 | 4.0 | (3.4) | 1.9 | (1.3) |
| LDCs | 4.4 | (2.2) | 5.5 | (2.9) | 6.8 | 5.6 | (3.6) | 0.8 | (−1.5) |
| East Asia | – | (2.1) | 6.6 | (4.0) | 8.8 | 8.9 | (6.4) | 5.4 | (3.3) |

*Per capita figures in parentheses; † per capita figures for 1970–79.
Source: UNCTAD, Trade and Development Report, various issues.

Table 10.6  Annual average flows of long-term capital ($ billion) from DMEs to LDCs 1951–1974

| | 1951–55 | 56–59 | 61–64 | 65–69 | 70–74 |
|---|---|---|---|---|---|
| Official | 2.0 | 3.3 | 5.6 | 6.6 | 8.0 |
| (Rate of growth, %) | – | – | (2.6) | (4.4) | (13.8) |
| Private | 0.7 | 1.4 | 2.6 | 4.4 | 9.1 |
| (Rate of growth, %) | – | – | (9.3) | (11.5) | (15.8) |

Source: UN, World Economic Survey, various issues.

of capital stock as α increases. The World Bank's *World Development Reports* show that for the period 1960–77, GDS rose from 20 per cent of GDP to 24 per cent for middle-income LDCs, the sub-group of LDCs which is more likely to depend on private rather than official overseas capital. Gross foreign saving (equal to gross domestic fixed capital formation minus GDS) remained constant at about one per cent of GDP, but since the data are rounded to the nearest one per cent little can be inferred from this about trends in $\beta_2$.

The flow of private investment into the Periphery is geographically very concentrated. While each national economy may have a foreign enclave of some magnitude, in aggregate terms the enclave is dominated by a small group of national economies. In 1974, for example, over 60 per cent of net direct investment in all non-oil developing countries (some $5 billion) was accounted for by seven countries: Brazil, Mexico, Singapore, Malaysia, Thailand, South Korea and Taiwan (Page, 1986). The five (relatively small) East Asian countries in this list accounted for nearly 25 per cent of the total.

The changing nature of overseas investments is shown in Table 10.7. (The figures are not significantly distorted by the inclusion of Japan which, over this period has been a minor recipient of direct investment.) The switch from primary production to secondary production could not be clearer despite the steady increase in petroleum investments. These changes are, of course, paralleled by a restructuring of overall production in LDCs and in LDC exports. The changing location of primary-product investment is also of interest. In 1950, 67 per cent of US FDI in primary products went to LDCs (70 per cent excluding petroleum). By 1980 only 26 per cent went to LDCs (35 per cent excluding petroleum).

The figures presented above are rather crude but not inconsistent with the general thrust of our arguments. An important outstanding issue concerns the direction of the change in the terms of trade. In the absence of technical progress but in the presence of Central wage pressure our model predicts declining Peripheral terms of trade, at least until such time as wage pressures can be fully relieved by overseas manufacturing investments (proposition 23). Different forms of technical progress will affect the terms of trade in different ways and there is no reason to suppose that these effects will either be mutually offsetting, thus leaving the declining trend in tact, or else

Table 10.7 US foreign direct investment in LDCs,* 1950–80, $ million

| | 1950 | | 1970 | | 1980 | |
|---|---|---|---|---|---|---|
| | Total | % | Total | % | Total | % |
| Petroleum | 2139 | | 6644 | | 10271 | |
| Food and materials | 2321 | | 4149 | | 5579 | |
| PRIMARY PRODUCTS | 4460 | 78 | 10793 | 56 | 15850 | 30 |
| Manufactures | 847 | | 5477 | | 17664 | |
| Finance and trade | 398 | | 2859 | | 19174 | |
| SECONDARY PRODUCTS | 1245 | 22 | 8336 | 44 | 36838 | 70 |

*including Japan
Source: Berberoglou (1987), from US, Department of Commerce data.

229

reinforce that trend. To that extent a prediction on the course of the terms of trade cannot be held with much confidence. In any case, the evidence on the terms of trade remains a subject of considerable dispute so that even if the prediction were confident the confirmation could not be. For what it is worth, a recent evaluation by Sarker (1986) finds that for the period 1953–72, the net barter terms of trade of primary products from LDCs relative to manufactures from DMEs were subject to secular decline. The net barter terms for LDCs as a whole to DMEs as a whole also declined but to a lesser extent. Quoting Singer (1982), Sarker emphasizes that the first of these trends obtained '*in spite of* the fact that the industrial countries maintained full employment and a steady and high rate of growth up to 1973' (italics added). The nature of the Emmanuel effect would suggest that the terms of trade declined not in spite but *because* of full employment in the DMEs.

A central part of the theoretical argument which is inadequately reflected in the discussion so far is that free international investment gradually displaces the Periphery's indigenous capitalist class and thus brings about the denationalization of its economy. Peripheral development, as we have seen, has been very rapid but the dependent nature of that development has not emerged clearly from what has been said. The precise form in which development occurs is a question more suited to concrete analysis of particular economies. It may, for example, be that capitalists and/or governments in East Asian NICs have been more successful than others in maintaining domestic economic control.[5] Latin America, on the other hand, has displayed much more clearly many of the symptoms of uneven development that are predicted by the theory. It is worth concluding this section with an extended quotation from Griffin (1969, pp. 147–8) on the impact of capital imports on the form of development in Spanish America:

> Under certain circumstances foreign capital, whether public or private, may fragment the economy, introduce monopoly elements into the society, discourage the development of a native entrepreneurial class, lower the domestic savings ratio, raise the capital–output ratio and cause subsequent balance of payments problems. This last problem can be avoided in part if foreign enterprises reinvest a substantial proportion of their profits in the host economy, but this, in turn, only causes further difficulties, *viz* growing foreign control of the economy and denationalisation of local industry. In Central America this process has already advanced very far. Foreign investment has penetrated not only into large

industries but into small and medium industries as well. This phenomenon has been associated with the acquisition by foreigners of established firms managed for many years by local businessmen. In effect, private foreign investment has converted small local entrepreneurs into rentiers and thereby retarded the development of an indigenous capitalist class.

## Final remarks

This brief flirtation with the facts hardly constitutes a rigorous test of the theory presented in the previous chapters. Nevertheless, the general histories of relatively undisturbed episodes of global accumulation appear to be roughly consistent with the main findings of the theory. A more serious challenge is posed by events in the last two decades. Among the more interesting recent phenomena in global economic relationships are:

- the increasing competitiveness in manufactures of the NICs;
- the rapid elevation of oil-rich countries to the status of major capital exporters;
- the crisis of indebtedness in much of the underdeveloped world; and
- growing pressure on natural resources.

Of these, the first and last appear amenable to analysis within the general framework of this book. It has already been suggested how the formation and growth of the NICs can be endogenized though the matter would certainly bear further elaboration. The impact of resource constraints in the presence of a Central labour constraint could give rise to complex short- and medium-term dynamics, but the long-run outcome remains intact (unless – or until – that itself is overcome by environmental catastrophe). More problematic is the emergence of OPEC. This represents a major structural shift in the global economy and short-run 'structural' models of the type proposed by Taylor (1983) offer greater insight into the implications of this development. At a theoretical level it would be valuable to see whether and how short- and long-run models can be made consistent with one another. The third issue, third-world indebtedness, has reached critical proportions following the recycling of OPEC surpluses at a time of rising interest rates. But it would be a mistake to think of it merely as a consequence of structural change. Growing indebtedness is, as we have seen, a secular phenomenon, a natural consequence of free global accumulation. A marriage of short- and long-run analyses might enable us to reach a more accurate assessment of this problem.

## Notes

1. Short-run or 'macroeconomic' models have received the attentions of econometricians. See, for example, Beenstock (1988) and Hughes-Hallet (1988).
2. Such an argument requires that the Periphery is not homogeneous; specifically, that extending the workforce in 'areas of recent settlement' is advantageous to capital.
3. For the same reason the Emmanuel effect need not hold when capital is imperfectly mobile. Indeed, in the present case it is reversed over the cycles, even though it remains valid in the longer run.
4. It should be remarked that such a trajectory will obtain only under certain conditions. Emigration reduces the labour supply at home, but by inducing a capital outflow it also reduces labour demand via $b(e)$. This is countered to some extent by the improvement in the terms of trade. The impact of $b(e)$ will be lower, the lower is the capital:labour ratio in the Periphery compared to the Centre (where 'capital' is measured in terms of the physical capital of the Centre).
5. Bienefeld (1981) compares South Korea's minimal involvement with foreign direct investment with Brazil's heavy reliance on overseas capital during their respective 'import-substituting' phases of development.

# Glossary of symbols

Where symbols are specific to a chapter, this is noted in brackets.

**Indexes**

$z$    ( = I,II) Countries [1,2]

$i,j$   ( = 1,2) Commodities; countries [3, onwards]

$W$   World average

$a$    Advanced sector of 2

$b$    Backward sector of 2

$e$    Enclave in 2

$I$    Indigenous sector in 2

$t,\tau$   Time

$\hat{a}$    refers to average values in dualized Periphery

**Variables and Parameters**

$\mathbf{A} = ||a_{ij}||$ Input:output matrix

$B$    Current balance = net capital outflow

$C_{ij}$   Consumption of $i$ in country $j$

$C_j$   Value of consumption in country $j$

$E$    Value of exports

$F$    Net foreign income from abroad

$G$    $1 + g$; public-sector capital stock [4]

$I$    Value of investment

$K$    Value of capital stock

$L$    Total employment

$M$   Value of imports

$N$    Total labour force

$R$    $1 + r$; foreign transfers [4]

$S$    Aggregate savings

$T$    Tax revenue [4]

$U$    Unretained earnings on enclave capital

$X_i$   Gross output of $i$; $\mathbf{X} = [X_1, X_2]'$

$Y_i$   Net output of $i$; $\mathbf{Y} = [Y_1, Y_2]$

$a_{ij}$   Input of $i$ per unit of $j$; $\mathbf{a}_j = [a_{1j}, a_{2j}]'$

$c_i$    Consumption of $i$ per worker

$e$    Materials input coefficient [3]; rate of emigration [10]

$g$   Rate of growth of natural resource supply

$k_i$   Value-capital:labour ratio in process/country $i$

$l_i$   Labour input per unit of $i$

$m$   Machine age [3]; $wl/p$ [9]

$n_i$   Rate of growth of workforce in $i$

$p_i$   Price of i; $p = p_1/p_2$; $p^T =$ international terms of trade [1]; $\mathbf{p} = [p_1, p_2]$

$q$   Rate of labour-saving technical progress

$r$   Rate of profits

$s_i$   Propensity to save out of profits by $i$-capitalists; $\bar{s}_2 =$ average savings propensity in Periphery

$t$   Machine age [3]

$u_i$   $U/K_i$

$v$   Rate of seepage of savings from $a$ to $b$ [5]; $L_1/N_1$ [6, onwards]

$w$   Wage rate (in terms of commodity 2)

$x_i$   $X_i$ per worker

$y_i$   $Y_i$ per worker

$z$   Cost of machine transport [3]; marginal grade of natural resource [6]

$\alpha$   Share of 2-capital stock owned by 1-capitalists ($= \epsilon\mu$ [4])

$\beta_i$   Ratio of overseas capital flow to $K_i$

$\gamma_i$   $G_i/K_i$ [4]; growth of real capital stock [6, onwards]

$\delta$   Proportion of firm's capital devoted to R & D

$\epsilon$   $K_e/K_a$

$\eta$   Relative measure of labours embodied, $(\lambda_{11} + \lambda_{21})/(\lambda_{12} + \lambda_{22})$ [8]

$\theta$   Rate of tax on profits [4]

$\lambda_{ij}$   Quantity of country $i$ labour embodied, directly and indirectly, in commodity $j$ [8]

$\lambda$   Labour–input coefficient in machine-using process [3]; Government propensity to accumulate [4]; $\lambda_{11}/\lambda_{12}$ [8]

$\mu$   $K_a/K_2$ [4]; Phillips curve parameter [6, onwards]

$\zeta$   Grade of natural resource [6]

$\pi$   Price of machine [3]; relative wage cost of commodities 1 and 2 [8]; $\Delta\pi =$ expected change in firm's profit [9]

$\rho$   Social rate of discount [3]; $R/K_i$ [4]; rent per unit of natural resource [6]

$\sigma$   Proportion of profits retained by firm [9]

$\omega$   $w_1/w_a$

# References

Amin, S. (1976), *Unequal Development*, Hassocks: Harvester Press.

Amin, S. (1977), *Imperialism and Unequal Exchange*, Hassocks: Harvester Press.

Bacha, E. L. (1978), 'An interpretation of unequal exchange from Prebisch-Singer to Emmanuel', *Journal of Development Economics*, 5.

Baldone, S. (1980), 'Fixed capital in Sraffa's theoretical scheme', in Pasinetti (ed.).

Barratt-Brown, M. (1974), *The Economics of Imperialism*, Harmondsworth: Penguin.

Beenstock, M. (1988), 'An econometric investigation of north–south interdependence', in D. Currie and D. Vines (eds), *Macroeconomic Interactions between North and South*, London: Cambridge University Press.

Berberoglou, B. (1987), *The Internationalisation of Capital: Imperialism and Capitalist Development on a World Scale*, New York: Praeger.

Bhagwati, J. and Brecher, R. A. (1985), 'Extending free trade to include international investment: a welfare theoretic analysis', in S. Lall and F. Stewart (eds), *Theory and Reality in Development*, London: Macmillan.

Bienefeld, M. (1981), 'Questions about NICs from a dependency perspective', in D. Seers (ed.), *Dependency Theory: A Critical Assessment*, London: Frances Pinter.

Blomstrom, M. and Hettne, B. (1984), *Development Theory in Transition*, London: Zed Books.

Braun, O. (1974), 'L'échange inégal', in G. Amoa and O. Braun (eds), *Echanges Internationaux et Sous Développement*, Paris: Anthropos.

Brecher, R. A. and Choudri, E. U. (1982), 'Immiserizing investment from abroad: the Singer-Prebisch thesis reconsidered', *Quarterly Journal of Economics*, 97.

Bruno, M. (1969), 'Fundamental duality relations in the pure theory of capital and growth', *Review of Economic Studies*, 36.

Burgstaller, A. (1985), 'North–south trade and capital flows in a Ricardian model of accumulation', *Journal of International Economics*, 18.

Burgstaller, A. (1987), 'Europe's industrialisation and colonial underdevelopment in the light of Ricardo's corn model', *Journal of International Economics*, 22.

Burgstaller, A. and Saavedra-Rivano, N. (1984), 'Capital mobility and growth in a north–south model', *Journal of Development Economics*, 7.

Cairncross, A. K. (1953), *Home and Foreign Investment, 1870–1913*, London: Cambridge University Press.

Cardoso, F. H. (1972), 'Dependency and development in Latin America', *New Left Review*, 74.

Chang, W. W. and Chiang, S.-H. (1986), 'A model of growth and trade in time-phased systems', *International Economic Review*, 27.

Chenery, H. and Keesing, D. (1981), 'The changing composition of developing country exports', in S. Grossman and E. Lundberg (eds), *The World Economic Order: Past and Prospects*, London: Macmillan.

Clifton, J. A. (1977), 'Competition and the evolution of the capitalist mode of production', *Cambridge Journal of Economics*, 1.

Darity, W. A. (1987), 'Debt, finance, production and trade in a north–south model: the surplus approach', *Cambridge Journal of Economics*, 11.

Dixit, A. K. and Norman, V. (1980), *Theory of International Trade*, Welwyn: Nisbet.

Dos Santos, T. (1970a), 'The structure of dependence', *American Economic Review, Papers and Proceedings*, 60.

Dos Santos, T. (1970b), *Dependencia y Cambio Social*, Santiago: Centre de Estudios Socio-Economicos.

Dumenil, G. and Levy, D. (1987), 'The dynamics of competition: a restoration of the classical analysis', *Cambridge Journal of Economics*, 11.

Dutt, A. K. (1988a), 'Monopoly power and uneven development: Baran revisited', *Journal of Development Studies*, 24.

Dutt, A. K. (1988b), 'North–south models: a critical survey', mimeo, University of Notre Dame.

Dutt, A. K. (1990), *Growth, Distribution and Uneven Development*, London: Cambridge University Press.

Edelstein, M. (1982), *Overseas Investment in the Age of High Imperialism: The United Kingdom, 1850–1914*, London: Methuen.

Eigen, M. (1971), 'Self-organisation of matter and the evolution of biological macromolecules', *Naturwissenschaften*, 58.

Emmanuel, A. (1972), *Unequal Exchange: A Study in the Imperialism of Trade*, London: New Left Books.

Evans, H. D. (1984), 'A Critical assessment of some neo-Marxian trade theories', *Journal of Development Studies*, 20.

Evans, H. D. (1989a), 'Alternative perspectives on trade and development', in H. B. Chenery and T. N. Srinivasan (eds), *Handbook of Development Economics* (volume 1), Amsterdam: North-Holland.

Evans, H. D. (1989b), *Comparative Advantage and Growth*, Brighton: Wheatsheaf.

Feinstein, C. H. (1972), *National Income, Expenditure and Output of the United Kingdom, 1855–1965*, London: Cambridge University Press.

Feinstein, C. H. and Pollard, S. (1988), *Studies in Capital Formation in the United Kingdom, 1750–1920*, Oxford: Oxford University Press.

Feis, H. (1930), *Europe: The World's Banker, 1870–1914*, New Haven: Yale University Press.

Findlay, R. (1980), 'The terms of trade and equilibrium growth in the world economy', *American Economic Review*, 70.

Findlay, R. (1984), 'Growth and development in trade models', in R. W. Jones and P. Kenen (eds), *Handbook of International Economics* (volume I), Amsterdam: North-Holland.

Frank, A. G. (1967), *Capitalism and Underdevelopment in Latin America*, New York: Monthly Review Press.

Gabisch, G. (1975), 'A vintage capital model of international trade', *Journal of International Economics*, 5.

Goodwin, R. M. (1967), 'A growth cycle', in C. H. Feinstein (ed.), *Socialism, Capitalism and Economic Growth*, London: Cambridge University Press.

Goodwin, R. M. (1986), 'Swinging along the turnpike with von Neumann and Sraffa',*Cambridge Journal of Economics*, 10.

Goodwin, R. M. and Punzo, L. (1987), *The Dynamics of a Capitalist Economy*, Cambridge: Polity Press.

Griffin, K. (1969), *Underdevelopment in Spanish America*, London: George Allen and Unwin.

Hirsch, M. W. and Smale, S. (1974), *Differential Equations, Dynamic Systems and Linear Algebra*, New York: Academic Press.

Hobson, J. A. (1902), *Imperialism: A Study*, London: J. Nisbet.

Hughes-Hallett, A. (1988), 'Commodities, debt and north–south cooperation: A cautionary tale from the structuralist camp', in D. Currie and D. Vines (eds), *Macroeconomic Interactions between North and South*, London: Cambridge University Press.

Imlah, A. (1958), *Economic Elements in the Pax Britannica*, Cambridge, Mass: Harvard University Press.

James, D. D. (1970), *The Economic Feasibility of Employing Used Machinery in Less Developed Countries*, Ph.D. thesis, Michigan State University.

James, D. D. (1975), 'Second-hand machinery in development: A comment', *Journal of Development Studies*, 11.

Kaldor, N. (1976), 'Inflation and recession in the world economy', *Economic Journal*, 86.

Kanbur, R. and McIntosh, J. (1988), 'Dual economy models: Retrospect and prospect', *Bulletin of Economic Research*, 40.

Kindleberger, C. P. (1962), *Foreign Trade and the National Economy*, New Haven: Yale University Press.

Krugman, P. (1981), 'Trade, accumulation and uneven development', *Journal of Development Economics*, 8.

Laclau, E. (1971), 'Feudalism and capitalism in Latin America', *New Left Review*, 67.

Lewis, W. A. (1954), 'Economic development with unlimited supplies of labour', *Manchester School*, 22.

Little, I. M. D. (1982), *Economic Development: Theory, Policy and International Relations*, New York: Basic Books.

Mainwaring, L. (1974), 'A neo-Ricardian analysis of international trade', *Kyklos*, 27.

Mainwaring, L. (1976), 'Relative prices and "factor-price" equalisation in a heterogeneous capital goods model', *Australian Economic Papers*, 15.

Mainwaring, L. (1980a), 'International investment and the Pasinetti process', *Oxford Economic Papers*, 32.

Mainwaring, L. (1980b), 'International trade and the transfer of labour value', *Journal of Development Studies*.

Mainwaring, L. (1982), 'A long-run analysis of international investment', *Metroeconomica*, 34.

Mainwaring, L. (1984), *Value and Distribution in Capitalist Economies*, London: Cambridge University Press.

Mainwaring, L. (1986), 'International trade in new and used machines', *Cambridge Journal of Economics*, 10.

Mainwaring, L. (1989a), 'Global accumulation with a dual southern economy', *Journal of Post Keynesian Economics*, 11.

Mainwaring, L. (1989b), 'World income shares and the terms of trade: A north–south growth cycle', *Bulletin of Economic Research*, 42.

Mainwaring, L. (1990), 'Self-organisation of world accumulation', mimeo, *Journal of Economics*, 50.

Marglin, S. A. (1963), 'The opportunity cost of public investment', *Quarterly Journal of Economics*, 77.

Metcalfe, J. S. (1984), 'Technological innovation and the competitive process', *Greek Economic Review*, 6.

Metcalfe, J. S. and Steedman, I. (1973), 'Heterogeneous capital and the Heckscher–Ohlin–Samuelson theory of trade', in J. M. Parkin (ed.), *Essays in Modern Economics*, Longman.

Metcalfe, J. S. and Steedman, I. (1974), 'A note on the gain from trade', *Economic Record*, 50.

Metcalfe, J. S. and Steedman, I. (1979), 'Growth and distribution in an open economy', in I. Steedman (ed.), *Fundamental Issues in Trade Theory*, London: Macmillan.

Molana, H. and Vines, D. (1989), 'North–south growth and the terms of trade: A model on Kaldorian lines', *Economic Journal*, 99.

Nove, A. (1974), 'On rereading Andre Gundar Frank', *Journal of Development Studies*, 10.

Ocampo, M. A. (1986), 'New developments in trade theory and LDCs', *Journal of Development Economics*, 22.

Page, S. (1986), 'Relocating manufacturing in developing countries: Opportunities for UK companies', *Economics Working Paper*, London: National Economic Development Office.

Palma, G. (1981), 'Dependency and development: A critical overview', in D. Seers (ed.), *Dependency Theory: A Critical Assessment*, London: Frances Pinter.

Pasinetti, L. L. (1960), 'A mathematical formulation of the Ricardian system', *Review of Economic Studies*, 27.

Pasinetti, L. L. (1962), 'Rate of profit and income distribution in relation to the rate of growth', *Review of Economic Studies*, 29.

Pasinetti, L. L. (1974), 'The rate of profit in an expanding economy', in *Growth and Income Distribution: Essays in Economic Theory*, London: Cambridge University Press.

Pasinetti, L. L. (ed.) (1980), *Essays in the Theory of Joint Production*, London: Macmillan.

Pigou, A. (1932), *The Economics of Welfare* (4th Edition), London: Macmillan.

Prebisch, R. (1950), *The Economic Development of Latin America and its Principal Problems*, New York: UN Economic Commission for Latin America.

Quibra, M. G. (1986), 'A note on foreign investment, the savings function and immiserization of national welfare', *Journal of Development Economics*, 21.

Ramsey, F. (1928), 'A mathematical theory of saving', *Economic Journal*, 38.

Robinson, J. (1966), *An Essay on Marxian Economics*, London: Macmillan.

Saigal, J. (1973), 'Reflexions sur la théorie de l'échange inégal', in S. Amin. (ed.), *L'echange Inégal et La Loi de Valeur*, Paris: Anthropos.

Samuelson, P. A. (1975), 'Trade pattern reversals in time-phased Ricardian systems and intertemporal efficiency', *Journal of International Economics*, 5.

Samuelson, P. A. (1978), 'Free trade's intertemporal Pareto optimality', *Journal of International Economics*, 8.

Sarker, P. (1986) 'The Singer–Prebisch hypothesis: A statistical evaluation', *Cambridge Journal of Economics*, 10.

Sau, R. (1978), *Unequal Exchange, Imperialism and Underdevelopment*, Calcutta: Oxford University Press.

Schefold, B. (1980), 'Fixed capital as a joint product and the analysis of accumulation with different forms of technical progress', in L. L. Pasinetti (ed.) (1980).

Schumpeter, J. A. (1939), Business Cycles, volume II, New York: McGraw-Hill.

Schwartz, S. L. (1973), 'Second-hand machinery in development; or how to recognise a bargain', *Journal of Development Studies*, 9.

Sen, A. K. (1961), 'On optimising the rate of saving', *Economic Journal*, 71.

Sen, A. K. (1962), 'On the usefulness of used machines', *Review of Economics and Statistics*, 44.

Sen, A. K. (1967), 'Isolation, assurance and the social rate of discount', *Quarterly Journal of Economics*, 81.

Silverberg, G., Dosi, G., and Orsenigo, L. (1988), 'Innovation, Diversity and Diffusion: A Self-Organising Model', *Economic Journal*, 98.

Singer, H. (1950), 'The distribution of gains between investing and borrowing countries', *American Economic Review*, Papers and Proceedings, 40.

Singer, H. (1982), 'Terms of trade controversy and the evolution of soft financing: early years in the UN: 1947–1951', IDS Discussion Paper 181, Sussex University.

Smith, M. A. M. (1974), 'International trade in second-hand machines', *Journal of Development Economics*, 1.

Smith, M. A. M. (1976a), 'Trade, growth and consumption in alternative models of capital accumulation', *Journal of International Economics*, 6.

Smith, M. A. M. (1976b), 'Second-hand machines: A comment', *Journal of International Economics*, 6.

Smith, M. A. M. (1979), 'Intertemporal gains from trade', *Journal of International Economics*, 9.

Smith, M. A. M. (1984), 'Capital theory and trade theory', in R. W. Jones and P. B. Kenen (eds), *Handbook of International Economics* (volume I), Amsterdam: North-Holland.

Solow, R. M. (1967), 'The interest rate and transition between techniques', in C. H. Feinstein (ed.), *Socialism, Capitalism and Economic Growth*, London: Cambridge University Press.

Spaventa, L. (1972), 'Notes on problems of transition between techniques', in J. A. Mirrlees and N. H. Stern (eds), *Models of Economic Growth*, London: Macmillan.

Sraffa, P. (1960), *Production of Commodities by Means of Commodities*, London: Cambridge University Press.

Steedman, I. (1975), 'Positive profits with negative surplus value', *Economic Journal*, 85.

Steedman, I. (1984), 'Natural prices, differential profit rates and the classical competitive process', *Manchester School*, 52.

Steedman, I. (1989), 'Time-preference, the rate of interest and abstinence from accumulation', in *From Exploitation to Altruism*, Cambridge: Polity Press.

Steedman, I. and Metcalfe, J. S. (1973), 'On foreign trade', *Economia Internazionale*, 26.

Steedman, I. and Metcalfe, J. S. (1977), 'Reswitching, primary inputs and the Heckscher–Ohlin–Samuelson theory of trade', *Journal of International Economics*, 7.

Sunkel, O. (1973), 'Transnational capital and national disintegration in Latin America', *Social and Economic Studies*, 22.

Sylos-Labini, P. (1962), *Oligopoly and Technical Progress*, Cambridge, Mass: Harvard University Press.

Taylor, L. (1983), *Structuralist Macroeconomics*, New York: Basic Books.

Taylor, L. (1986), 'Debt crisis: North–south, north–north and in between', in M. P. Claudon (ed.), *World Debt Crisis: International Lending on Trial*, Cambridge, Mass: Ballinger.

Thomas, B. (1954), *Migration and Economic Growth*, London: Cambridge University Press.

Thomas, B. (1958), Migration and international investment', in *The Economics of International Migration*, London: Macmillan.

Thomas, B. (1967), 'The historical record of international capital movements to 1913; in J. H. Adler, *Capital Movements and Economic Development*, London: Macmillan.

Thoumi, F. E. (1975), 'A Theory of the optimum age to import a durable good, with reference to the Columbian case', *Journal of Development Economics*, 2.

Todaro, M. P. (1970), 'Some thoughts on the transfer of technology to less developed nations', *East African Economic Review*, 2.

Toye, J. (1985), '*Dirigisme* and Development Economics', *Cambridge Journal of Economics*, 9.

United Nations (1949), *International Capital Movements in the Inter-War Period*, New York: UN.

Valenzuela, J. S. and Valenzuela, A. (1979), 'Modernisation and dependence: Alternative perspectives in the study of Latin American development', in Villamil (ed.) (1979).

Varri, P. (1980), 'Prices, rate of profit and life of machines in Sraffa's fixed-capital model', in Pasinetti (ed.) (1980).

Velupillai, K. (1979), 'Some stability properties of Goodwin's growth cycle', *Zeitschrift fur Nationalokonomie*, 39.

Villamil, J. J. (ed.) (1979), *Transnational Capital and National Development*, Hassocks: Harvester Press.

Vines, D. (1984), 'A north–south growth model along Kaldorian lines', *Discussion Paper 26*, London: Centre for Economic Policy Research.

Williams, J. H. (1929), 'The theory of international trade reconsidered', *Economic Journal*, 39.

# Author index

# Subject index

244 *Dynamics of Uneven Development*